# UNEVEN
# GROUND

FOR MARY

# UNEVEN GROUND

by
PAUL JAMIESON

Friends of the Owen D. Young Library
St. Lawrence University
Canton, New York
1992

ISBN  0-9634028-0-3

Printed on recycled paper

Grateful acknowledgment is made for permission to quote letters from friends and the writer's pieces in St. Lawrence University publications and in the Katonah Museum of Art's *Forever Wild,* 1991; thanks also to Richard Kuhta, St. Lawrence University librarian, for originating the plan to publish this memoir, to Chris Jerome for the gift of her professional expertise as editor, and to Nathan Farb for the use of his photograph of Elk Lake as cover design.

# FOREWORD

THE RADIUS of Paul Jamieson's fame is short, in comparison with that of some other men and women, but solid. It embraces two principal groups, occasionally overlapping, who will be the primary audiences of this autobiography: alumni of St. Lawrence University from 1929 to 1965, the years chronicled here; and enthusiasts of the Adirondack Park who have witnessed his flowering as hiker, canoeist, writer and crusader over the last four decades. Devotees of autobiography as a genre will also find pleasurable reading between these covers.

The mileage markers of his life do not set him off, particularly, from the rest of us. There have been no elections to high office, no headlines in the international media. And yet he's done much, quietly, that distinguishes him. Paul Jamieson was raised in Iowa before World War I. He couldn't wait to leave, for he had, he realized later, "an affinity for uneven ground," of which there was a profound dearth in that Corn Belt state, as well as a bad reaction to its fundamentalist doldrums. There followed higher education; girlfriends; sojourns in Europe during its 1920s golden age of literary and cultural vitality; marriage to Ruth Kirby; settling in to a career in college teaching, interrupted by a stint in the service, stateside in World War II; growing infatuation with the wild mountains, forests and rivers of the Adirondacks; retirement; and commencement, almost without design, of a second career of writing about the Adirondacks and campaigning with courtesy, persistence and force of character for the region's preservation.

Thus did the Midwesterner grow into Europhile and Emerson-like American, from lover of Romantic literature to lover of writing about wild places. The fruit of this latter work runs to over 100 items, including articles, essays and reviews (many collected in his *Adirondack Pilgrimage*); book chapters and introductions; the widely acclaimed anthology *The Adirondack Reader*, a one-book library on the Adirondacks; and the equally well-regarded guidebook *Adirondack Canoe Waters: North Flow.*

Nearly self-sufficient all of his life, Paul Jamieson has stood up to deans, dogma, now death itself without fear. He confronts his past in like manner, writing candidly of youthful explorations into sex, his agnosticism-approaching-atheism, campus politics, attraction to the wife of a young colleague. He is unequivocal in his restrained outrage that many Adirondack canoe routes, once open to the public, have in essence been stolen by selfish private landowners, with a wink from spineless state officials. His portrayal of his efforts to reopen these routes, and to save what he can of Adirondack wilderness for the benefit of future generations, is a profile in determination inspired by optimism. Lest the reader think his life is only ponderous abstractions, he also writes with the clarity that has become his trademark of humorous interludes, of bridge games with cherished Canton friends, of the pain of Ruth's losing battle with Alzheimer's disease.

True to his lifelong preference for simplicity over ceremony, he has asked that there be no memorials upon his death. But no person departs this world without leaving memorials, however unintentioned. Some leave wealth or goods. Paul Jamieson will leave words and deeds. *Uneven Ground* will become his memorial.

—Neal Burdick<br>January, 1992

# CONTENTS

# I  CUCUMBER  HEAD

I WAS THE FIRST BORN, on August 1, 1903, of John M. Jamieson and Stella Young Jamieson. My father was a graduate of Simpson, a small provincial college in Iowa. Though he spent an extra year there to take his master's degree, he continued through life to have trouble with the negative contraction of the third person present tense of the verb *do*. I picked up this solecism from him, and it was not till a teacher in a high school class stopped me with a smiling invitation to correct "he don't" that I learned better. Years later, when I found the same colloquialism in Byron's *Don Juan* and even in a novel of Virginia Woolf, I was able to excuse my father.

My mother's education ended with high school in rural Adair County. She was one of twelve siblings of an Iowa farmer. Her brothers became in their turn Iowa farmers, whom we used to visit in various parts of the state. In a beauty contest staged by Indians, I believe a Sioux tribe, she was judged the prettiest girl in Adair County, and indeed she kept her good looks into maturity.

During my first seven or eight years we lived in a house directly across from the State Capitol on Grand Avenue in Des Moines. My father worked in the State House, as it was known, becoming the deputy secretary of state. My memories of that time are scanty. When, a few years ago, the minister of the Unitarian-Universalist Church here in Canton asked several members of the congregation to submit brief sketches of their childhood to become the core of a sermon, I wrote the following, based on the odd genetic fact that whereas my parents and grandparents were all brachycephalic, the shape of my head was quite different—like a cucumber, my mother said.

Where is that *petite madeleine* and cup of tea? The taste of one with the other evoked in Marcel Proust a stream of childhood memories that fill many pages of *Remembrance of Things Past*. I have not found the key to such a flood. My early years were underprivileged. I grew up in flat country amid the alien corn. Des Moines was a city then, but the corn pressed in on the suburbs threatening to smother them. I have heard that there is a second crop now, soy beans, to relieve the monotony, but then it was all corn, corn, corn. In the Iowa countryside two levels prevailed, the flat ground and the level of the corn tassels. By August the tassels, responding to rich Iowa gumbo, were above eye level. You were imprisoned in monotonous walls of corn. Iowa was not the place for me. I was born with an affinity for uneven ground.

Maybe it was the shape of my head. My parents said that it was shaped like a cucumber. Since I was their only child for the next thirteen years, this was a serious matter to them. While that article was assumed to be still malleable, they tried to mold it into roughly human shape. They were not very successful. Anyone with a head as uneven as a cucumber is not going to take to flat country.

In Des Moines there was the semblance of a hill if you looked up at it from the depression a muddy river had cut. On top of this hill stood the State Capitol with its gold dome. Architects, I have heard, consider the building a monstrosity, but to me it was the most glamorous thing in sight. During my early years we lived just across the street from it, and between our house and the capitol grounds was a streetcar line. When I was three or four, the streetcar got in my way. For a few yards I was trundled along in front of the cow-catcher. The fact that I was dirtied but uninjured Mom always attributed to the astrakhan coat she dressed me in and the tam o'shanter hat. After that episode Mom was reconciled to my cucumber head. She thought I had been spared for some good end. She kept repeating this on birthdays and other occasions till the passing years undermined her faith.

My next vivid memory, dating perhaps a year later, relates to a visit to the Iowa State Fair. An aunt and uncle were visiting us from their three-hundred acre cornfield near Ottumwa, and Dad must have thought the occasion deserved something better than a ride on a crowded streetcar or interurban. He rented a horse and surrey. My memories of the Cow Barn, the Hog Barn, and the Midway are very blurred. But clear and stark is the image of what took place on the return trip. While still miles from home, the horse dropped to the ground in a sprawl, whinnied pitifully, and breathed its last. I don't recall what measures Dad took to get us out of that fix, but he was a resourceful man.

Not all memories of my first ten years are unpleasant. My favorite sport was not marbles or catch but climbing to the cupola of the Capitol dome. That dome was one of the highest elevations in Iowa. A friend of my later years made it the first project of his retirement to scale the highest elevations in every one of the lower forty-eight states. As I recall, it took him just ten minutes to ascend the tallest hill in Iowa. It took me much longer to climb to the top of the Capitol. Once there, you could look out over the sprawling city to the cornfields beyond. It wasn't the view so much as the way up and down that thrilled me. Halfway up, there was an arcade around the base of the dome, from which you could look down on the miniature figures of the Governor and his staff crossing the rotunda. But the great thrill was the spiral stairway that ascended the dome, bending inward with its curvature, all in a region of dim light from window slits and of stressful girders. Here alone (at least in pre-puberty years) was there romance in Iowa. If there is anything in my experience resembling Proust's pastry and cup of tea, it is Piranesi's drawings of the architecture of Rome, especially his imaginary prisons with their shadowy multi-leveled interiors and stairways leading to infinity.

During the summer of my tenth year Mom and I spent a month's vacation in Colorado. We walked most of the way up Pikes Peak, first amid the conifers and columbine and then over the scree above timberline. This certainly beat the dome of the Capitol. It left me dissatisfied till, sixteen years later, I settled down for the rest of my life in a country of three dimensions: a country of woods and waters upthrust by lateral and subterranean forces, split in fault zones, and gouged, grooved, and molded by the glacier into a treasure trove of kettle holes, drumlins, kames, valley trains, and eskers. This gloriously uneven ground is the right country for a cucumber head.


I have few pleasurable memories of childhood and early adolescence. Growing up in the corn-and-bible belt, as Mencken used to call Iowa and its sister states, ran counter to natural instincts. Things took a turn for the worse when Billy Sunday, the evangelist, came to town and changed the lives of my parents. Previously they were not church goers. But Billy Sunday converted them, and they joined the church of the Disciples of Christ, a denomination strong in the Midwest and close to the fundamentalism of Billy Sunday. I of course had to follow along with baptism by immersion, Sunday school, church services day and night on Sunday, and sometimes a Wednesday night service. There was little to appeal to the mind and senses of the young in that church. Sundays became days of dreaded obligation. Learning to cope with this world is burden enough for a boy without at the same time preparing for the next. I acquired a distaste for organized religion that has remained with me for life, buttressed in college by the writings of agnostics and atheists. In recent years this distaste has abated a little as Ruth led me into the Unitarian-Universalist Church in Canton. In this church you are not constrained to believe anything in particular.

If as Freud held our phobias are traceable to the wounds of childhood, I have a ready-made explanation for my stage fright. In one of the Sunday evening services of the church we attended, children were coerced into reciting parts of the Bible they had memorized in Sunday school. I forgot my lines in midcourse, stammered, and fled the pulpit to the laughter of the audience. Though doubtless good-natured and indulgent, that laughter seemed hostile to me. Whether this was the origin of my lifelong phobia for public speaking I can't say. But when asked to speak outside the classroom, I have usually managed to find excuses. On the few occasions I could not avoid, my performance was marred by nervousness. This was a handicap in my profession till, in the last fifteen years before retirement, I turned to the writing of professional articles and was rewarded by two promotions in a few years.

Weekdays too were not much better than Sundays. Classes were all right, and I liked several of my teachers. The schoolyard was my problem. I didn't like body-contact sports. I ducked challenges to fight. The nadir of my career as sissy came the year we moved into a blue-collar neighborhood of East Des Moines. My father had bought a house there as a real estate speculation. We were to live in it for a year while it was being renovated and then sell it. That was a long year to me. The school I attended was a roughneck one. My mother continued to overdress me, and my fine clothes were a red flag to the barbarians of that school. They chased me home with taunts of "sissy," though I took to the back alleys to elude them. One day, however, when I was roughed up by a school bully, I surprised myself by fighting back. We gathered an audience, intrigued by the spectacle of a sissy's using his fists. My tormentor gave me a bloody nose, but I landed a good one that blackened an eye. When we broke off, the fight seemed pretty much a draw, and for a brief moment I thought I had redeemed myself. But that ring of howling barbarians, seeing blood, mocked me for my dripping nose. Their taunts got to my sensibilities, and I broke into tears. So all the advantage I might have gained was whisked away. I was a sissy indeed and might as well learn to live with it. The nearest I ever came to fighting after that was bouts with a punching bag in the cellar.

*The Sissy*

It was a relief to move out of that neighborhood. I have the vaguest memories of the house we next lived in, still in East Des Moines. But the next move was a drastic one. We left East Des Moines for a new development on the outskirts of West Des Moines. There were zoning provisions. Lots had to be an acre or more in size. For three summer months we lived in a large partitioned tent on a wooden platform on our new lot while our house was being built, to an architect's design, in the Spanish mission style my mother favored. My parents must have been counting on an enlarged family, for the house had four bedrooms and a maid's room on the third floor. I watched all stages of the construction, probably to the irritation of carpenters and masons. Less exciting was the duty I settled down to of operating the push mowers of those days on an acre of lawn.

Those were prosperous years for my father. He was no longer deputy secretary of state but state binder. That is, he had a monopoly on folding all pamphlets and binding in cloth all books generated by the state government and the state university and colleges. There was also a state printer. Both plants were owned by the state in an odd arrangement that gave the Republican governor (always a Republican in those days) plums to pass out among his supporters. It wasn't necessary to know anything about printing or binding. Competent foremen in the two plants saw to that side of the business. A lifelong friendship developed between the printer and my father. In concert they had a good deal of flexibility in setting charges to the state. Perhaps they went a little too far, for after two three-year terms my father served, the offices of printer and binder were abolished. At that time my father bought the bindery from the state and continued running the plant for the rest of his life. He got most of the state contracts, but under the less lucrative system of competitive bidding.

In the new home (I was twelve at this move) pressures on me eased. I was not the only sissy on the West Side. There were as yet only a few houses in the new

*Jamieson home in Des Moines*

development, and just two neighborhood boys, brothers, of about my age. We became fast friends. They lived in the most elaborate of the new houses, a mansion really, for their father was owner of a large plant that made cardboard shipping boxes. I was somewhat in awe of their mother, who on most of the occasions I saw her was sitting in a patrician pose at a secretary on the upstairs landing.

We had lived in the new house only a few months before Mother gave birth to a girl. Ruth was a pretty, placid, well-behaved child who seldom interrupted my reading or home work on evenings when I was baby sitter. Our maid, a rangy Swedish girl, preferred to spend her evenings out. Having acquired a Kodak, I began to fill the family album with snapshots of baby sister. This pastime redoubled two years later when Mary was born. With her perpetual smile, lively spirits, and habituation to the camera, she was even more photogenic than Ruth. My sisters, thirteen and fifteen years younger than I, were too young for close companionship during the remainder of my years at home. Later I returned home from the East to attend Ruth's wedding to a St. Louis man. After giving birth to a daughter, she died at twenty-six of a ruptured appendix, the cause of my father's death two years earlier. Mary, soon after her marriage to a Drake University graduate, moved to Los Angeles. We have kept in touch over the years. Since my wife's death in 1989, Mary is the person to whom I am most closely attached by affection, love, and mutual interests. We spend two weeks together each year.

Just a five-minute walk from the new house, there was an undeveloped woodland of several acres on the outskirts of the city. I used to go there often with the two neighborhood boys, alone, or with Mother, who taught me the names of the succession of wildflowers. I liked those woods, a foretaste of the vaster Adirondack woods I was to explore in later years.

The new house, the new sister, and the woodlot fill my memory of the next two years to the exclusion of the school I attended in seventh and eighth grades. After turning fourteen, I attended West High. It was two and a half miles distant for walking and farther by streetcar, which involved a transfer downtown. I usually walked to school in the mornings and returned home by streetcar or with my father in the Hudson. During most of my high school years I worked after school at the bindery and on Saturdays, usually operating the folding machine. I developed the habit of saving for future enjoyment. Mother had made me an offer of five hundred dollars if I refrained from dating girls until I was eighteen. In later years I questioned her judgment in making this offer, but at the time the money was a powerful lure, and we both kept our side of the bargain.

I believe I was thirteen when an episode occurred that may have prompted Mother's offer. We were visiting my maternal grandparents in Greenfield, Iowa. At the same time an older sister of Mother's and her daughter Betty were also visitors from their farm in South Dakota. My grandfather had moved into town and left his nearby farm to one of his sons. Betty and I had the run of that farm. She was a pretty girl of sixteen. Iowa summers are hot and sultry. Betty wore a loose smock with a low neck revealing generous glimpses of two dewy, fully developed, snow-white hillocks untrammeled by a bra. I was unwilling to part with that oft repeated vision. I was determined that Betty and her mother should visit us forthwith in Des Moines. This was the strongest volition of my life so far. When my aunt and my mother deemed the proposed visit impractical, I threw a tantrum that may have convinced Mother that the wilder impulses of puberty needed to be reined in.

Earlier visits to my paternal grandparents were more placid. Before they too retired and moved to Des Moines, they owned a general store in a small town, Montgomery, in the northwestern lake district of Iowa. The store was a spacious one with groceries in one wing, dry goods in the other, and a meeting hall above where square dances were held to the music of local fiddlers. I had access to the candy counter, the crock of pickles floating in brine, and the pickled pigs' feet. The latter was a gustatory delight that I've never been able to duplicate since in what used to pass for pig hocks in New York State but has since quite rightly disappeared from menus and markets. Another taste sensation of those summer visits was frog legs, which I used to watch jump in the frying pan as my grandmother cooked them. I became quite adept at catching frogs with fat thighs in the surrounding fields.

Our first car, a Maxwell, was always breaking down. It was followed by a succession of more reliable Hudsons. With the car came mobility. Father bought a summer camp on a lake in northwestern Wisconsin near Lake Superior. The lake, originally called Sucker, was renamed Lake Des Moines, for the primary residence of the seven camp owners. We spent a good part of our summers in camp on a diet of blueberries, northern pike or bass, and muffins. Mabel, our maid, accompanied us. She fell in love with the caretaker of the seven camps and eventually left us to marry him. I spent a good deal of time alone, often crossing the lake in canoe to the undeveloped shore and either reading or pecking away at my portable typewriter under a favorite Norway pine on a knoll above the lake. Beautiful surroundings, however, were of no avail. Though I had decided I wanted to be a writer, I recognized even then that the stuff I turned out on the portable was worthless day-dreaming. I swam a little but didn't enjoy fishing, which occupied most of my father's time during his briefer visits to camp. One summer we had as guest a friend of my own age, Everett George, a classmate in both high school and college. With him I had my first experience running a river in canoe on an overnight trip down the Namekagon.

Reading occupied much of my spare time in those pre-radio and TV days. As I graduated from Tom Swift, the Rover Boys, and Horatio Alger, I turned to the popular novels of pre-World War I days. Lacking contact with the opposite sex, I was led to believe that girls remained virgin before marriage; that indeed they were too delicate and ethereal for the sexual act as I then understood it from sub rosa readings and experiments in masturbation. That is why all the novels ended at or before the marriage ceremony. This lingering notion made me a slow learner when in college I began dating. During high school the fictional ideal was embodied for me in a girl named Mary, whom I passed in the halls but never spoke to till we were seniors at Drake University. Even as my reading tastes improved by acquaintance with English and European masters of the novel, the sentimental fiction of the first two decades of the century continued to control my conception of girls as nearly devoid of sexual appetites. A final awakening did not come till my junior year in college.

During my high-school years there was little discernible progress in other ways except perhaps in the quality of extra-curricular reading. I lived too far from West High to participate in after-school activities. The teachers were competent, but most of them failed to arouse in me any enthusiasm for their subjects. One exception was a geometry teacher in my sophomore year; hers was the only math course in which I ever showed much aptitude. Another was my fourth year English teacher, who had a more lasting influence. The English teacher in my junior year required a speech. On the day I expected my turn to come, I tried to decamp. A male teacher stopped me at the exit and obliged me to return to class. My turn did not come that day, and at the next class meeting I had to face the ordeal. Somehow I got through it, but my nervousness must have been obvious. This experience and others in later years failed to overcome my stage fright. When I received an invitation to attend the fiftieth reunion of my high-school class, the specter of having to render a vita, however short, at the banquet would have prevented my attending even if I had had agreeable memories of those days.

The prohibition on dating put a premium on deferred pleasure, and one of the consequences was working at my father's bindery or at a cod-liver oil bottling plant in the same building and saving virtually all I earned. The work was monotonous, but I endured it. Thrift is one part of the puritan ethic that has stuck by me. By the time I turned eighteen and entered college I had saved about twelve hundred dollars. This was augmented by my mother's tribute of five hundred. The future seemed bright.

## II  COLLEGE AND GIRLS

BUT NOT YET. Aside from a few movie dates with the visiting niece of one of my mother's friends, I was to have no serious relationship till my junior year in college. Deprivation had become a habit. Besides, Mary, though a classmate of mine in college too, obviously had a steady boyfriend. And all the other girls on campus appeared too plain or too attached for a promising fling at first love. I had the money, but my peers had snatched the girls—the flaw in my mother's system.

I had wanted to enter the University of Wisconsin. This desire led to the first real "scene," or revolt, I remember ever having with my father. The year was 1921. He had suffered reverses after two postwar years of investing heavily in farm and ranch lands while America was still feeding a devastated Europe. He had borrowed heavily and was now left with devalued, unsalable properties and large debts as the boom came to a sudden end and real estate values collapsed. He could not afford, he said, to send me away to college. I would have to live at home and attend Drake University. As the fall term began, my bitterness over this disappointment lasted two or three weeks. Then, to my surprise, I began to like Drake and make a few congenial friends.

College brought a scholastic awakening. For the first time I had a strong incentive to study, and my average grade for the first semester was close to A; in the second, a few A pluses brought it to better than A. This entitled me to a tuition scholarship for the remainder of my college years. I was at the head of my class in the Liberal Arts College and was elected to Phi Beta Kappa in my junior year, an honor accorded to one male and one female student at Drake.

In my sophomore year I was under the spell of three professors, Morehouse in astronomy, Martin in philosophy, and Lewis Worthington Smith in English. Morehouse had discovered a comet, which was named for him. He presided over a good observatory located on the heights of the golf and country club just three blocks from my home. I spent many enchanted nights scanning the heavens. For several months I toyed with the idea of majoring in astronomy till I realized the advanced mathematics such a major would entail. Martin too was a strong advocate for his subject, and so was Smith in English, a smiling, white-haired, white-mustached gentleman who enjoyed a reputation as writer and was for a time president of the Iowa Authors Association. As students of the postwar era we were in the habit of belittling his poetry as a sentimental hangover from an earlier generation, but he nevertheless had our respect as a published writer. By the end of my sophomore year I had decided to major in English and minor in philosophy.

In 1981 a graduate student addressed a query to me about Professor Smith, the subject of her dissertation. My answer, which sums up the academic side of my years at Drake as well as characterizing Smith, is as follows:

First, let me correct a date in your letter. I graduated from Drake in 1925, not in 1939. Those extra years of longevity may explain gaps in my memory and alert you to check whatever facts can be verified. I knew LWS both as teacher for three years and as colleague for two, 1926-1928, when I returned from Columbia University with a master's degree.

The Liberal Arts College had a strong faculty in my time. LeCoq in French, Clark in history, Herriot in sociology, Martin in philosophy, and Smith in English were strong personalities with quite positive reputations among us students. LeCoq, an expatriate to escape the draft in World War I, had such a passion for French literature that he continued to write articles and monographs about it long after his retirement; he sent copies of them to my wife, who had been one of his best students. Martin later went to the State University in Iowa City. I took nearly all his courses. Watching him think in a seminar on Kant was fascinating; I've known no one else whose thinking was so visual. I came near majoring in astronomy too, since Morehouse was an inspiring interpreter of the universe in class and at the observatory. Clark and Herriot were not so congenial to me. Clark went in for "primary sources," which seemed to me dryasdust and badly written. Herriot had a bagful of picturesque locutions which dazzled for three or four weeks into the term and then became dull and repetitious. He would have been more in his element running for political office.

Into this competitive arena of individualists came LWS with his patrician manners, his reputation as "Iowa author," and his modified Socratic method of teaching.

Smith taught no freshman classes, but in my first year I had indirect contact with him through a young instructor on his first teaching job. He was a little uneasy in it, particularly I think in having to use a small text by LWS which called for close analysis of literary texts. Its emphasis was on sense impressions. It broached a set of symbols ($s_1$, $s_2$, etc.) to use in evaluating the effectiveness of images in descriptive passages. At the top of the scale, I believe, was the pregnant metaphor that sets up a chain of associated images in the reader's mind. Then we were supposed to aim at this optimum effect in weekly themes. The young instructor was rather literal minded but conscientious. He felt he needed guidance. So one week he asked LWS to read and comment on a batch of themes. I tried hard to impress the great man, according to my lights (we had been warned to do our best), but I'm sure there were no pregnant metaphors in my theme. It came back with the faintest of praise: "This is good in its way"... and then went on, in neat script, to detail deficiencies. Since becoming an English professor myself, I have wondered at the energy of a man who would undertake to read and analyze a colleague's themes in addition to his own heavy teaching and writing load.

LWS's classes were large, the more popular ones ranging up to forty or fifty. Teachers from the city high schools poured into his late afternoon classes. As far as my evidence goes, he read all papers and exams himself. And yet he somehow had the reserve energy to keep up a writing career on the side. He also directed an active English Club, which often met at his home. In spite of this heavy work load he never seemed pressed or distracted. In my mind's eye he is always smiling, a slightly condescending smile perhaps, for he knew how to keep a certain distance between himself and importunate students. Although a little under average height, he was a handsome figure with his prematurely white, abundant hair and white mustache. For several of us he personified the literary life. Although we didn't read his poetry or essays, we respected the niche he had carved for himself in "creative writing," as well as textbooks. Jim Duncan's characterization of him as a Victorian gentleman is apt. He was at home in what critics have called the genteel tradition in American letters, with its intellectual home in the New England of the late nineteenth and early twentieth centuries.

You say that Jim terms him a puritan. I would agree so far as the ethical side of puritanism is concerned. I don't know whether he had any religious affiliations, but if he had, they must have been nominal. His orientation seemed to me that of a secular humanist.

The twenties were a decade of disillusion with the institutions that had failed to prevent bloody World War I and of rebellion against the puritan tradition. LWS knew as well as anyone the intellectual temper of the times. He kept abreast of the literary scene, though he may not have condoned it. In his course in the modern novel he knew he must recognize the winner of the Nobel prize in literature, Anatole France. So he chose the early, innocuous *Crime of Sylvestre Bonnard* for reading and class discussion instead of the novels of France's wicked old age, which put him on the RC Index. I remember LWS's warning to me not to read these later subversive novels when I told him how much I had enjoyed the *Crime*. I wonder how he would have handled, in later years in that course, Dos Passos, Joyce, Hemingway, Fitzgerald, and Faulkner, who were just then beginning their careers.

One can hardly blame him for being a man of his generation. I admired him and thrived under his teaching, collecting a string of A+'s, junior Phi Bete, and a

Roberts Fellowship to Columbia. On the first day of class he would hand out a multipaged set of precisely worded questions. Then with each assignment he would write on the blackboard the numbers of the questions we were to consider for each assigned poem, essay, act in a play or section of a novel. Most students ignored these questions in reading the assignments and depended on improvisation if called on. But I deliberated on them and had my answers pat for class discussion, waiting till mine was the last hand to go up to give the expected answer. I starred till confronted with unfair competition. My adversary was Phil Stong, about five years older, a graduate I believe of the State University in Iowa City, and already a published "Iowa author," though his best seller, *State Fair*, was some half dozen years down the road. (I wonder what LWS made of that!) The class which Phil invaded, working toward his master's, became an eloquent colloquy between him and LWS, in which I was left biting my nails; I believe I slipped back to an A that term.

You ask about Mrs. Smith. She was a shadowy figure on the occasions I visited their home for meetings of the English Club or other purposes. I believe it was in my senior year that I gave her driving lessons, and at that time I was too preoccupied with other concerns to be a close observer of a middle-aged woman. She did dress rather exotically, as you have heard. She had probably been beautiful as a girl, but at that time her figure was too matronly to appear so to me, conditioned as I was by the campus sylphs in their flirty skirts. Her chief attraction was that of an enigma. She seemed moody and discontent, perhaps a little hypochondriacal. Preoccupied as he must have been with professional duties and writing, LWS was probably not an attentive husband or father. There was one daughter, Marjorie, a few years older than I but still living at home, who had allowed herself to become fat and unlovely, though her parents were both personable. I don't think the Smiths had an active social life, though they exchanged visits and dinners with the family of the prominent Des Moines publisher Gardner Cowles.

When in the fall of 1925 I and a classmate became candidates for a master's degree at Columbia, LWS wrote a letter of introduction to the head of a big New York publishing house, and shortly after we arrived in the city we received invitations to lunch at a Central Park West apartment, where we met a few friends of the publisher, including Stephen Vincent Benét, with whom my friend, a better tennis player than I, spent the rest of the afternoon on a private court. This impressed me with LWS's pull—a big publisher willing to invite a couple of jejune midwestern graduates to dine with house writers must have wanted to keep LWS on his active list.

My contacts with LWS when I came back to Drake to teach were less frequent and close. Our classrooms and offices were in different buildings. But he was my department head and my relations with him were always cordial. The first year I taught only freshman classes. The second he gave me a seminar in Comparative American Literature, with the idea that we might collaborate on a textbook in that field. I looked forward to this, but nothing came of it because that year was my last at Drake.

LWS was an excellent teacher. An atmosphere of courtesy and lively interest prevailed in his classes. His method of close textual analysis antedated the New Criticism and was excellent discipline for literary scholars. I don't want to mar the image I have of him by reading much of his writings. You may have reason to query whether he diffused his energy. His writing may have been more manner than matter. His desire to be a man of letters probably outran his capacity. I doubt whether he had a subject he felt passionately about. As for the limitations of his tastes in literature, they were understandable for one of my present age. With me obsolescence set in with the Beat Generation. English professors should be subsidized so they could retire comfortably, say, at 55. That is not to say that LWS had too little going for him after that age. What he was was enough.

As for your question about his influence on the next generation of writers, there were two novelists-to-be in his classes in the mid-twenties, Phil Stong, graduate student, and Tom Duncan, a year behind me. I knew Phil only casually but Tom quite well. Tom knew he was going to be a writer while the rest of us undergraduates were floundering in uncertainty. The only son of a well-to-do widow willing to subsidize his early career as writer, he was already leading the literary life with an assurance we others envied. Pipe smoking in his Des Moines home, he gossiped by the hour with me and others about books, writers, and his own writing; he dated girls from all milieus of the city for the experience as well as the fun and summed up their quirks and physical attributes in neat phrases. Phil and Tom, like me, thought LWS was failing to keep abreast of the time spirit. There was no possibility of hoisting him into the age of sexual liberation and disillusion with institutions. Nevertheless, we respected him as a teacher, Phil perhaps most of all. I never heard him say anything disrespectful about Smith.

I can say that LWS opened my eyes to writing as an art. Nothing gives me greater satisfaction, after the first, second, or third drafts painfully produced, than what Philip Roth calls "turning sentences around." LWS gave me a thrust in this direction, and I like to think that a few of my pieces meet his standards of prose style, in spite of their paucity of pregnant metaphors.


During my first two years at Drake I was too much preoccupied with fitting myself into the role of scholar to pay much attention to girls. Except for Mary, who never seemed to lack for male companions, the girls I saw in my classes and in the halls had no particular appeal. They all seemed flawed in one way or another. And how did one go about asking a girl for a date anyway? Shyness and lack of savoir

faire combined with low incentive to defer my first love affair to the second semester of my junior year. And then it was the girl who made the overture.

Maybe it would be more accurate to call Clara "woman." She was twenty-six to
my twenty. She always wore a hat on campus. But I cling to "girl," loveliest and
most connotative word in the English language, to designate any female I'm fond
of, no matter what her age.

One day in the hall between classes, Clara spoke to me. Immediately it seemed
that here was someone I should have noticed before. Strange, how beauty lights up
a girl once she speaks to you.

Clara was a special student at Drake. She had graduated some years earlier from
Iowa State University. Now she was living at home in Des Moines with her parents and younger sister and brother. She was between jobs downtown and was
occupying the hiatus by taking two or three courses at Drake with professors of
reputation, like Martin and Smith.

I have forgotten what Clara said that day in the hall. Whatever it was, it seemed
perfectly natural and right. Clara was versed in the ways of the world. From start
to finish our relationship personified innocence and experience. Maybe it was this
reverberation in my first love affair that accounts for my addiction to the novels
of Henry James, in which unformed Americans of both sexes encounter the old,
wiser, more sophisticated society of Europe only to find that innocence, however
attractive it may be superficially, has its drawbacks; may even lead to disaster.

Why did Clara speak to me that day? I don't know for sure. But later she told
me that in her philosophy class Professor Martin had held up a leather-bound term
paper of mine and, in that thinker-looks-into-the-future demeanor that so impressed
us students, had said, "He will go far." (Even philosophers can make mistakes.) His
evidence was a longer paper than he was accustomed to receiving and one I had
bound in board and morocco at my father's bindery; the title was lettered in gold
leaf on the front. The quality of the binding was excellent, whatever that of the
contents, and so I was given a boost in Clara's eyes.

Her speaking to me that day was incendiary. I must have fallen in love at her
third word. I asked to drive her home that very day. With the nest egg I had saved
from vacation and after school work at the bindery, I had bought a secondhand
Buick roadster in good condition. Walking the two and a quarter miles to campus
had been too time consuming for the scholar I had become. Few students had cars
then. Now, at St. Lawrence, a residential college, nearly two thousand parking
spaces have been constructed for twenty-three hundred students. But in 1924 I had
a distinct advantage, which I now began to realize, over the other men in my class.
Slowly it dawned on me that I had cachet with almost every girl on campus. And
on second thought, it might well have been the car that sparked Clara's overture
that day rather than Professor Martin's off-the-cuff prophecy.

The car was in fact the only resource of the muddled adolescent I was then, a condition described by Graham Greene in his autobiography, *A Sort of Life*. "As we grow old we are apt to forget the state of extreme sexual excitement in which we spent the years between sixteen and twenty....What a mess those inexperienced years can be!"

I was in a state of euphoria, whether escorting Clara to secluded balcony seats in one of the movie palaces of those days, driving through the cornfields, or on weekends dining at a downtown restaurant. Parked or running, the Buick was accessory to romance. Clara settled into it with the assurance of a lap cat. Often she waited in it till my class was over, or I waited for her in my double role as chauffeur-lover. On drives out of town I looked, often in vain, for a scrap of woodland beside running water. Even if found, it was gated and fenced. One warm moonlit evening we crawled through barbed wire to spread a blanket under a leafy canopy of oaks. Soon an irate farmer appeared to send us packing. Boy-and-girl is devil incarnate to a dour Iowa farmer. But I was hardly aware of these limiting circumstances till I moved to New York, where state parks in most areas favor the designs of lovers. In Iowa land was too valuable for corn to waste on public amenities.

*Paul and Clara*

Dinners, mileage on the car, corsages, and other gifts accelerated the depletion of my capital far in excess of the rate of accumulation. One fine spring day as we passed Professor Martin on campus, he asked with a smile, noting Clara's corsage, "What is the occasion?" "No special occasion," I replied proudly. Love catapulted scrooge into spendthrift.

My progress as lover was slower. Clara led me gently and by considered degrees through the stages of petting as then practiced by Iowa boys and girls, stopping short of the big bang, for in those days we knew little of contraceptives. Once, however, Clara guided my middle finger to her dewy cleft. In that moment my education about girls took a giant leap forward. There was nothing like this in those romantic Edwardian novels I had read. The experience was a mixture of fascination and repulsion. The odor of female arousal, an atavistic survival of life's emergence from the sea, when first encountered by an aesthetic young man, just then a disciple of Walter Pater, seemed so disharmonious with the embroidery of romance and roses we have inherited from the troubadours and embellished since that my adjustment was slow. But sex is a stronger force than aesthetics, and fascination overcame repulsion in due time.

I thought, wouldn't it be nice to marry Clara at some distant day when I had caught up with her twenty-six years and had a means of livelihood, as yet undetermined. Older men marry young girls; why not the other way around? Would Clara be willing to wait?

She knew my mind on this subject, but I did not know hers. This ignorance, however, was no real threat. Everything went smoothly till near the end of the spring term at Drake. Then Clara made a strange proposal. She wanted me to meet her dear friend Christine, a student in the Education College at Drake. This didn't strike me as necessary or desirable. But Clara kept insisting. Christine, she said, was lovely, I would like her; just ask her for a date and you will see. Finally I agreed to be introduced. Yes, Christine was indeed pretty and she was just my age and asking her for a date proved remarkably easy.

I fell in love with Christine too. Twenty long years of deprivation and belated discovery that girls attract in a variety of ways combined to prolong adolescence and cast me in the role of Cherubino. For three or four weeks I dated both girls, separately of course. Christine was saying with a concerned little frown that she didn't want to hurt her friend Clara, and I agreed. I didn't see any reason why Clara would be hurt. I was more attentive to her than ever. Being in love with two such charming girls simultaneously was paradise—a fool's paradise, as it turned out.

Suddenly there were only two of us left. Clara withdrew abruptly, permanently, and without explanation. When I phoned, she hung up. When I wrote, she did not answer. When I hovered about her home in the parked Buick, she never appeared. I was devastated. Christine was devalued in my eyes. It was only Clara I wanted.

I had been an open book to Clara, she a closed one to me. More months, years, of exposure to the randomness of life, the bruised feelings we heedlessly inflict on others, the misfits in personal relationships were necessary before I understood why Clara had broken off.

That summer offered little encouragement to the natural resilience of youth. Monotonous work at the bindery left me open to tremors of loss and regret. I dated Christine infrequently and with diminishing satisfaction. She was a poor substitute for Clara's depth and maturity. Wounds did not heal till the fall term of my senior year when I renewed male friendships with Everett George, Eugene Page, Lazarre Courtright, and Ralph Jester. I worked on the campus newspaper and yearbook and on the founding of a professional fraternity chapter; I continued to garner A's and A+'s.

Slowly it dawned on me that Mary, my classmate since high school, seemed

*Drake University classmates:* from left, *Eugene Page, Paul Jamieson, Everett George, Lazarre Courtwright*

to lack the attentions of a steady boyfriend. As I found out later, he had transferred to the Naval Academy at Annapolis. So one day I asked her for a date. She accepted.

The prettiest girl in the senior class, Mary was tall, slender, fair-complexioned, with dreamy blue eyes and dark brown hair trained in wisps over her brow. She was the youngest daughter of a Drake biology professor under whom I was taking a course in Heredity and Environment. I was welcomed in their home. It was there that I first learned to dance, to victrola music, under Mary's expert tutelage.

In temperament Mary was as placid as Clara had been animated. She liked quiet pleasures, such as dancing to slow music, being read to, drives in the country, tranquil, measured kisses, picnics. Her temperament set the tone of our relationship, one of playing at being in love rather than love itself. Occasionally we attended dances, one of which was a costume ball for which Mother made me a fair imitation of the dress of Gainsborough's Blue Boy (my aesthetic phase lingered on). Mostly we preferred to be alone.

At last, in country drives, we found a woodlot of respectable size about thirty miles from the city. Wildflowers grew there and a lazy river meandered by. In the spring and summer months we spent many afternoons and early evenings there, always with a book to read aloud and a picnic lunch. Between chapters in a novel we kissed or waded in the river. In deepening water Mary lifted her skirt higher than strictly necessary over long, shapely legs. Afterwards as we settled on our blanket, in tribute to this Diana of the woodlot I kissed her thighs just as high as she had revealed them but no higher. This was the boldest sexual gesture that ever took place between us. Though Mary came after Clara and Christine, she was a virginal first love of my high-school fantasies.

One late afternoon, as we were spreading out our lunch, the owner of the woodlot and his wife appeared. I braced for another eviction. But this farmer did not look like the archetypal American Gothic of Grant Wood (an artist to whom my family was distantly related). As introductions confirmed, he was a Drake graduate and had taken courses under Mary's father, whom he greatly admired. We were given a welcome so long as we always closed the gate.

Although Mary may not have been formally engaged, she was committed to the Annapolis man, and a few years later she married her naval officer. But it is unseemly for a girl in her senior year in college not to have an attentive lover. For Mary I was that substitute. For me she was a fantasy engendered six years earlier, now enacted and realized. For both of us, a happy senior year and following summer. Our parting in the fall was without pain and with only mild regrets. We agreed to write and did so with diminishing frequency. Six months later, in New York, I drifted into another affair—with Mary's older sister.

## III  NEW YORK AND ENGLAND

A FEW YEARS BEFORE my graduation a wealthy Des Moines widow had left an endowment for several fellowships to Columbia University from Iowa colleges and universities. As the winner of one of these Lydia C. Roberts fellowships, I left for New York in the fall of 1925 to study for a master's degree in English. Accompanying me were two of my classmates, Eugene Page, also a candidate in English, and Stephen Slaughter in history. Gene and I roomed together in a two-bedroom suite in Furnald Hall on campus. Both Gene and Steve have been lifelong friends, Gene till his death at sixty-five and Steve, who died early this year (1991) after returning from the East to his native Missouri.

For us two roommates it was a busy year of cramming as well as writing the master's essay. That year there were nine hundred candidates for the two advanced degrees, including a large number of Southern girls ripe for a fling in the big city, and a graduate faculty that was a small percentage of that number. An overburdened faculty had installed a short-answer, so-called objective test at the end of the year in order to lighten the work load. The emphasis was on literary history and biography from *Beowulf* to modern times. Having studied under Professor Smith, whose approach ignored biography and touched lightly on literary history but emphasized close study of texts, Gene and I were ill prepared for that exam and had to begin our English studies over again. We became adept at memorizing facts, but the effort left little time to enjoy the city, at least in the first semester.

Gene's major field was the eighteenth century of English literature, mine the nineteenth. We soon discovered that the most entertaining lecturer in the department at that time was Carl Van Doren in American literature. Along with a sizable group of the nine hundred, we attended his lectures faithfully the first semester in a large amphitheater classroom. In the second semester our attendance on lectures tapered off, even in the field of concentration, as we learned we could advance our interests more effectively in independent study.

I have no warm feelings toward the faculty of that time or the system at Columbia. Relations between candidates and faculty were remote and impersonal. Interviews had to be arranged well in advance. Professor Wright, head of the graduate faculty in English, was the nominal director of my work on an essay on the ethics of Thomas Hardy's novels. I saw him for just three brief interviews. When I handed in my essay early in the spring term, he said he would read it and give me a summons; I was not to contact him. Time passed without a call from his office. Finally, in desperation, just four weeks before the final exam, I asked his secretary for an appointment. There was another wait of about a week before I was admitted to his office. He looked vexed. Why didn't you come sooner? he asked. Of course, he had forgotten the contents of the essay. He said it was all right and dismissed me. Since he had penciled in a few suggestions for alterations and the manuscript was not intended to be a final one, I had to retype it in the remaining three weeks of the term, time I could ill afford to spare. My impression of the English graduate faculty at that time is that they were more concerned with publications to buttress their reputations than with educating the next generation of scholars. Gene and I passed the dreaded exam, however, and won our degrees in the spring of 1926.

The New York of the twenties, before drugs and muggings, was an exciting place to be. Late at night, when I could study no more, I used to walk down Broadway or on Riverside Drive wondering about people's lives in the tall apartment houses. It was a productive time in the theater. When houses were not sold out, blocks of tickets were sent to Furnald Hall and made available at discounts to graduate students. In this way I saw a few revivals and new plays. I recall especially my excitement over Eugene O'Neill's *Desire Under the Elms*, a new kind of theater for America. Also affordable were standee tickets to the top balcony (wasn't it called Nigger Heaven in those racially insouciant days?) of the Metropolitan Opera in its old location.

But a new love affair was the principal excitement of my year in New York. In her letters Mary had been urging me to meet her older sister, Helen, who was working in the cosmetics department of Lord and Taylor on Fifth Avenue. She was living close to the Columbia campus in a single room of a widow's apartment. Subletting to students was a common practice on Morningside Heights.

I remembered Helen from passages in the halls at Drake. She was a senior while Mary and I were sophomores. She had been conspicuous with her mop of red hair, her escort (often more than one) of boyfriends, her gaiety and liveliness. For weeks I hesitated, wondering whether a graduate student deep in books was up to all that animation. But now, according to Mary, Helen was lonely in the big city and would enjoy meeting someone from back home.

It was early spring before I got around to phoning Helen. New York springs are seductive and so was Helen. We met once or twice a week for the next two months, often spending the evening in her small room or walking and sitting on park benches in Riverside Park across from the blinking Mazola sign on the Jersey shore. On a few occasions I met her at the employee door at Lord and Taylor's as she emerged from work, and we had dinner downtown. Mostly we talked. Helen was very articulate. Once again I fell under the spell of an older girl, whose thoughts and feelings were a new book to read, a new world to explore. I too was replete with new experience. Amidst talk and kisses we fell in love.

Meanwhile Steve Slaughter interested me in joining him on a cattle boat from Montreal to Liverpool. He wanted to spend the summer in Germany learning the language. Passage was said to be free both ways for those who tended cattle on the outgoing voyage. This proposal appealed to me as an opportunity to visit the Thomas Hardy country and the Lake District of Wordsworth, two current literary enthusiasms. I had a little money left over from my fellowship and prior savings, about $400. In those days the dollar was worth several times what it is now and, I thought, there would be no boat fare to pay. So I signed up with Steve for the cattle crew on a boat transporting five hundred Angus steers to Liverpool in those days before refrigerated freighters, when slaughtering took place at the country of destination rather than source.

We left New York at the end of the term, about May 20, on the Delaware and Hudson line along the eastern fringe of the Adirondacks, our first sight of a region that was to mean much to both of us in later years. After boarding our ship, we were segregated from the regular crew in the bowels of the prow, a dark, badly ventilated hole where thin mattress pads were stretched over narrow boards to serve as bunks. A sharp class distinction existed between the cattle crew and the regulars. We got the worst of everything in quarters and board. A regular diet of cabbage stew was unpalatable to most of us till we had carefully extracted the angleworms. We all lost weight on that voyage, what with the unappetizing food and seasickness.

The cattle crew was a mixed bag of thirteen or fourteen men from various parts of Canada and the United States. One was an itinerant preacher from the Northwest Territories who insisted on leading us in prayer and Sunday services as we sprawled on bales of hay on deck. This uplift was overbalanced by vociferous profanity in a mixture of dialects in that age before radio and TV had homogenized vernaculars. Some of the talk was unintelligible to Steve and me but fascinating. It was our first contact with the raw natural man.

Days were long on the cattle boat. We were roused at four in the morning to feed the cattle for two hours before breakfast; we fed them again in the last half of the afternoon. The rest of the day was passed in gazing out to sea for schools of whales or porpoises and in lazy talk. We were three days on the broadening St. Lawrence as shores passed from sight. We finally rounded Newfoundland into the open sea. As we hit ocean swells the cattle crew began to drop off one by one till, at mid ocean, only four of us were left to do all the work of feeding and of cleaning up after sick steers with watery eyes and drooling jaws. Steve was one of the worst sufferers, now prone on a stack of hay daylong. I was spared—if that is the right word. We four worked like demons the last half of the trip. Now I understand why fourteen men were signed on to do the work of a dwindling number of survivors. Steve had grown up on a Missouri farm, working in the hay field, tending cattle, while I, the city boy, was the one who had to do his and my own share of the work tending those woeful Angus steers. It is a one-upmanship that in later years I've made the most of.

In spite of the casualties among the cattle crew, the regulars pronounced it an easy trip with a good tail wind most of the way. We sighted land early one morning as we rounded the green fields of northern Ireland, entered the Irish Sea, and finally in early evening docked at a Liverpool wharf. The voyage had taken ten days, less than average time for that ship, so there was an excess of feed left over. We were not released till we had unloaded leftover bales, backbreaking work. Finally, about midnight, Steve and I left ship to look for a hotel near the harbor. The first person to greet us on English soil was a prostitute covering the wharfs. "Do you want a woman for the night, boys?" A warm welcome in a foreign land, but in our present condition all we wanted was a bed with springs and mattress and no woman in it.

The next morning, a Sunday, I left our hotel room while Steve was still sleeping to look for a restaurant. To my amazement, all restaurants were closed. It was only after I had returned to inform Steve that we would have to do without breakfast that I learned of the good British custom of bed and breakfast on the premises, an amenity now spread to most civilized lands. Our breakfast in the hotel was a substantial one too.

Before leaving ship we had been warned of a two-week deadline for free passage back to Montreal. This was new, alarming news. Now that we were here we didn't want to leave in two weeks. We would have to economize if we were to pay return passage on a liner.

After a day in the drab industrial city of Liverpool long before the Beatles enlivened it, Steve and I parted, he for Germany, I for a tour of England. It was the summer of the general strike in England. The trains were not running, at least on regular schedules. Even if they had been, I would have chosen, for economy's sake, self-propelled travel. I bought a good secondhand bicycle and headed north for a literary pilgrimage in the Lake District, the sites of Wordsworth's poems and his homes in Grasmere and Rydal Mount. I ascended Skiddaw, highest peak in the Lake District. The climb was less arduous than struggling to understand the dialect of two Scottish ladies with whom I was marooned in a pension in Grasmere for two days of continuous rain.

Descending from the mountains, I made my longest one-day trip of ninety miles to Preston, an even drabber city of red brick row houses and industrial filth than Liverpool. In early morning in my hotel room I was wakened by the clatter of wooden clogs on cobblestones as laborers went to work.

I learned to avoid the industrial towns. Chester and north Wales were redolent of a more gracious and picturesque past. Then on to Litchfield, Dr. Johnson's birthplace, to Stratford, and Oxford. I intended to bike into London, but within forty miles of the city traffic became so heavy and threatening that I turned aside. Much to my regret I have never visited London. I turned toward the rural country of the southwest and another literary pilgrimage to the sites of Hardy's novels, all of which I had recently read and annotated for my master's essay. The last three weeks of my tour were spent in the counties of Wilts, Dorset, Devon, and Somerset. This was a country of sharp contrasts: Salisbury Cathedral and Stonehenge, austere heathlands and lush gardens in villages of winding lanes and thatch-roofed cottages. The dourness of Egdon Heath was offset by the voluptuous beauty of a girl clerk in a Dorchester bookshop, an incarnation of Eustacia Vye. But I had no pretext for approaching her other than to buy a book, and since Helen was still in New York and my funds running low, at the end of six weeks I went to Southampton, sold my bike, and booked third class passage with immigrants on a liner out of that port.

As I arrived in New York, Helen was about to quit her job at Lord and Taylor's and return to Des Moines for a visit to her family. I too had an urgent need for home since my funds were exhausted. I had to wire my father for a loan to cover rail fare to Des Moines and one other expenditure he would not have approved of if he had known. Helen and I decided to return together but to enjoy four more days in New York before doing so.

One evening we took the Hudson River excursion boat upstream and back at midnight to the 125th Street pier. There was an orchestra on board. We danced for hours. On the last night Helen, fully packed for the trip home, left her room on Morningside Heights, and we booked a room in a Broadway hotel. With shaky hand I signed the register "Mr. and Mrs." with a fabricated address in Syracuse. Would the clerk be suspicious? Even my apparent nervousness did not ruffle his aplomb.

It was a night of discovery. Though Helen set limits on our love making, there was much to discover for both of us—the heights of sensation reached by the entwined contact of two epiderms. For me, the night was an immersion in the world of the senses. For Helen, articulate as ever, a similar revelation.

On the train back to Des Moines, I spoke of marriage once I had got established. Her reply, which I was to hear several times over the next few months, was "I love you too much to marry you." This was a paradox not to be taken seriously, I felt. All I needed was time, a good job, and persistence. But I was wrong.

During Helen's vacation of about a month at home, we saw much of each other. Mary too was at home. One afternoon the three of us sat on a blanket in the backyard with cakes and soft drinks. The affectionate teasing and bickering between the two sisters was a charming thing to witness. Perhaps on Mary's part there was a little pique in it, now that Helen had appropriated a former lover, however expendable he was.

That summer Helen or Mary (to my chagrin I've forgotten which) finished a linoleum block she was making for me as a bookplate. I had given her the theme for a triptych, a quotation from some forgotten author (I cherished quotations in those days, jotting them down in a notebook now lost) about the tension in a scholar's life between ascetic and erotic impulses. I liked to fancy that I was experiencing such tension, but in reality oscillating between books and girls was very easy. Anyway, it was a lovely bookplate. At the left was a monk bent over his study desk; in the middle, crouched in an attitude of intense struggle, a male figure with one hand on a pile of books and the other shading his eyes from the vision on the right; on that right, a slender, naked girl, exquisitely carved, parting hair as long as Mélisande's with outstretched arms. My attachment to that plate began to wane as the theme came to seem overdramatic and as the two sisters receded into the past. Two years later a student made me another, a simple profile of my cucumber head, which gradually replaced Helen's or Mary's. How degrading it is not to remember which. I dug the plate out of an attic trunk to examine it, but the only name on it is mine, not the maker's.

As late as April of my year in New York I was uncertain about a vocation. Gene, my roommate, had signed up with a teacher's agency and, after an interview, had a job lined up in a northern New York college. About the first of May I received an offer from Drake of an instructorship in English. This seemed to point the way. One of the conditions, though not mandatory, of the Roberts fellowship was that the recipient should return to Iowa for at least two years. I felt I should honor this, though the salary offer of $1,300 was lower than the one promised Gene. I discovered later, in talking with colleagues who had begun teaching about the same time, that the range of $1,200 to $1,500 was standard in Midwestern institutions. Some fifty years later, following my retirement, institutions learned that they could get away with tuition increases twice the rate of inflation and hence establish a salary scale comparable to the disposable incomes in other professions. I accepted the Drake offer, *faute de mieux*, and most of the time I have not regretted this contingently determined vocation. My old ambition of a writing career had to be given up or deferred, for I lacked a subject I felt strongly enough and knew enough about to write well. Until those conditions could be met, a teaching job with a steady income was the reasonable choice.

As Helen left Des Moines for her next job in Chicago, we agreed to write and to see each other again during my Christmas vacation. I was fortunate during that first term not to have the distractions of a demanding love affair. Christine was always available, always compliant, never exigent, but she was not a distraction and accepted long intervals between dates without question. My schedule was the heavy one of those days: fifteen hours (seventeen in the following year) a week of class meetings and weekly themes to correct for over one hundred students.

## IV  IOWA AGAIN


I FACED THE BEGINNING of the fall term at Drake with dread. Would I be adequate? Would my old stage fright return to hobble me? And so it has been at the start of almost every academic year. But nervousness soon wore off, and my lifelong shyness before audiences has hampered me in the familiar milieu of the classroom just to the extent of inhibiting the histrionics of some popular professors. I have never been a character about whom students gossip in the halls. But I was competent, often enthusiastic, and over the years I learned how to hold students' attention.

As agreed in an exchange of letters with Helen, I left for Chicago a few days before Christmas for what was to be a week's reunion. Actually I saw her for only one evening after her day's work. Some love affairs just fade away. This came to a crashing end that one evening, all because of a random coincidence. The day of my arrival Helen had received from her former lover, a medical student at I believe Johns Hopkins, a telegram announcing that he was arriving the following day to spend the holiday season with her. She had not anticipated this. I learned now the nuances of her remark "I love you too much to marry you." I learned the primacy, the necessity, of the other man. I was to clear out at once, Helen insisted. And five hours of wrenching argument proved that she meant it. Neither before or since have I known such concentrated emotional turmoil as on that evening in Chicago, and the days and weeks that followed brought little relief from the ache of lost love and the sense of my weakness in yielding to dismissal.

There was a brief sequel. In the following spring Helen phoned me one night at two in the morning. She was now in Des Moines. In a voice of desperation she said that her medic had found some of my letters in her Chicago room and read them during her absence. Now he threatened to confront me in my office that very day. "Deny everything," Helen said—words seared on my memory.

Trying to put myself in his place, I doubted that, on reflection, he would come. Having pried into personal correspondence without permission was a vulnerable stand from which to confront a rival. Some of my letters of the previous fall may not have distinguished between reality and fantasy. But if he should come, I was prepared to deny, truthfully, the worst he might have assumed from those ardent letters. Time, in the resilient age of the twenties, had healed my wounds; there was already another girl. Helen was receding into a grateful memory. If her future was at stake, as her call hinted, I would do as she wished. An interview with a jealous lover was not a pleasant prospect, but I remained in my office that day later than usual, till 5:30. He did not come.

Mary and Helen were fine girls. I do not blame them for the slight deception of withholding from me the extent to which each was committed to another man, nor for preferring that other to a college instructor with a salary of $1,300. Having grown up in a college professor's home, they were familiar with privations that three sisters (the oldest, whom I never knew, had married and left home) were constrained to endure. Mary's naval officer and Helen's physician had better prospects as providers than I, as well as having been first on the scene.

I have lost track of Mary, but have known something of Helen's future through occasional items about her husband in the New York *Times*. He became a prominent physician in New York City, for many years the health commissioner. His lengthy obituary appeared a few years ago. He had traveled extensively in Europe. Presumably Helen had accompanied him. They had two sons. His death occurred at age eighty-four; Helen had predeceased him by two years. From these facts I reconstructed a good life for her with ample means, a role in the art and social life of the city, foreign travel, and the raising of two devoted sons. I hope it was that way with her.

Early in the spring term of 1927 Professor Smith and his daughter, Marjorie, approached me with a novel proposal. Marjorie was then governess to three girls living alone in a big house on a Des Moines boulevard settled by the old wealth of the city. Their parents were living in Chicago. Marjorie thought that the girls were ready for a little discreet male companionship. Her suggestion, supported by Professor Smith, was that I should select two personable young men from my freshman English classes and ask them to accompany me some night for an introduction to the three girls and an evening of dancing in the ballroom of their house. Marjorie would be the chaperone. I would join her as such and also be an opposite to one of the girls.

Marjorie gave me a briefing on the history of the family, and I found out more later. The father was a retired rear or vice admiral in the Navy. The mother was a Chicago sculptor, considerably younger than he, who had been his mistress before his divorce from a first wife. The two older girls were born out of wedlock. There had been a messy scandal in puritanical Des Moines. In consequence the three daughters had never attended public schools. They had received spotty education from a succession of governesses in the Des Moines home while most of the time their parents lived in Chicago. The father and two associates were engaged in planning a Chicago skyscraper, and the wife had her studio there. These facts had an irresistible appeal to my imagination: three Mirandas marooned in the city on a desert isle of scandal.

Reality seldom matches the absoluteness of imagination. The first setback came when I surveyed my freshman classes and found no candidates worthy of the occasion. (If it had been the following year, a bonanza one in male students, I would have had no problem.) But then there was something wrong with every boy in those classes. The choice I finally made rested mostly on the quality of the themes I had received. I knew that writing ability did not preclude social gaucherie. But at least my two choices came to class shaved, clean, and good mannered. They were not handsome but certainly not repulsive in appearance. My doubts revived, however, when neither of them showed much enthusiasm over the situation as I explained it. I feared that they were clods without imagination. They had not read *The Tempest*, and neither Mirandas nor scandal had much appeal for them. But they did turn up. As their instructor I had some hold over them.

The large size of the house and its furnishings overawed at least one of the freshmen and impressed me. There was wealth here. The girls were excessively shy. Conversation did not flow. Only one girl, the middle in age, showed any responsiveness. To liven things up, Marjorie led us all into the ballroom and put some music on the victrola. We exchanged partners. The youngest of the sisters, Betty, aged fifteen, was taller than either of the two freshmen, awkward, and brittle. The oldest, Adele, twenty, was short, plain, and tense in the arms of partners. The middle one, Sarah-Katherine, eighteen, was not only a yielding, light-footed dancer, though shy, but had a figure and face to set me dreaming.

Gladly I would have danced with Sarah-Katherine all evening. But since I had drafted my freshmen for an evening of doubtful success, I felt obliged to sacrifice her to them. So I danced with the tall gangling one and the short plain one, trying to break them into compliance, while the two boys exchanged dances with Sarah-Katherine.

Clearly there was only one Miranda here. One evening of sacrifice was quite enough for me. Anyway, it wouldn't do to make rivals of the two boys for the one eligible girl. I was going to have to jettison the freshmen, even if it spoiled Marjorie's plans.

That is what I did. They did not complain; they asked no questions at the time. I think they were relieved to be out of it. But years later, while I was in Des Moines administering my father's estate, I met one of them in the offices of the Des Moines *Register and Tribune*, where he was city editor. With the brashness of a newspaperman he asked me point blank whether I had ever seen those girls after that one night. "A few times," I muttered, and let the matter drop.

Quite a few times. Evenings in the big house became more and more frequent as spring wore on. This was a new kind of love. Previously I had known only girls processed through college in the standard educational mill. Sarah-Katherine (Sieur-Katherine in the family after her little girl rendering of her name) was a child of nature, I felt. And I was a privileged character in literature, shifting modes from the classic simplicity of *Daphnis and Chloe* to the psychological romanticism of Bernardin de Saint-Pierre's *Paul et Virginie*. Sieur-Katherine seemed adaptable to either mode.

What do you do with a child of nature? If you are a young English instructor with a rage to educate, you write on the near blank slate letters that may never be expunged. I read aloud to the three girls passages from favorite authors. Marjorie absented herself from most of these literary evenings. The girls accepted passively whatever literary fare I chose. Occasionally I danced with each in turn in the ballroom. But this could not go on forever. My preference for Sieur-Katherine was plain enough to the others, and my desire to be alone with her overwhelming. We began to retire to the loveseat in the ballroom and, as spring advanced, to the back porch or the spacious lawn sloping down to one of Des Moines' two rivers. Often I walked the two miles from my house to theirs. Sieur-Katherine would meet me halfway, and we would walk on hand in hand.

I discovered the charms of naivety in this eighteen-year-old girl who had never known the presence of a young man in the Des Moines home. At first, in our private talks in the darkened ballroom, her responses were short and breathless, but soon timidity gave way to eagerness. Our talk became intimate and interspersed with kisses. Her naivety was an eloquent defense against liberties, but limited progression was unavoidable. I cupped a breast at first outside her blouse, then inside. Weeks later Sieur-Katherine herself took the next wordless step by dressing without a bra, which had no practical function anyway.

There were flaws in this idyll. I felt guilty about the two neglected girls. Adele did not seem to mind. To me she seemed the resigned spinster. But Betty had spirit. One evening she declared that she was going downtown and attempt a pickup. This horrified Adele, and Sieur-Katherine and I were able to dissuade her. Another interruption was the father's arrival for a week's visit to his daughters. He was an affable, self-possessed, handsome man in his upper fifties, master of his fate, captain of his soul. He brought the great world into that cloistral household. Things outside were just "tremendjous," a favorite adjective of his. The boom going on in that decade (it was still two years short of the fatal crash of 1929) was tremendjous, and so was the office building he was planning in Chicago. Our talk was mostly about neutral affairs, in which I followed him lamely, for at that time I was not a reader of newspapers. There was one item of a personal nature, however, that he pried out of me—my salary at Drake. Thirteen hundred dollars was obviously not on the tremendjous scale fitting to those times or to relinquishing the family's crown jewel. My admission must have played a part in my downfall.

I had returned from a New York vibrant with new movements in the arts and letters expecting to be awash in the dull and prosaic in my native city. Instead, in that extraordinary household I was caught up in a love affair with reverberations through the ages from classical to romantic times, at least in my imagination. Another revelation of that spring semester was a mission Professor Smith wished on me, though it had been expected of him. I was to read a long poem in blank verse that a city businessman had submitted and then visit the writer in his home for a criticism of the work. I read that poem in competent verse with growing astonishment and chagrin. It was a philosophical poem quite above my level of understanding, though I had waded through Kant's *Critique of Pure Reason* under Professor Martin. The only thing I was prepared to say with assurance was that, in the present state of enlightenment, I didn't think it publishable. Good as it was, it lacked the popular appeal and epigrammatic terseness of Pope's *Essay on Man* (the only poetic work I thought to compare it to) and would be beyond the comprehension of the common reader (myself). On visiting the address, I was ushered into a large room with a grand piano and walls lined with books. We talked for an hour or two. I felt distressingly young and inadequate. He quickly sounded my depths but tried to conceal his disappointment. In the course of our talk it transpired that he was a real estate agent. I had lightly assumed from reading *Babbitt* that all Midwestern real estate agents were philistines. Could this be Des Moines?

Sieur-Katherine's father had inspected me. It was now the mother's turn. I was invited to visit their ranch in Colorado in late June. They had left earlier by motor. Mother and daughters met my train in Glenwood Springs. They had brought bathing suits with them for a swim in the mineral-water pool in that town, and I was invited to join them before the drive of fifteen miles to the ranch. I had no swim suit with me (it was prior to the day of simple trunks for males) and had to rent an ill-fitting, flabby one at the bathhouse. Depleted after a demanding social and workaday first year of teaching, I weighed barely 120 pounds and cut a skinny, angular figure for the mother's inspection. Sieur-Katherine, on the other hand, was a vision in her snug-fitting one-piece suit, *jeune fille en fleur*. As I gazed at her rounded perfection, a resolve seized me, I must have this girl. There were no tempering afterthoughts, such as how acceptable I might be to the family and whether a child of nature would be a suitable lifelong mate in academic circles.

The ranch brought a reversal of roles. In Des Moines I had been the disturbing and commanding presence. Here, after many a summer's residence, the girls were the habitués inducting a novice into the ways of the country. Practiced equestrians, they introduced me to horseback riding. There were four good riding horses in the stables, just enough to go around. As I recovered from sore joints and learned to respond to the rhythms of varied gaits, we went farther afield on the bridle paths of the valley and up into the foothills. Occasionally we dismounted, tethered the horses, and rested on a wooded knoll. One such day I complained of an itching sensation in my armpit. Sieur-Katherine immediately took charge. "Let me see," and she looked under my arm. Spotting a wood tick, she ordered that we go at once to a doctor. So we all mounted and rode to the office of the local doctor. He extracted the tick and congratulated me on the early discovery before possible infection set in.

In all innocence, proud of their prompt action in the affair of the tick, the girls told this story to their mother. Her reaction was unexpected. She scolded Sieur-Katherine for the indelicacy of looking under a man's arm. There were to be no more such familiarities. She ordered Adele and Betty to constitute a vigilance committee and accompany Sieur-Katherine and me at all times. Our corner of the ballroom in Des Moines was liberty itself compared to the prison that now closed about us in the vast open spaces of ranchland.

During my second week at the ranch a new guest arrived, a bachelor cousin of about thirty. He was my enemy from the start. I sensed that he was plotting with the mother to keep Sieur-Katherine under vigilance. Snatching moments alone became harder than ever. Finally Sieur-Katherine devised a plan of desperation. The ranch house was a sprawling one-story building with a loft over one section. I occupied that loft, while all the others slept downstairs. The cousin's room was directly below mine. Sieur-Katherine proposed that she slip quietly upstairs to my room early in the morning, bringing the dog with her. If the cousin were awake and heard movement on the stairs, I could say that the dog was my early morning visitor. This plan seemed utterly rash to me. The stairs were of old, creaky wooden treads, I pointed out. Her cousin would hear two different sounds, the click of the dog's toenails and the creak of her heavier tread in slippered feet. Besides, the dog had never come up to my room; why now? And how was she to explain her absence to her sisters?

Attempts to dissuade her failed; maybe I didn't try hard enough. She came with the dog. The clickings and creakings were quite audible to anyone who happened to be awake. We had little solace from the escapade: for me, a momentary thrill at the image of this girl in her nightgown, for both an anxiety-ridden ten minutes of closeness as we lay side by side, whispering faintly in each other's ear. Then she withdrew with the dog. I heard her on the stairs. The cousin heard. That morning he asked me about the commotion. "The dog," I replied as coached. He looked disbelief.

The consequences were soon apparent. The atmosphere in the ranch house turned chilly, talk over the dinner table strained. I realized that my welcome was up. To put a good face on things, I said I must leave on the morrow in order to prepare for a new course in the fall. As we parted at the railway station, I mustered all my politeness to thank the mother for a wonderful two weeks, knowing all the time that I had failed inspection by her.

I saw Sieur-Katherine only once after that. The family stayed at the ranch late into the fall, the date repeatedly postponed. This, I concluded afterwards, was to give the mother time for a cure. I wrote regularly once or twice a week to Sieur-Katherine, but the intervals between her ever briefer replies grew longer and the tone colder. They finally returned to Des Moines in late October. I was called to the house for an orchestrated finale. The mother remained in her room upstairs, and the three girls received me, not now as they once had. Sieur-Katherine said that she could not see me again. I begged to be alone with her, but the sisters, as instructed, would not budge. Sieur-Katherine offered to return my letters, this too as she had no doubt been instructed. I refused to accept them. Burn them, if you will, I said, hoping, however, that she might keep them as a witness on my behalf.

I have often wondered what happened in that extraordinary family. The Chicago skyscraper, I believe, was scheduled for completion in 1930, shortly after the stock market crash and the beginning of the Great Depression, not a propitious time for the opening of an office building. Some years later when I was home from the East for a visit, Mother told me that Sieur-Katherine (or some other lost girlfriend?) had called and asked for me. By that time I was married or about to be. I had almost forgotten the image of the girl by the poolside in Glenwood Springs and the nightgowned girl in the ranch-house loft. Is it a defect in life or a blessing that persons and things that have meant so much to us come in time to mean so little? So little till now, sixty-three years later, as I write these memoirs or listen to an intensely emotional opera, such as *Eugen Onegin*, about a failed love affair.

My teaching career spans thirty-nine years from 1926 to 1965. Eight of those years were leaves of absence: one for study and travel abroad, three for graduate study toward the doctorate, three for service in the U.S. Army in World War II, and one to complete work on a book. My second, and last, year at Drake was in hindsight the most stimulating of all. I had a salary increase of three hundred dollars, generous in those days. And Professor Smith offered me, in addition to freshman and sophomore courses, a course for upperclassmen in Comparative American Literature. He proposed that we collaborate on a textbook in that field. While teaching, I would gather material for the book. Finding parallels between American and foreign texts and noting cultural differences were an absorbing venture. Nothing came of the textbook because I left Drake at the end of the school year, but that course was of interest to me and I think to my students. We groped our way together.

Another stimulus came from five outstanding freshman men, who banded to-gether in a clique I called the Ardent Sons. Never since have I had such a congeries of talent and enthusiasm in a single year, especially of male students. At St. Lawrence the better students, in literature courses, were more often girls, whom I had little contact with outside of class. With the Ardents I lunched in the campus vicinity and exchanged visits at their homes and mine (four lived with their families in the city). Only seven years older than the youngest of the group, I still had enough youth in me to join in their verbal high jinks, though the fast pace often left me trailing.

Blithe Andrew Stewart (Stewie), full of high spirits, was the star punster. He had drawing talent and entertained us with cartoons. He made my second linoleum-block bookplate. James Duncan was the only country boy of the group, from Clearfield, Iowa. He was the quietest and I think a little humble in the fast company of city boys, but perhaps the most appreciative of acceptance by the group and opportunities at Drake. In a letter over a year later he wrote from Clearfield: "I ran into an article written by my grandfather. It was in a prose worthy of Melville. And this from an old farmer who never was in a schoolhouse. And it is I, two generations later, with less than no genuine ability, who am exposed to the magnificent succor of books and the right kind of friends." Jim was a better writer than he thought. He eventually became professor of journalism at Drake.

Hugh Duncan (Hughie) was the Gargantuan wit, outsized in both body and zest. His talk was concrete and vivid. But when he wrote he became a different person, reaching for nebulous heights of abstraction. I urged him to write as he talked, but this seemed impossible for him. The book he eventually published showed that he never outgrew this habit. He was a voracious student, however. At the beginning of his junior year, when he decided to stay at Drake instead of transferring to Northwestern, he wrote to me, "We know now what we want. Drake doesn't have all of it, but we're going to take all we can get."

The more serious Ardents were Webster Peterson (Petie) and Donald Campbell (Nod). They were the best writers. I looked forward to reading their themes each week. In his sophomore year Nod fell in love and began to write love poems, which he quoted in letters to me. In his junior year he left Drake to transfer to Harvard. At first he was disappointed with the change. But a few months later he wrote, "One leaves here and never ceases talking about the place, simply because nothing one finds later in life absorbs the whole body, mind, and spirit. I mean, not unless it can be created from within."

The Ardents tried to promote an affair between their French teacher, Ruth Jane Kirby, and me. But during the whole of that year I was too much preoccupied with shaping a new course and with the Ardents themselves to consider further involvements. Instead, I fell back on an old, undemanding girlfriend, dating Christine at wide intervals.

I corresponded with the Ardents through 1930. One of the letters I have kept was composed by all five of them, each typing a separate paragraph or two and challenging me to determine which was which. Aside from reading a book by Hugh Duncan, I didn't have further contacts until 1959, when I received the following letter from St. Paul, Minnesota, from Petie:

May 5, 1959

Dear Ruth Jane and Paul:

I think I have adequate excuse for a little sentimentality, for addressing you by your first names, and for reminding you of someone left over from the twenties. In the course of trying to induce my daughter to choose college instead of a job or marriage to a hot-rodder (she has tentatively chosen college on condition I make it a good one in California) I reassured her on the happiness of college days, and recalled that my first few weeks in college were the most miserable of my life, but were soon followed by several months that were the happiest.

Reflecting on my own words, I grew very sentimental over the fact that I had lost touch with the people who brought me that happiness, and even with the man who furnished the first start toward it. Also, I realized that I had never gotten around to expressing to any of them what I owed to them.

And that though I read *Hydriotaphia* at least once a year, and never without a glow, remembering the thrill I got when Paul rolled off "And now since these dead bones," etc. and explained that these words were in the rhythm of clods dropping onto the coffin. (I can still quote the passage from memory, down to *"Sic ego componi versus in ossa velim."*)

So I went over to the Hill Reference Library and found you both in the *Dictionary of American Scholars*, and I write in confidence that professors don't change their addresses much oftener than legal writers.

I told Mary that in case of a choice, she should try to get a younger professor (who might have a little more enthusiasm, I hastened to explain when she grinned). I was thinking of Paul when I spoke, and of Max Edwards when she grinned. But afterward I wondered whether I might not have been dead wrong in my advice. I thought of some of the younger specimens I have come in contact with, and their Eliot-Richards brand of neo-classicism, neo-orthodoxy and neo-pedantry, and I thought that there was a good chance that Paul has been able to keep the spark going despite thirty years of a drizzle of adolescents.

Which is worse, the unenthusiastic majority of students or the enthusiastic minority who never seem to accomplish anything with their enthusiasm? But I may be talking through my hat; you both had better senses of humor than I, and perhaps it hasn't bothered you, though the fear of it was one of the things that kept me out of teaching.

Anyhow, I certainly wish I could send Mary east, instead of west. To take English under Paul and French under Ruth Jane would be enough college education for anyone.

But education and college aside, I'm getting old enough now to realize what just kindness, to any kid, means. And as I mentioned above, I never got around to telling what that meant to me. The extra time spent, the encouragement, the milk and grapes in Paul's backyard, the letters and the book (which I still prize) from Europe, the restraint when my father blew his top and caused trouble—not wasted, I hope.

Even intellectually, your efforts may not have been entirely wasted. I deliberately renounced literary ambition many years ago, but have lately resumed a little writing just to get things off my chest, dull and didactic but with a little room for artistic quality. Meanwhile, I have turned out plenty of printed words; and if you will accept for your own purposes, as showing your teaching wasn't wasted, the consolation I have devised for myself, you are welcome: my work does require a little imagination and skill, it is about the best of its kind, and it will have more permanence than 99.9% of the more ambitious things that get printed. It is a safe bet that my writings will be read with interest, and be of value, a hundred years from now.

But you may not even have heard what my work is, or much about me. The short and simple annals of the poor, then: studied law for lack of anything better in the depth of the depression; disliked practice of law and came to West Publishing Co., the country's leading lawbook publishers, in 1937; married '38, divorced '53; two daughters: Karin, 21, mentally defective, and Mary, 17, in high school, beautiful blonde, interested in art and boys.

My parents are in Oklahoma City; did you know that my father got over his prejudices which caused him to raise hell with Morehouse, to the point that he actually quoted the horrid Walt Whitman freely and approvingly in his novel *Trumpets West*? (This novel was praised by Rascoe and even by Malraux, who himself sought an interview with my father; but the publisher went broke immediately after publication and it never got anywhere.) My younger brother Edwin is a leading psychiatrist, clinical director of Washington State Hospital; my youngest brother Erik, born during my first week at Drake, is a chemical engineer for Northrop Aviation, active in the satellite and missile business.

I kept contact with most of the Ardent Sons to some extent, up to a few years ago, and will try to re-establish contact. My last contact with Hugh Duncan was about '53, just after his book (*Language and Literature in Society*, University of Chicago Press) was published. I visited him in his beautiful modern home in Flossmoor. He had given up teaching in disgust (at the racketeering in the profession, not the kids) and had developed a very sensible combination of writing and free-lancing in the real estate business. He was nuts over architecture and Kenneth Burke, and not at all enthusiastic over auld lang syne. His book was pretty good; but it was supposed to be sociology, and if that's sociology, so is *Tristram Shandy*.

Jim Duncan survived the navy, tried teaching at the University of Alabama, couldn't stand the Southern atmosphere including the miasma of race tension; returned to Des Moines and got into radio and television, including a Drake job. Lost touch with him in the '50s.

Don Campbell was editor of the Mexican-American Chamber of Commerce magazine, then on the embassy staff, then in 1955 founded a school of business administration using the new Harvard case-method system. The last I heard from him, in '56, he reported success in this venture. He transferred his "ardency" to the Quaker religion, but his son and daughter Tonio and Clara are apparently Catholics. My friendship with him retained more warmth in the long run, though I had been more congenial with the others before; I was more like him in being fundamentally serious-minded, than I had admitted to myself.

Which gives me the note to close on. I do feel serious-minded and sentimental now. As I have indicated, comparing my daughter at 17 and myself at 17 when I met you, and hoping that she will somehow get something of the sort I got from you, and fearing that the chances are poor. The personal kindness, and despite the withering of Cabell, Machen, Mencken et al., the real intellectual value. We sneered unjustly at the L. W. Smith school and its excursions in Arcady; the social-conscience boys of the '30s sneered unjustly at us; now they are being sneered at themselves, also quite unjustly. But there is a continuum underneath all these changes of fad, and you put us in touch with it, as I'll bet you are still doing with the kids of the '50s.

Belated thanks and best wishes.   Petie


The trouble Petie refers to as caused by his father led to my resignation from Drake. I had intended earlier to go abroad for a year, but had kept open the option of applying for a leave without pay. Late in the spring semester Peterson senior intervened to convince me that a teaching career at Drake would go against the grain.

Anatole France was a popular novelist worldwide in the twenties. Early in the decade he had received the Nobel prize in literature. My introduction to him was in a course in the modern novel in which we read the innocuous early work *The Crime of Sylvestre Bonnard*. Professor Smith warned me against reading the novels of France's old age. Of course, I went to the Drake library to look for them. They were not there. I began to buy them for my own collection. Their spirit was congenial to young men growing up in the twenties; one of freethinking, skepticism toward established institutions, and pleasure-seeking characters unhampered by puritanical inhibitions. Petie had read *Penguin Island.* I lent him my copy of *The Revolt of the Angels.* His father read it too and, as Petie says, blew his top. He took his outrage to Morehouse, then president of Drake.

I have long since outgrown my taste for Anatole France. So too has nearly everyone else, except maybe for that gem of a short story, "The Procurator of Judea." To refresh my hazy memory of *The Revolt,* I have just now skimmed through it. There are the usual scenes of adultery, *de rigueur* in the later novels; the scoffing at the established church, the parade of esoteric learning, the bland irony. It is not a good novel. The characters are stock figures, the thought superficial, the narration halting, and the symbolism explicit rather than suggestive. What I was in the twenties, bound up with my old enthusiasm for this book, now seemed just one of those dead selves that we scatter behind us on the march to the body's death. Petie speaks of a continuum. Maybe so.

President Morehouse summoned me to his office. He was no longer the inspiring professor of astronomy I had known as an undergraduate but the administrator apprehensive about public relations. He enjoined me to be cautious about lending or recommending books to students. And he directed me to call on the senior Peterson in a downtown office and try to mitigate the damage. He may have counted on my innocent looks.

I did as ordered but resented it. If the father had a complaint, he could visit me in my office, I felt. At that time Peterson was the editor of the magazine *Better Homes and Gardens,* published in Des Moines, a suitable location for a magazine flattering bourgeois complacency. I have forgotten most of our conversation. I remember that he was courteous, not accusatory, but firm in the conviction that *The Revolt* was not a suitable book to put before the young. He underestimated the good sense of his son. He seemed to me the embodiment of what H. L. Mencken was saying at that time in denigration of the Midwest—its fundamentalism and its suspicion of anything new in arts and letters.

Even my classroom turned suddenly uncongenial in those last days of the term. It was in a new building, the Bible College, with available space for the overflow of other colleges. All the furnishings were brand new and shiny; carvings on the armchairs were few or missing; there was no scholarly patina in that room. And on the walls were posters of winged angels. I don't know what they were doing there in that stronghold of the Disciples of Christ. Perhaps some irregular theologian with idolatrous leanings toward Rome had put them up. (The Ardent Sons quipped that during my tenure of that room the angels had lost their virginity.) I wanted out. If I was going to teach, I wanted it to be in a liberal atmosphere where books in the college library were not censored and there was no interference from parents and administrators. By sheer luck I found such a place.

## V  EUROPHILIA—MUNICH AND PARIS

WHILE LIVING ABSTEMIOUSLY at home from the summer of 1926 to June of 1928, I saved half of my two-year salary, enough, I thought, to finance a year abroad. The course in Comparative American Literature had stimulated my interest in foreign literatures, which I wanted to pursue. I had taken French for two years but no German. Before leaving I equipped myself with a German grammar and dictionary and enrolled by correspondence in a summer class for foreigners in the German language at the University of Munich. In early June I sailed from New York on the Holland-America line.

My memories of that year abroad are assisted in part by an intermittent diary I kept. There are gaps in it of as much as two months, so that while parts are more fully documented than I could wish, exposing the jejune observations of an American innocent abroad, other parts with no diary entries are hazy in memory. This being so, I take the liberty of being selective, writing only of what still interests me and seems part of that continuum, which Petie refers to, of self-education, and not just another dead self.

The first five or six weeks on the Continent, with no diary entries, are largely irreclaimable. Only a few strong impressions stand out in memory: the satisfying foreignness of the windmills and dikes of Holland on the approach to the port of Rotterdam; the art museums of The Hague and Amsterdam, with their wealth of Rembrandts and other Dutch artists; the canals of Amsterdam and Delft; an overflight of Holland, my first in commercial aircraft; in Germany the aspiring Cologne cathedral; castles on the Rhine; the medieval towns of Rothenburg, Dinkelsbuhl, and Nuremberg; a Bach concert in Stuttgart, at which an American concert pianist, Guy Maier, in the seat next to me, invited me on a certain date to an evening party for his German students at his villa in Munich, where he spent the summers teaching piano. I attended that party. Much beer flowed from a cask and much music from twin grand pianos played by the host, his wife, and the German students. The little English of the students and my little German hampered conversation, but the music was glorious, and the beer, well, it was Münchener.

I loved Munich from the start. My first diary entry is dated July 24, 1928; this was already one or two weeks after the beginning of the summer course for foreigners. I had attended several classes for a large number of enrollees, about eighty or ninety. We all met together for a short lecture and then give and take between the witty professor and the no less witty, it seemed to me, students, most of whom had had two or more years of college German. Their glibness with the language intimidated me. I dreaded being called on from the roll the professor held lest I be at want for words and wit. So in that first entry I note that I'm dropping out of that class and studying German on my own from books. That is what I did over the next five weeks, starting with the simple German of Grimms' fairy tales and proceeding to Schlegel's *Lucinde*, Novalis, Heine, Goethe, and later in Paris, Nietzsche. What I wanted mainly was a reading knowledge, and that is what I got in those weeks in Munich and the following fall in Paris. My ear for foreign languages has never been good, but I have progressed far enough in German and French readings to acquire a sense of the spirit of those languages and of individual authors, so that the original texts yield a richer experience than the translations.

Many of us foreign students lived in a dormitory, some distance from the University, called the Hansaheime. Meals were served there, at which in theory German was spoken. English and American students outnumbered other nationalities, however, and much of the time English was spoken. Some did try out their German in simple, declarative sentences but with fractured grammar and often a confusion of words. A droll Canadian named Anderson, whose reading knowledge of German was better than that of most of us, mocked the quality of our German by a deliberate confusion of words and imitation of our faulty phonetics. His mock serious manner and projectile enunciation often sent the table into spasms of laughter. Once he tried to make a Hungarian teacher of German understand his German for "psychoanalysis," and although she did not, he said with great assurance and satisfaction: "Sie *verstehen. Die Fräulein Doctor von Hungar* immer *versteht mish. Ish sehe es in ihre Ohren.*"

For me the Canadian became a kind of role model. He was several years older, probably in his mid thirties, had traveled much abroad, combined scholarship with an ability to entertain, and was, I felt, an internationalist, embracing Western cultures. Once when he passed an English student from Oxford and me, engaged in an argument over relativism and the moral imperative, Anderson corrected my quotation from Protagoras—a plural to a singular noun but significant in altering the sense. When the Canadian and I visited the Alte Pinakothek and I waxed enthusiastic over a Rubens, he said that he never praised a thing while looking at it. In that case, I said, he would make a poor lover. That was no part of his ambition, he rejoined. Just then I was inclined to agree. We were both enjoying the freedom of bachelorhood, he for a longer time than I. Love and its sequel marriage tie one down. He seemed enviable in his commitment to the single life. At another time he chided me for preferring Wagner to Mozart in the operas we were attending. I have retained my enthusiasm for Wagner but have come to understand his view of Mozart as the more civilized composer and to appreciate *Don Giovanni* as perhaps the greatest of all operas.

That summer there was a Wagner-Mozart Festspiele at the Prinz-Regenten Theater in Munich. It lasted about five weeks in late July and August, with some outstanding German singers such as Gertrude Kappel. The Wagner operas began at four and lasted till about 9:30. In the long intermission the audience wandered through the gardens of the theater and had dinner in the theater restaurant. It was an amiable way of accommodating the great length of the *Meistersinger, Tristan und Isolde,* and the *Walküre,* all of which I attended along with two Mozart operas. It was in the Prinz-Regenten Theater that my love of opera began. I had seen two or three productions at the old Metropolitan in New York, but it was the concentration of witnessing five operas within one month, performed in a smaller and more intimate theater and preceded by the reading of the librettos, which confirmed that love. I understand what Wagner himself said about *Tristan*: "It is and remains to me a miracle. It will always be incomprehensible to me how I could make such a thing." Creators like Wagner, whatever his failings as a social being, and Goethe and Rubens have something godlike about them. The conviction grew on me during my year abroad that what counts most in the sum of human achievement is masterworks of the arts and letters. And Europe was the progenitor of most of them.

We residents of the Hansaheime enjoyed also the pop culture of Munich. We went to variety shows and to two immense beer gardens, the Hofbräuhaus and the Löwenbrauerie, where fat Germans guzzled in cellar, terrace, hall, and gardens in time to music. Particularly glorified sots in the *keller* sang beery songs in which we tried to join.

Adjacent to the Hansaheime was a large park bordered by the Isar River and called the English Gardens, apparently after the English fashion of natural gardens started in the late eighteenth century, when some gardeners went so far as to plant dead trees in imitation of nature. Munich did not go that far, but it did eschew here the formal, geometric designs of the French tradition. I enjoyed walking there in the evening, sometimes with Fräulein "Nil," an English expatriate who lived in Rome (she got her nickname by refusing to speak German at table). One weekend, as a special treat, an excursion to the Bavarian Alps was arranged. I left the crowd at a guesthouse on the Eibsee and wandered alone around the emerald lake overlooking the white comb of Zugspitz, highest peak in the range.

Diary, Aug. 26, Sunday: I am sad this evening, whether from leaving Munich tomorrow or just having seen Ibsen's *Ghosts*. The latter was a typical German performance rendered with naturalness in parts, with fire and demonstrativeness in others—strong contrasting effects. The ending was overdone, as if the audience must be left with no lingering doubts of Oswald's madness and Frau Alvin's dilemma. Oswald utters *"Sonne, Sonne"* an unconscionable number of times, and his mother goes into hysterics. All this is much like a German critic's suggested "improvement" on Landor's "Rose Aylmer":

A *year* of memories and of sighs
I consecrate to thee.

Goodbye to princely München. One more walk in the park by moonlight.

Aug. 27, Monday: Augsburg. I feel I've found the heart of Germany here. The town is beautiful in typical ways. Many old medieval buildings are still standing among stately modern ones. Narrow, winding *Gasses*, faced with medieval fronts, give way to handsome boulevards. The fountains are numerous and exquisite, in rococo style. There must be fifteen or more, all playing. The figures are delicately carved and have a rich variety. A spring issues from the mouth of a nymph, the hair of another who is wringing it, from a jug by which a third is washing her feet, and from the breasts of several others. Other streams issue from a serpent's head held by a nymph and from the mouths of swans held by cupids.

Aug. 29, Wednesday: I left Ulm this morning and discovered that an eight-hour, fourth-class train journey can be pleasant. Most of the way I had an entire compartment to myself. The train passed through the valley of the Danube. High wooded hills alternated with sheer limestone cliffs, on the crests of which stood castles. This Germany, the picturesque country and towns, and the *Geist* of the people suit me well. Tonight I am enjoying the luxury of hot water from the tap in my spacious room overlooking Titisee in the Black Forest.

After a stop in Strasbourg, I reached Paris on September 3, where I was to spend the next four and a half months. Paris is seductive in September and October before the rains set in. Sunny, mild days succeed one another as if the fine weather would never end. I spent two nights at the Pension Parisiana, Rue Tournefort on the Left Bank, long enough to make the acquaintance of an American girl, whom I later had trouble shaking. She helped me move to the Pension des Grandes Écoles on Rue Cardinal-Lemoine, where all the rooms of two floors opened on a quiet, beautiful garden court. Today it is hard to conceive of the modest costs of those days of the 1920s in Paris, when the dollar exchanged for twenty-five francs. Those nearly ideal living quarters in the Grandes Écoles, including breakfast and lunch, came to just under forty dollars a month. No wonder Paris was then the haven of American expatriates. Hemingway, Fitzgerald, Gertrude Stein and others who later achieved fame were also there in 1928. I must have brushed elbows with some of

[ **41** ]

them at their favorite bistros. Simone de Beauvoir, then in her last year at the Sorbonne, may have attended some of the lectures I did that fall, and Sartre was at the École Normale Supérieure, but I was unaware of them. It was an exciting time to be in Paris.

I began to explore on foot that inexhaustible city. The Seine divides two cities, one smelling of fish, the other of perfume and petroleum; the Left Bank of the students, artists, intellectuals, and the old aristocracy; the Right Bank, of the bourgeoisie and new aristocracy. I spent many hours browsing along the book stalls of the Seine and in the book shops of the Left Bank. Paperback books sold for a fraction of a dollar, and craftsmen in small book binderies would bind them artfully for a dollar or less. Used classics in bindings, some of them annotated by former students at the Sorbonne, like my copy of Montaigne's *Essays*, were available at bargain prices. For me Paris was a city of books. I bought enough to require the purchase of a large trunk to ship them home in. Having worked in a bindery, I felt I had some original ideas about bindings and gave special instructions to workmen in two small binderies. Among these were gifts for the Ardent Sons, according to their choices of French or German classics. Another was Joyce's *Ulysses*, for Stewie, still banned in the United States and available only in the Paris edition. I had to conceal it carefully in the bottom of the trunk to get through customs in New York.

Although the fall term at the Sorbonne was not to begin for about six weeks after my arrival in Paris, there were a few foreign students in my pension. A talk with a German student from Heidelberg is more significant to me now, in the light of subsequent history, than it was then. He spoke of the German creative spirit as something perpetually becoming, always in the making, and pointed to *Faust* as an incomplete artistic form, deliberately unfinished in order to suggest future becoming. This incompleteness contrasts with the French love of pure form, even at the expense of content. The well-bred Frenchman shows this love of form even in his conversation, which is rounded, urbane, and formal but devoid of ideas. The well-bred German, on the other hand, is likely to be formless in his conversation but fertile in suggestion and ideas. Germany is the creative, masculine country, France the feminine, conventional one. Germans do not read their classics much, Frenchmen cling to their Corneille, Racine, and Molière because of sheer delight in form. Germans are interested in the movement of ideas. Nietzsche is the most complete expression of the German spirit, with his strength, creative force, abundance, drive, and expansiveness. As a stylist he is often considered superior to Goethe in Germany. Practically all modern tendencies in that country spring from him. Heine, whose poetry I liked, this German student assured me, is considered superficial in Germany. His Jewish mode of mixing romance and irony is contrary to the German spirit.

Then we got around to politics. Like most of his countrymen, he said, he considered America's entrance into the first World War, a struggle which was not hers, rather contemptible, motivated mostly for the protection of financial interests in France and England. Socialism was growing rapidly in popular favor in Germany. France is decadent. England is too except in politics. Germany is the forward-looking, creative country of Europe.

In the light of the subsequent rise of Hitler to power, the triumph of national socialism, the second World War, and the holocaust, it appears that this German student of 1928 had the makings of a storm trooper. *Deutschland über Alles.* But at the time I thought his remarks profound.

He soon left for Heidelberg, but I found a more lasting friend in Wong, a Chinese student, who was soon to enroll in the Sorbonne for the full academic year. I marveled at his command of English—the English of Oxford, where he had also studied. He said that his countrymen readily acquire European languages, as well as literary and historical knowledge of the West, because of their highly trained memories. All Chinese students are disciplined to memorize the dates and events of the long history of their country and cannot affirm that they know their literature until they know it by heart. It follows that seeing or hearing a foreign word once suffices for retention. Wong admitted that memory may be overdeveloped at the expense of originality. But then, what do the Chinese need with new thought? Everything is to choose from the long past. New combinations of the old make China's revolutions, inventions. An imperialism of culture has succeeded in binding together the vast provinces of China. The idea of progress in his country is to imbue all people with the best ideas and images of the best literature, a formulation that reminded me of Matthew Arnold's definition of culture, "the best that has been known and thought in the world." Wong spoke of the objectivity of Chinese poetry. Nature images mean the same thing to all because of literary associations, and thus a symbolic language has developed. The Chinese love of nature has none of the self-centered egotism of the romantic nature poetry of Europe, but is objective, homogeneous, and universal.

Wong's talk about his country gave me a sense of China as very old, very wise, and very weary. But there was nothing weary about Wong himself. He could talk with interest and intelligence about almost any subject. After studying in England and France, he intended to spend a summer in Italy and then a full year in Germany for an introduction to the best thought of Europe. Along with his grace of mind, earnestness, and objectivity, this added fire of learning, and living what he learned, made Wong one of the most vivid personalities I have ever met.

Another acquaintance of my early days in Paris was an American of about my age, Bent. He worked for an American firm with branches in Europe and had just been transferred from Oslo to Paris. Never having studied French, he was trying to get a speaking knowledge through contact with the night life of the streets. We met at a restaurant. The second evening I saw him there he was accompanied by a *fille de joie*, Lucie, whom he had told me about. He invited me to sit at their table. Lucie was a pretty girl and full of verve and spirit. As I learned later, she had come to Paris from the provinces, Normandy, and had slipped into the only employment she could find. She had fallen into a routine, rising at noon, combining breakfast and lunch at one, bathing in the Seine in the afternoon, dining at seven at the Source or the Aline, and then repairing to the Jockey on Montparnasse at 9:30, where she usually picked up her bedfellow for a rendezvous at 11:30. Bent offered to share her with me, but he had given me such a graphic account of the social diseases one might be exposed to with a freelance girl of the streets that he had succeeded in frightening me, if not himself. For the time being, I said, I would like to join them at dinner and thereby learn a little street French as antidote to the classics I was reading.

We met at dinner the next few nights. Lucie was temperamental, alternating between annoyance with us for failing to understand her patois and affection, real or professional. In her limited English she would say, "I love you, God damn, be nice to me." When I told her I wanted to learn French from her, she responded with verve: *"Moi, je suis professeur, n'est-ce pas? Voilà! Une leçon! Entendez."* So, as Bent was paying for her nightly services, I felt I should compensate her for dinner-hour lessons. When she pointed with a *moue* to her run-down shoes, I offered to buy a new pair. She accepted with alacrity. One evening she rated nationalities in their qualifications as lovers. Americans, she said with a wink at Bent, were pretty good, but the best were Persians. The dinners went on for about ten days. Just as I was beginning to fall under Lucie's spell and consider a shift to her night routine, Bent rushed into my room at the Grandes Écoles one afternoon and said, "Drop that girl. She's given me the clap." He had just come from the American Hospital. Sometimes the accidents of life work in our favor—just *my* favor in this instance.

As the fall term at the Sorbonne was about to begin in mid October, I moved from my pension to a nearby hotel on the same street, Rue Cardinal-Lemoine. The Grandes Écoles was solidly booked by student reservations. My room in the hotel was just thirteen francs a night, or fifty-two cents. It was a large room but sparsely furnished with a single chair, a desk, and a double bed. Central heating was minimal. As the nights grew colder, I wore my overcoat as I read French or German classics at the desk. But there was a hot plate on which to make tea when Wong visited, tea brewed according to his instructions and with a brand he recommended as the best to be found in Paris. As I described this mandarin tea ceremony to the Ardent Sons, they wrote back ribbing me for failing to take advantage of the bibulous opportunities still denied to them under Prohibition.

Another occasional visitor was a Boston girl named Elizabeth. After walking the streets or visiting the museums and other landmarks till we were both tired, we had tea in my room, one of us sitting on the bed for lack of an extra chair. Although there were opportunities, I never made a pass at Elizabeth. She was never Betty to me, or any of the contractions of her name—always Elizabeth. Tall, erect, almost beautiful, she had a patrician air that proclaimed *noli me tangere*. I obeyed this unspoken mandate, and she seemed to appreciate my restraint, for we continued to see each other until I left Paris for Italy in January. There was a month's interruption in our meetings during which she suffered from bronchitis, brought on perhaps by our damp November walks. During that month we corresponded by *pneumatique*, that Parisian facility that brought the whole city within an hour's reach until the telephone became ubiquitous. She was well taken care of during her sickness at the home of family friends on the Rue d'Assas, where I used to call for her. She had the advantage of family connections or relatives in France and Wales. The previous summer she had spent at a chateau on the Brittany coast with the French nobility for companions, and the friends she was living with in the city introduced her into Parisian society. During the Christmas holidays she left Paris briefly to stay with relatives in Wales on a country estate. On returning, she told me of fireworks, hunts, and hunting balls. She described a partridge hunt she had taken part in. In the woods along a cleared runway, the squires concealed themselves while servants worked toward the center of the clearing from the two ends, flailing the ground, making weird calls. The birds, avoiding flight, hustled along the ground until they reached the compressed center, where they were forced to take flight. The squires then called "Ovah" and fired with precise aim that seldom missed. The following night a hunters' ball was held that lasted till five in the morning, resurrecting the "merry England" of Shakespeare's time.

I did not have Elizabeth's social advantages, but she and I had in common the fascination Europe held for us. The Americans I met during that year in Europe fell across a broad spectrum, at one extreme of which were the complainers that no good ice cream, or other icon of American culture, could be found on the Continent. They wanted to get home as soon as possible. At the other extreme, where Elizabeth and I fitted in, were the potential expatriates, wanting to stay until the need to make a living forced them to return home, or the stock market crash of October 1929.

Elizabeth was not forced to return, except for brief visits to her parents in Boston. Over two years later, when I was again in Europe, I met her at a railway station in Paris. Each of us was accompanied, I by my wife-to-be, who was traveling with me that summer, Elizabeth by a handsome Frenchman. She was the first to show recognition. I was slower because she was no longer the Elizabeth I had known but a transformation, elegantly dressed, tastefully made up, supple, gracious, warmly smiling—no longer the proper Bostonian. Was it Europe that had transformed her into this desirable woman at ease in the world, or the Frenchman?

Lectures at the Sorbonne were open to whoever cared to attend, or one could enroll for a tuition fee of four dollars. I attended several series, Lichtenberger on Goethe, Regnier on the French drama, and Cestre, the authority on American literature, on Emerson. About the latter I remark in my diary that I would not grudge ten years of effort to acquire his lucidity of explication. Regnier was the favorite of all foreign students. His large classroom, adorned by frescos of nymphs and graces, was regularly filled. He made a commanding figure with his abundant gray hair, his cutaway coat, faultlessly pressed trousers, and brocaded cravat. He was the artist in narration of the legends on which French classical dramas are based. Eyelids drooping, lips caressing his words, he made madrigals of explication, music of the French language. He was fertile in wit and humor. As he lectured on Corneille, Racine, and Molière, I went to performances of the plays, mostly at the Odéon, occasionally across the Seine to the Comédie Française. Performances were frequent, for the French never tire of their classical drama.

Reading the plays beforehand, I was able to follow dialogue in the theater. I saw twenty dramatic performances, three each by Corneille and Racine, six by Molière, two by de Musset, and one each by six other dramatists. I also attended three symphony concerts; one performance at the Folie Bergère, obligatory for Americans; the National Opera for *Parsifal* and two ballet performances, one by the Diaghilev troupe and the other featuring Ida Rubinstein in premiers of Stravinsky's *Baiser de la Fée* and Ravel's *Bolero*.

Several pages of my Paris diary are devoted to descriptions of my favorite paintings in the Louvre. I quote just one because it reflects what I made of the French classical spirit. The painting is Poussin's *Enterrement de Phocin.* "A multitude of objects is presented, temples, waterways, processions in single file, a rectangular group carrying the coffin, valleys, sky, trees, etc. All objects fall into geometric groups, which in turn compose a large geometric pattern of parallel lines regularly bisected. This might be a scene in a Corneille or Racine tragedy and recalls Fontenelle's wish to constitute the geometric mind as the basis of all action. All is order and perfection of contour, a world in which men perform to the last nicety the rituals of birth, prayer, marriage, and death. Yet so artful is the hand of the painter that one scarcely perceives his improvement on nature. The leaves, turned over in a breeze, are carefully silvered; the trunks, in spite of their symmetry, seem natural in form. Nature has been imitated, but here it has been sublimated into the formal moulds of the French spirit."

Diary, January 17, 1929: As the time approaches for leaving Paris, I realize how much I love its narrow, crooked streets [in the Latin Quarter] and its vivid throngs.

Life is richer and more varied here than in the States. Tradition gives a sacramental quality to daily duties, rites, and pleasures. The density of population, high cultivation of the social life, the habit of living in the streets, the stimulus of being surrounded by beauty in stone, garden, and painting, the rich accumulation of tradition through the centuries, pomp and pageantry, the jostling together in the small continent of Europe of people so widely diverse as the French, German, and Italian—all these make for abundance and variety of living.

I was turning into a Europhile—another self to be eventually overcome.

## VI  EUROPHILIA—ITALY

O N JANUARY 20, 1929, I left Paris for southern France and Italy.
Marseille, where I spent three days, was a city of contrasts between the
majestic harbor setting and the filth and animation of the streets. All nationalities of the Mediterranean—Turks in fez, Arabs, Italians, Spaniards,
Greeks—streamed along the streets and around the quais. Vendors, sleight-of-hand
performers, and fortune tellers competed for the pay of sailors just off their ships.
One evening there was a brawl in the bistro where I took my *café au lait.*
Muscled sailors, rushing out on the sidewalk, hurled chairs at one another. In sharp
contrast with these street scenes were the opulent white villas, terraced vineyards,
red cliffs, eucalyptus, pine, palm and cypress groves as my train to Nice wound
around headland and harbor of the Riviera. Nice, in preparation for the carnival,
was a city of many colored lights, some in the form of bunches of grapes festooned
over the streets, others figuring dancing girls. There were no contrasts here as in
Marseille. Nice was the opulent resort of the capitalists of Europe.

Leaving the train at Monaco, I walked to Menton through changing vistas of sea,
villa gardens, and mountainslope. My next stop was Genoa, where I spent the
afternoon and evening wandering the palatial streets of this modern Italian city. I
soon discovered that prices were higher in Italy than in France, and that all tourist accommodations were taxed. To live within my budget of four dollars a day was
going to mean dispensing with some comforts, such as adequately heated rooms
and three square meals a day. Pensions provided breakfast and dinner. For lunch
I learned to get along simply with figs, delicious Italian figs that were cheap in the
markets. Goethe, in his *Italienische Reise*, which I read as I traveled, counted as
not the least of his pleasures in Italy the genius of the fig, his favorite fruit.

Hugging the rugged coast of the Italian Riviera, the train ride from Menton to
Pisa must be one of the most beautiful in the world. To Spezia the electrified train
passes through innumerable tunnels, some of them with arched openings giving
fleeting glimpses of the sea. The day was sunny with cloudless blue skies. From
Spezia to Viareggio we passed through the vineyards and olive groves of a valley
which sloped gradually down to the sea on one side and rose to a mountain range
on the other. In the foothills were pine forests; above them, brown and purple

heather; and towering over all, a jagged crest of white marble. Gray villages, some fortressed and all crowned with towers, were tucked in fissures of the foothills. Larger towns rested on plateau summits. Among these was Carrara. It occurred to me suddenly that this was the country of Pater's *Marius the Epicurean*, a book that had fascinated me while, as a junior in college, I went through a stage of aestheticism in which I expected prose to verge on poetry in rhythmic and phonetic effects. Here was Marius's country villa, White Nights. And that evening I copied in my diary from memory Pater's sentence of cadenced verbal music: "The little glazed windows in the uppermost chamber framed each its dainty landscape—the pallid crags of Carrara, like wildly twisted snow-drifts above the purple heath; the distant harbor with its freight of white marble going to sea; the lighthouse temple of *Venus Speciosa* on its dark headland, amid the long-drawn curves of white breakers." The scene before me matched that sentence in beauty. As the train passed through this valley for one hour, Italy, in prospect for me, seemed one gigantic art museum.

A stop of three days in Pisa brought discomfort during the winter nights in an unheated room and euphoria during mild sunny days. The leaning tower and the cathedral, over-advertised tourist attractions, meant less to me than country walks under umbrella pines through this elysian valley of the lower Arno. There were no discordant notes. All images caressed the eye, and the whole seemed the conception of some Italian Renaissance painter rather than a real landscape. I visited the house where Galileo was born and the palace occupied by Shelley shortly before his death by drowning off the coast. A local merchant I complimented for his good English said that he had learned it by reading Shelley and eating roast beef.

A warm night train ride to Rome, in spite of missed scenery, was preferable to another night in a cold pension room in Pisa. As moonlight faded into a Homeric rosy-fingered dawn and the train followed the windings of the Tiber into the city, I saw the sunrise over the Seven Hills. Taking care this time to choose a comfortable pension room for a three-week stay, I had the luck of locating a large well-furnished one with running water and ample central heat.

At dinner the first night in my pension I sat near an old gentleman with a resonant voice, fair complexion, white hair and mustache, and large girth. Soon he was joined by a pretty woman I judged to be his daughter. They fell into animated talk, interrupting each other, laughing, and talking fast because they had so much to say. The woman, also of fair complexion, had smiling eyes and a wide mouth that curled over rolling Italian vowels. Emotions played freely over her mobile features. Another man, presumably her husband, joined the two a little later with a child of three or four, who had the olive complexion of the father and the mother's regular features. New occasion for emotional display. The husband was just as lively and flexible as the old gentleman. What a rich emotional life those people led, I thought. Though many Italians I met in the course of the next several months were more reticent, this family, through whom life flowed like a river, typified for me the Italian character.

I shall not bore my sister, the one most likely reader of these memoirs, with details of my rambles among the antiquities of Rome, but touch on a few highlights that don't necessarily represent the best the city has to offer; just the best that I was prepared to take at that time. Rome, where pagan and Christian cultures flourish side by side, is the maternal city of Western civilization. It makes formidable demands on one's capacity for appreciation. As of now I don't think I did it justice.

The great number of churches is daunting. I visited several until I tired of frescos of the virgin and child. St. Peter's was different of course in the awe its great size and opulence inspired. My stay in Rome happened to coincide with the celebration of the seventh anniversary of the coronation of Pope Pius XI. Almost every day there was a spectacle of some kind in Rome, but this one was significant because it marked not only the anniversary but also a reconciliation between church and state after several years of strained relations between the Pope and Mussolini.

I followed throngs through the streets to the church. Royal and Papal troops were stationed around the entrance. Free tickets were distributed by guards. The crowd was prodigious. An English priest near me said that St. Peter's holds sixty thousand people, but that day I believe the capacity was exceeded. I squeezed into a position halfway to the transept, edged as close as possible to the line of guards clearing a passage through the center, and waited. The Papal procession entered. The Pope, seated in state on a throne carried on the shoulders of porters, was dressed in a white and yellow robe. Heralds trumpeted. The crowd broke into deafening *Viva Papa - Viva Papa.*

After a long ceremony the same procession withdrew from the church. I was within two yards of the Pope as he passed, waving his hand in benediction. The Ardent Sons replied to my description of this event with the following jingle:

> Why did the Pontiff bless you twice?
> Why, he looked at you, and in a trice
> Saw a soul ribald, unregenerate,
> Scoffing, ironical, almost degenerate;
> And mercifully brought down from heaven
> A blessing for your soul unshriven.
> Then he passed, but came back by
> And observed again with infallible eye
> That here was still an intellectual rake
> And that the first time didn't take.
> And lo, he blessed you again, oh, thank'ee
> *In nomine Patris et Filii et Spiritus Sancti.*

Pageantry was not over for the day. Signs posted on street corners announced a Fascisti gathering in Place Quirinal before the Royal Palace at seventeen o'clock. This was to betoken the reconciliation with the church. Again I joined the crowd. The King, Queen, and Mussolini appeared at the hour announced on the balcony of the palace overlooking the square, Mussolini bareheaded, the Queen waving her handkerchief to outbursts from the crowd.

The Christian art of Rome that impressed me most was, of course, the Sistine Chapel in the Vatican. Only Michelangelo among Italian painters had sufficient passion and sublimity of soul for the subject of the creation depicted on the ceiling. In the frescos of the Creation of the Sun and the Moon and the Creation of the Earth, I wrote in my diary, "The sweeping gestures, the stormy furls of drapery, the attitude almost of rage represent a spirit driven by a fury of creative power....The Creation of Man is more serene. The spark of generation animates merely the fingers and arm of man. The rest remains supine, to be animated by growth and experience in the new world....Among these many figures of passion, rage, and power there are three or four of pure beauty and serenity, such as the Delphic Sibyl."

Michelangelo the sculptor was best represented for me by his Moses in the museum of the Capitolino. "The power, patriarchal dignity," I wrote, "the massive rugged face, combined with the living folds of drapery, display the fullest effect of marble to simulate the living being. The Moses breathes torment of soul, fiery dominance over outer forces, and stern will to power."

It was the pagan art of Rome, however, that occupied most of my attention. In the museum of the Capitolino it was not the Moses that drew me back several times but the marble Venus standing alone in her octagonal enclosure of pale blue and gray walls. The beauty of the setting and of the statue itself on its revolving pedestal is breathtaking. With apologies for the flossy prose, I quote from my diary in fairness to what I was then: "This morning I saw my Venus for the last time with mixed feelings of adoration and regret. She more than any other monument in Rome expresses for me the serene beauty of ancient Greco-Roman art. A second Pygmalion, I have endowed her with life. Each time I approach the shrine I have the illusion of her bending from an upright posture to the inclination of modesty the sculptor has given her. She arouses empathic sensations of reaction and interaction. I pause at the threshold, held off by her pout of vexation at being surprised in the bath. But then I realize that she courts admiration, and, being alone with her this morning, I revolved her on her pedestal, savoring all aspects, including the callipygian."

The Villa Borghese and the Farnesine Palace were also pagan oases among the Madonnas of Rome. In the Borghese, fauns, bacchantes, and satyrs abound in the statuary, along with Bernini's *Apollo and Daphne*. In the gallery of paintings on

the second floor I found my favorite in Rome, Domenichino's *Hunt of Diana.*
(Remember, I'm confessing the taste of my twenty-fifth year.) I went all out in
describing this canvas: "It is a symphony of grace and movement, of girlish
naiveté, of life in nature, of silken gowns and gleaming flesh. As well as a complex
harmony of flowing movement, the canvas is no less a complex harmony of color.
Each maid has her own peculiar emotion. The two faces to the left express, in
different ways, the sympathy of onlookers. The dainty crouching figure with open
mouth and upraised palm expresses wonder at the skill of her companion, who has
just hit the mark. The girl in the act of drawing her bow (most graceful gesture of
the painting) has expectation in her eye. The face just behind her beams with the
excitement of the hunt. The childish figure sprawling in the water is one of sen-
sual contentment. The girl to the right adjusting her sandal is evidently the
*précieuse* among Diana's maids, indolent, remiss, vain, perhaps dreaming of another kind of hunt. The girl at Diana's right has evidently made a startling discovery. She alone sees the eavesdroppers hidden at the far right. Domenichino
depicts her first reaction, surprise, soon to be followed by outrage. The concealed
male faces add a touch of humor and balance the dynamic currents of impulse that
race from one side of the canvas to the other. The figures in the background, more
statuesque, blend into the Tuscan landscape. The action, directed inward from both
sides, balances slightly left of center in the commanding upright figure of Diana
herself. No analysis can account for the spirit of the painting, its charm of naiveté,
of youthful joy." Goethe might have had this painting in mind, or literary works
in the same spirit, in a remark to Eckermann in *Gespräche mit Goethe,* which I was
reading just then and quote in my diary: "*Wir Neueren fühlen wohl die grosse
Schönheit eines solchen rein natürlichen, rein naiven Motivs, wir haben auch wohl
die Kenntnis und den Begriff, wie es z'machen wäre, allein wir machen es nicht,
der Verstand herrschet vor und es fehlet immer diese entzückende Anmut.*" That
quotation, it seemed to me, was a true characterization of the pagan art of Rome
descended from ancient times or revived in the Italian Renaissance.

While in Rome, I had a packet of letters from home, Mother, Father, and two
sisters. The one from Mary, who was just ten, I admired for its precision and
transparent feelings:

We got a new car but its only 5 passenger but it has a place for a trunk in back. It
has baloon tires it is a hudson as usual the front seat lifts up and you put your tools
there. Daddy says there is enough snow for ten years for him. It is snowing now.
Ruth got off all day today the lucky thing then she goes back for her report card
at 9 o'clock and then comes home and I don't think that very nice do you. I think
I will pass in fact I know I will. I will write and tell you if I do. We had a spelling
test today of 40 words and I got 100. What do you think of that as you have always

thought I was such a *dumb* speller. now you know I am not, don't you. Did you say you were going to bring our watches in May. Frances Huff is my violin teacher she had a contest and I won it.

Yours truly, Mary

On February 22 I left Rome by train for Florence, with a stopover of one night at Orvieto, perched at an elevation of 355 meters and ascended by funicular. My first impression of Florence was of dirt and splendor. I had the good luck of engaging a room in the Pensione Caselli. Although there was no central heat in the old building, no running water in my room, the room was large and well furnished and fronted on the Arno just three doors from the Ponte Vecchio. A space heater operated by coins kept me comfortable on cold days. The Caselli was frequented by English-speaking people, and in its moderate-sized dining room there was lively conversation not only at individual tables but across the room from table to table. Florence I shall always associate with sociability during the sunny days of that advancing Italian spring.

Having bored you, Sis, with much twaddle about the art of Rome, I'll skip lightly over the many hours I spent in the museums, churches, and palaces of Florence and concentrate on the sociability,

*Sisters Ruth* (left) *and Mary c. 1927*

so different from my solitary wanderings in Rome. Among the guests I came to know at the Caselli were Edgar Slaughter, vice consul at the American Consulate; Miss Smallwood, a middle-aged Englishwoman and world traveler; Hebe, a tall, robust, handsome American girl; Miss Reed, a clerk at the American Consulate; Miss Stewart, a kindly, sentimental Australian; Wilkinson, who harangued against cruelty to animals; a garrulous American woman who had escaped from Tama, Iowa, at the age of two and had since lived in many countries; Martelli, a good-looking American art student; and Joyce Melville, a sprightly English girl, whose easy good humor and gay chatter set the tone for the whole dining room when she was with us and not in nearby Greve.

Most of these people knew one another well before I arrived and had a common fund of experience to call on. At first, I was tongue tied and shy in that lively dining

[ 53 ]

room. But as I got to know the others in small groups of two, three, or four on sight-seeing walks or evenings at theater or opera, I began to loosen up and enjoy myself. After dinner in the evening we formed small groups: Miss Smallwood, Martelli, Melville and I for a cinema or opera; men alone in Slaughter's room, where we admired his books and listened to his poetry; and walks about the city with Martelli, who taught me to appreciate Florence as the most intellectual of Italian cities. I visited his studio at the top of the same palace (reputedly the oldest in Florence, built in the tenth century) as the pensione, which was in a remodeled wing. I admired Martelli's paintings of nudes (he said that Italian women were the best proportioned in the world) and his etchings. I watched him make a zinc plate from one of his drawings. We went up on the roof for a grand view of the city. By early March I wrote: "I'm beginning to love Florence with intimacy and passion. Surely no fate could be happier than owning or even renting for a time one of the sequestered villas on the slopes of Fiesole hill." I read Dante in an English translation.

But the overriding impression that Florence left with me was not indigenous; not the Botticellis in the Uffizi, not Michelangelo's *David*, not the aspect of Fiesole heights. It was Miss Melville's rippling chatter, restrained ever so little by English poise and what she called her "old-fashionedness." I had never heard anything like it. I told her that she reminded me of a character in the *Forsyte Saga*. She said that she hoped she was not like Fleur—the very character I had most in mind. After a shopping expedition one afternoon, we visited the Strozzi Palace. She had met the present Duke in the home of her employer, an Italian sculptor of Greve who had married an English wife and whom Miss Melville was serving as governess to the children. The English-speaking guard in the Strozzi, hearing that she knew the Duke, gave us a tour of the art. She was charmed by a small bronze elephant. The guard remarked that Barnum's Jumbo, reputedly the largest elephant of record, had been killed several years earlier in a railroad wreck. "How dreadful," Miss Melville exclaimed; "the poor dear! The train must have come off rather badly too." She was full of piquant, oblique angles on objects and events. Her trips from Greve to the Pensione Caselli set her all aglow with pleasure. Just then she was trying to decide whether to stay on as governess in Greve or return to London in answer to a call of a friend who wanted her to keep house and care for the children during an absence in America. As we got around to ages, Miss Melville said that she was twenty-six and intended to stay right there. She had a strong intuition, she said, that there was a happy destiny before her.

Her running comments and translations as we attended Donizetti's *Don Pasquale* made a good performance doubly enchanting; I likened this mixture in my diary to a Russian salad full of happy surprises. She said after the performance that she had decided to accept my "very American" proposal (to me, an Iowan, it seemed very European) that she accompany me to Venice on her way back to England week after next. She wanted to do Venice properly on her first trip there with a gondola ride, a full moon, and a congenial companion. But she wondered whether I was "honest." Miss Smallwood, who was with us, supported my character and together we persuaded her that I was quite harmless. At the cafe after the opera we clicked glasses of mandarinas to the Venetian adventure. I felt that I too had a happy destiny before me in the near future—a gondola ride on the Grand Canal and a pretty girl who chattered delightfully, even if she was a bit old fashioned and would probably behave like Norina in *Don Pasquale*; she had whispered to me at one point in the opera, "She is refusing to go to bed with him."

Two days after the evening at the opera Ed Slaughter and I left Florence on a Saturday for a train to Greve and then a walking tour to Siena. We missed the ten o'clock train and had to wait for the next one at two. Climbing up the Chianti valley, we had beautiful views back over Florence and of vineyards, olive groves, cypress and umbrella pine woods, and the gray masonry of farms and country villas. Slaughter told me about meeting Ezra Pound and Norman Douglas. He described the author of *South Wind*, a seminal book for those of us experiencing the liberation of the twenties, as a robust, ruddy-faced, vigorous man with a booming voice and the appearance of being extravagantly sexed. Douglas was living in Florence at the time.

Our slow, local train reached Greve at four thirty. Slaughter insisted on sampling Greve wine, which he called the best in the world. We stopped at a trattoria where he was acquainted and drank quantities of white and red. I was light headed and wobbly till our walk sobered me down.

The distance from Greve to Castellina, our one overnight stop, is twenty kilometers, and it was five in the afternoon when we started out afoot. Both of us were practiced walkers, however. Following the Chiantigiana Road, we walked through a landscape of dreams, of contours so voluptuous, vegetation so lush, that it seemed habitat for the pagan demigods. As the obscurity of twilight settled down, I could imagine satyrs chasing nymphs under the cypresses and pines and through the vineyards.

Our road eventually ascended to the crests of the hills overlooking the darkening Chianti valley and distant hill towns. Only four cars passed us in that early stage of the motor car, but we frequently met peasants on foot or in horse-drawn carts, twisted by labor and mellowed by sunshine and Chianti wine. They were softspoken, courteous, as they directed us and parted with a "*Buona sera, Signori.*" The stars began to appear, but enough light lingered that we could make out the broad outlines of the landscape. Approaching Castellina, the road ascended straight toward the constellation of Orion through a draw in the hill; we seemed to be stepping into the sky.

Castellina is an ancient fortified hill town with just two rows of houses along the main road and a medieval fortress, which served then as the only inn and gave the town its name. As we approached at eight-thirty the vaulted passageway of the old castle, with an iron-barred window over it, Slaughter said that on his last visit he had seen a pretty young woman with a child in her arms framed in the window, a Madonna. The window was dark as we approached, but the next morning we looked up and saw a withered old hag peering through the iron bars. I chided Slaughter for his taste in Madonnas.

Slaughter knew the family and insisted, against demurrals from the landlady, that we have dinner in the kitchen, where the family was assembled. It was a large, high-ceilinged room with unpainted stone walls hung with shiny copper kettles and pans. At the table in the center sat a young man painfully forming the characters of a letter he was writing. Across from him sat a shriveled old woman, yawning over a piece of knitting. An immense fireplace, raised a foot above the kitchen floor, was deep and wide enough to accommodate stone benches on both sides for three people each. An old man sat on one side and a boy of about eight on the other with a meager fire of twigs and sticks between them. We dined at the center table on spaghetti and pork chops while the family looked on.

In my room on an upper floor I found a "priest" in my bed, a crock of burning coals suspended in a wooden frame in the shape of a rocker. The contraption, intended to take the chill off sheets, made a bulge in the covers as if a fat *padre* was occupying the bed, as Slaughter explained to me next day.

In the morning I rose early to see the sunrise. From the Castellina hilltop two wide valleys fell away to east and west. Clouds of mist filled the lower hollows and looked so much like the sea that I had to convince myself of a location far inland. As the sun rose long shadows lingered across the glorious valley to the east, mingled with patches of golden sunlight. Distant hill towns came slowly into view across a panorama of vineyards, olive groves, and old stone farmhouses, some converted into villas of the well-to-do. This was the rich Tuscan landscape of Italian Renaissance painters. It raised a question in the mind as to which came first, a real landscape to be faithfully copied in art or the vision of the painters as model to be copied by several generations of an artistic people improving on nature. It was a humanized landscape, very different from the wild American forest that later won me over.

The best way to traverse this country, as Slaughter had assured me, is as we were doing it, in a leisurely walk. We still had twenty-five kilometers before us to Siena. Hardly a tenth of a kilo on that elevated road did not have some object or vista of interest. We had occasional views of the towers of San Gimignano or Siena. "I have never," I wrote in my diary, "absorbed so much beauty in so short a time," and wondered why people chose to live elsewhere. We admired especially a huge pile of masonry that we took to be a monastery until it was explained to us as the Villa Campari, owned by a wealthy family. I dreamed of owning it some day and spending my old age looking out over the smiling Chianti valley where the earth gods of the ancients can be assumed to survive if anywhere in the modern world. Slaughter held forth on the superior beauty of old things, the mellowing effect of centuries of weathering on stone, something we do not have in America. He praised even the "beautiful old haystacks" we passed, an oxymoron I teased him about for the rest of the way to Siena. We reached our goal in midafternoon.

Before leaving by train for his job in Florence, Slaughter arranged for my pension room in the Flora at a reduced price for his promise to direct visitors at the Consulate to this place. I saw him off with regret. I would miss his company on my continued walk to San Gimignano.

Walking back through town that Sunday afternoon, I witnessed an annual sporting event of Siena University. First there was a chariot race, the charioteers dressed in Roman togas. Following this was a funny contest of twelve students, six from the law college dressed in tan frock coats, snug trousers, and preposterously tall blue hats; and six medics in red coats and tall red hats. Both teams were mounted on balky mules. They slowly approached each other. Whenever the mules could be persuaded to a near encounter, the riders lashed out with short whips with the object of knocking off the silk hats. The hats were firmly fastened under the chin, however, so that it was usually the rider who was unseated, tumbling in his glad garments under the mule's belly.

In Francis Marion Crawford's *Saracinesca*, which I picked up at a bookstore, I came across the following quotation: "The chief object of most Italians is to make life agreeable; the chief object of the Teutonic races is to make it profitable.... Hence the Italian excels in the art of pleasing, and in pleasing by means of the arts." So it seemed to me during my brief stay in Siena and on my walk through the lowlands of the Chianti valley to the hill town of San Gimignano with its fourteen towers, a Manhattan of the Middle Ages.

My room and meals in the Pensione Cisterna, a converted old palace, were the best accommodations I had in Italy at the moderate rate of thirty lire a day. The well-furnished room had hot and cold running water, central heat, and a private balcony jutting out over the cliff at the edge of town. The first evening I sat there six of the fourteen towers were silhouetted against the western sky on one side and the Chianti valley on the other. I spent another day exploring the town before setting out again, on foot, for Certaldo. Here I found the house in which Boccaccio died, a melancholy brick building with a few narrow slits for windows, sad place for the teller of merry tales to meet his end. Certaldo depressed me, and I was glad to entrain for Florence and the Pensione Caselli.

Florence seemed ideally beautiful under a cloudless blue sky, and on a street near the Caselli I saw the face of Botticelli's *Venus*—the same oval head, wistfully quizzical eyes and faintly pouting mouth. A letter from Miss Melville awaited me. It confirmed our plans to leave Venice the following Monday, March 18.

Miss Smallwood, pander to our escapade, saw us off at the railroad station. By the time we passed through Pistoia we were on a first name basis, Joyce and Paul. She told me the story of her ten months as governess to the Romanelli family. Romanelli was a combination of sensitive artist and crude natural man. Shortly after her arrival he had begun maneuvers to seduce her, pleading the illness of his bedridden wife and his sexual frustration. For ten months Joyce was subjected to advances from a man physically repulsive to her. Once he surprised her in the bath, the door having no lock. Henceforth he added to his demands for sexual gratification the request that she pose nude for him. She had told him to go to hell, but he persisted in both pleas till she could stand the strain no longer in that hermetic country villa near Greve. Yet she was still a little remorseful over leaving the dying mother and the two children. She had not told this story to anyone else, not even to her mother.

If we were to do Venice properly as Joyce had ordered, time was of the essence. She had just three days there before she had to leave for a new job as governess in London. To do Venice properly, each of us had to bend a little but not too much. I was pledged to be harmless, not another Romanelli; but still, less reserved than my normal self. Joyce had to break some of the barriers of her old-fashionedness. This delicate coming together worked to perfection during our three days. If not the first act of her intuited happy destiny, at least Venice must have been for her an orchestral overture. Almost from the first hour in the city my reserve melted away and for three days I chattered in the mode of unconsidered trifles I picked up from her. Why are you not always like this? she asked.

She did her part. In our pensione on the Riva Shiavoni, not far from the Piazza San Marco, she sent a message to my room by the waiter who served her breakfast, asking that I join her. I found her in bed in a décolleté dressing gown, face unmade, tousled hair, and looked on while she ate breakfast. This ritual was repeated all three mornings. In the States we have a coarse word for this behavior, but it is inappropriate here.

She wanted to see Venetian glass made on the island of Murano. So we threaded narrow, labyrinthine lanes across the oldest part of Venice, crossing bridges and passing under arcades. Joyce was ecstatic. From one gracefully arched bridge we looked down on a barge loaded with fagots and a crooked old man carrying them up the stairs from the canal. In another lane was a neatly arranged fruit stand with a steaming crock of roasting apples beside it, subject for an impressionist painter. We stopped in the square of San Giovanni e Paolo, a church as austere as San Marco is opulent, to buy two chocolate bars (my treat) and two ice cream cakes

(Joyce's) from a vendor. As we ate by the fountain, urchins of the neighborhood gathered round, too polite to beg and too many for our combined resources to respond to their envious looks. Guilt turned to merriment as we left the square.

In Murano we saw plenty of wine-colored glass in windows, but the hour was apparently that of the siesta or the day a holiday. All the doors we tried were locked but one. Opening it, we faced the dozing figure of a glass maker on a couch. Retreating, we laughed till tears came into our eyes. The scenes and events of that first full day seemed exquisitely funny, picturesque beyond belief. They engendered a spontaneous intimacy between us that was to last all three days and seemed to me quite Italian. On the vaporette going back to Venice, Joyce said, "Tonight I'll let you kiss me." A half dozen Italian heads on the crowded boat turned in our direction as if sensing some portentous announcement, and it was portentous for a girl who, she admitted, viewed kissing as the first step toward marriage.

We had not one but two gondola rides, the first a three-hour affair by day. Joyce was charmed by our gondolier, dressed in corduroy pants, black flannel shirt, and sombrero and sporting a thick mustache. His manner was gentle and insinuating. We stretched our legs out, snuggled close, and congratulated ourselves on being in that particular place at that time. The gondolier, respecting our privacy, whispered the names of the palaces we passed, one of which he invited us to inspect at the absent owner's consent. Joyce bubbled over the Madonnas, I chose the Suzannas to admire. Back in the gondola, we held hands and the gondolier now observed silence. We finally returned to the Piazzetta S. Marco more than ever pleased with Venice and each other. As he helped Joyce out, the gondolier murmured in the sweetest voice, "Please no forget kind gondola man who take you so nice trip and show you so many nice ting and give him something for leetle bottle beer." And of course I tipped him ten lire on top of the agreed fare of thirty lire.

I had turned spendthrift as the occasion seemed to demand. When Joyce said she wanted to dance, I agreed. She donned a green evening gown and I my black suit and we went in search of music on the Piazza about nine o'clock. At the Martini we danced to all the waltzes and sipped champagne till two in the morning. Though the evening cost me a scandalous 104 lire, I assented when Joyce suggested another dance at tea time in the same place.

On her last night in Venice, under clear skies and a moon, if not quite full, at least plumply gibbous, we went for a second gondola ride in the small canals, this time drawing a fat, gruff, good-natured gondolier. We held hands and kissed to the lulling glide of the gondola skillfully maneuvered around sharp bends in dark canals. As we passed under an arched bridge, an ironic pedestrian paused above us to sing a few bars of "Con Amore." Finally we emerged on the Grand Canal, where a barge hung with a dozen lanterns was moored under a palace-hotel. Its occupants were serenaders. We drew alongside and a couple of five-lire pieces, in installments, wafted to us "Ave Maria," "Sole Mio," "Con Amore," "Ramona," and then again, at Joyce's request, "Ave Maria."

We shopped the next morning, her last, visited the Ducal Palace once more, and talked about the future. There was a cloud on her happy destiny. She wanted children of her own, instead of caring for other people's. But in her country with a whole generation of young men decimated by trench warfare in WW I, the fate of her countrywomen was too often prolonged waiting for the right man. About ourselves, we agreed that we were not yet totally in love but that another two days in Venice would probably suffice, if we had them. She wanted me to come to England that we might picnic in the meadows and dangle our feet in the streams. "You would feel more *real* to me there." I saw her off at the station in the afternoon.

Brief as our Venetian interlude was, I have valued it over the years. It seems a work of art three days long, wrested from contingency, created in full control by two people trying to please each other.

During the remainder of my stay in Venice I copied in my diary the letters I wrote to Joyce. Some excerpts follow:

I had no idea four days ago that I should be so lonely after your departure. "Companions on the way" was your expression, and I accepted it, savoring the idea of a quick intimacy quickly eclipsed. But a dozen questions about your trip home need urgently to be answered, and I shall find it hard to wait for the promised Milan letter. In the meantime I poke about among the stones of this beautiful graveyard; and meet your request for a chronicle of my remaining days here, though I'm afraid that the excitement of your homecoming will have lessened your interest in canals and gondoliers....When I returned to the Aurora last night, the Grizzly One met me with a consolatory smile and ushered me into your room, muttering "*Tutto, tutto.*" He had moved all my things into your room, including toothbrush and note you sent up to my room Tuesday morning....After dinner I walked with my loneliness, setting out for the Campo San Giovanni e Paolo where we tantalized the urchins of the neighborhood. Of course I got hopelessly lost (the canals seem to change places at night) and it was after midnight when, thinking myself near the Rialto, I emerged on the Piazza....Today dawned fair. I took a long walk in the morning, finding lovely spots to show you on our next Venetian rendezvous. Late in the afternoon I sauntered into the Piazza to stumble on Events. The first five-year regime of the Fascisti is about to expire and the election is scheduled for Sunday. The Piazza was brilliant with flags, and the municipal band, bright blue plumes dropping from hats, was playing divinely. A genuine Venetian crowd was there, filling the Piazza, and the pigeons in even greater numbers. Many of them zeroed in on a child of two, scarcely able to stand, who was trying to feed them.

They alighted on his head, perched on his shoulders, and pecked at his hands; he was fairly smothered by flopping wings.

The oriental splendor of San Marco was dazzling in the setting sun. I am beginning to love it, as you did, and as I love all the rest of the incomparable Piazza, where each visit reveals something new. Now I look at the details, the minarets, the mosaics, the four prancing horses over the door of San Marco. And I've discovered that, amid the acanthus leaves of the thirty-six capitals of the Ducal Palace, grave faces of children, saints, and personifications of the virtues peer forth, each capital different from any other. I'm not sure I would have noticed this on my own. You see, I'm reading *The Stones of Venice* by your eloquent countryman....

Would you believe it, Joyce, I've found one entertainment in Venice that is free. Moving pictures in the Piazza. Last night an enormous screen was hung from the top of one of the facades opposite San Marco. From nine to eleven-thirty Venice witnessed a pictorial display of the accomplishments of the Fascisti regime in the last five years and learned that work, heavy breeding, physical training, and economy were the highways to national wealth and individual welfare. There followed in rapid succession views of a powerdam in Sicily, a boys' camp near Verona, a factory in Milan, a row of tenements in Naples, a foundling hospital at Genoa, a grinning Tuscan peasant family of nineteen, a hygienic baby of Siena, etc. When the name of each city was flashed on the screen, the whole crowd breathed ecstatically "Napoli," "Roma," "Siena," "Milano," and a great shout went up at "Venezia." Mussolini's oily face moved through it all, drawing applause and much lifting of hats. Between each of the four parts the lamps of the Piazza were relighted and the band played the national anthem. High political fervor....

Partly cloudy all day; the sky cleared about six, just in time for the facade of San Marco to catch the rays of the setting sun. The Piazza, under a slate blue sky spangled with rosy tuffs of cirri, was more than ever beautiful. The Fascisti, bearing brilliant banners, marched in and the din became horrific. While the municipal band played the last scores of *Pagliacci*, the two Fascisti bands played a boisterous march, and the mighty bells of the Campanile tolled. The band stubbornly persisted in finishing *Pagliacci* to the end in a triumph of discord....

I wish you might have stayed over until today. All the gods have mingled their art to fashion a perfect day. This morning a soft, silver fog hovered over the islands and the Grand Canal, hovered so low that the towers and domes emerged above to shimmer in the sun, wisps of fog coursing around them. The air cleared about ten, and now Venice floats on the sea in bright, warm sunshine. I am quite sure that this is the most beautiful city in the world....

The Fascisti carry the election, for another five years, by 8,500,000 votes to 130,000 opposed....

This morning I visited the Ducal Palace again, enjoying all of it but entranced as before chiefly by the grace of the three Tintorettos *Bacchus and Ariadne, Three Graces and Mercury*, and *Minerva Rebuking Mars.* Along with the *Europa* of Veronese, those paintings compose a museum room unequalled anywhere I have been. Not even the Sistine Chapel has impressed me more.

This afternoon I went by steamer to the Lido, an almost deserted place just now with its long rows of unoccupied bath houses and hotels. I walked along the beach looking for shells and gazing at the sea, gray-blue in the afternoon haze. Anchored in the distance was the *Rotterdam*, on which my passage back to the States is booked. It is apparently on a homeward lap of a Mediterranean cruise, disembarking its passengers here for a day or two. When I returned to the city, I found them in the Piazza, which is now beginning to fulfill its function as the open air drawing room of all Europe. The fact is that I'm lonely today, and that you are an essential part of Venice for me. I should not have stayed so long after you left.

Joyce and I continued to correspond through the summer after my return to the States. From her first letter awaiting me in Milan, I was struck by the labored flatness of her writing as compared to her lively, supple talk. The letters were awkward, inexpressive, even slightly solecistic. I remembered that she had grown up in Preston, where her mother still lived, and I recalled the one night I spent there during my bike tour of England in 1926. Preston was then a hangover of Dickensian England, a sweatshop industrial city of grimy brick row houses, belching factories, and workers in wooden clogs clattering on the streets at six in the morning on the way to a long day's labor. Though Joyce talked like Mayfair, she wrote like Preston. And in the absence of propinquity, the schizoid letters came uppermost for me. Besides, by summer's end, I became interested in another girl, one who like me did not want children. Correspondence with Joyce tapered off as I prepared to go East for a new job. I hope that she found the right man, had her several children and her happy destiny, and sometimes remembers Venice gratefully, as I do.

There is little to tell about the next six weeks of my European trip after I left Venice at the end of March. On the way back to Paris I stopped for one or two days in Padua, Verona, and Milan. Taking the route through the Simplon Pass into Switzerland, I stopped at Vevey, Lausanne, and Geneva as the winter snows were melting in the mountains. It was not an ideal time to see Switzerland, but I found Lake Geneva beautiful, especially at sunset over the Savoy Alps. What interested me most was the literary associations with the lake and its environs—Rousseau, Voltaire, Madame de Staël, Gibbon, Byron, and Shelley. I visited some of the scenes associated with them. And in Lausanne I bought wristwatches for my two sisters, aged ten and twelve.

In Paris I renewed contacts with Wong and Elizabeth and again attended lectures at the Sorbonne. As spring was breaking over the city, attendance at lectures was tapering off. If you wished to find students in pairs, a good place to look was the Luxembourg Gardens. One professor remarked with mock sadness that it was a losing fight of professors at this season against *les tendances charmantes.*

After ten days in Paris I began a leisurely trip in the Loire valley with stopovers in the chateau towns and in Chartres. In the latter town I met an old acquaintance from the Pensione Caselli, the American girl and drama student, Hebe, whose surname escapes me. We toured the cathedral together, even to a walk on the roof, and everywhere Hebe's comment was, "How dramatic!" I think she considered it an ideal setting for a play. From the Loire valley I went directly to Cherbourg, where the *Rotterdam* put in to take passengers from France.

My passage home was arranged to coincide with the original date of the wedding of my Drake classmate, Eugene Page. I was to be his best man. However, I had received word in Florence that the marriage had been moved up to February, with Everett George as best man. Everett, another Drake classmate, was then a medical student at McGill in Montreal. Gene had taught English for two years at St. Lawrence University in northern New York. His bride was a St. Lawrence graduate of 1927. Gene had taken a leave of absence for 1928–29 to begin studies for his doctorate at Columbia, and, as I arrived in New York, he and his bride were in an apartment near the campus on Morningside Heights. Before returning to Des Moines, I visited them there.

I was all wound up with Europhilia. Everything in Europe was superior to its counterpart in the States, except perhaps the ice cream; I was willing to concede that much to fellow countrymen. Gene and Helen said later that I was quite eloquent. They listened patiently throughout the evening. Just for the record, I wish I had a tape recording of that harangue. I cannot reconstitute it now, for it was the expression of a self that was slowly to die over the next decade of repatriation. Now it is chiefly by reading or rereading a novel or the autobiographical writings of Henry James that vestiges of what I was then rise to the surface. But as for desire to turn expatriate, there is no longer a trace. The America I came to know with my next job, and where I have lived ever since, is the right place for the continuum.

## VII  GO EAST, YOUNG MAN

O N ARRIVAL IN DES MOINES in late May, two stark realizations bore in on me. I was without funds. I had no job lined up for the fall. I vaguely recall working again in the bindery for pin money. It was late to be job seeking as a college professor. Most appointments for the academic year are arranged in the preceding spring term and ordinarily require an interview. I had been abroad at that time. I enrolled with a teachers agency and waited. Professor Smith at Drake offered me a job with an increase in salary, but I was more than ever determined to break ties with Drake. About the first of August I had an offer through the agency of a job in a small North Dakota college. This was unattractive, but time was getting short.

As I was on the verge of accepting the North Dakota offer, I had a phone call from Eugene Page. He told me of an opening at St. Lawrence University with a salary of two thousand a year. Would I take it? I accepted at once. The usual interview was waived, for Gene had spoken for me with the department head, Clarence Gaines. This opening had come about belatedly when Owen D. Young, St. Lawrence alumnus, chairman of General Electric and world statesman, had funded an expansion of the English Department on condition that two years of English be required of all students. Young was a strong advocate of the humanities and especially of English. I believe that he attributed much of his own success to his command of a flexible, forceful style in speech and writing. He was one of the most articulate public figures of his time. Since he was chairman of the Board of Trustees of the University, he had his way in most things. The English Department benefited, but I have known a science professor to explode: "What I want is for Owen D. Young to get his foot off my neck."

During the summer I renewed association with the Ardent Sons. I had a gift book for each of them, usually one I had bought in paperback and had bound to my specifications at a Paris bindery. Once again, they urged me to get acquainted with their French professor at Drake, Ruth Jane Kirby. We would have a lot in common, they insisted. Well, why not? A French teacher might understand my Europhilia. And besides I remembered her as an attractive young woman during the two years we had both been on the faculty at Drake.

Ruth had grown up in Boone, Iowa, where her father was editor of the local newspaper, till in her mid teens the family moved to Des Moines. She was a Drake graduate of the class of 1922; though only two years older than I, she had skipped a grade in public school and had graduated three years earlier. After her graduation she taught French in a teachers college in Kansas. Then she went to Columbia University, in the same year I was there, for a master's degree that would qualify her for a post at Drake. She had been an outstanding student of Professor Le Coq, head of the French Department. She had spent three summers in France studying at the universities of Grenoble, Clermont-Ferrand, and Paris. In the summer of 1929 she was living at home with her father, now secretary of the Fitch Company of Des Moines, makers of a popular brand of shampoo. Her mother had died a few years earlier of breast cancer. Her two brothers, both younger, were graduate students in chemistry at Iowa State College (now, University) in Ames.

In my affairs thus far I had fallen in love almost immediately. This time was different. The growth of love was slow and steady, keeping pace with a sounding of character. The final commitment came a year hence after a reluctant surrender of what in Munich had seemed the superior advantages of bachelorhood—freedom, irresponsibility, travel, and multiple choice. But there could be no denying that Ruth was the most felicitous of my loves thus far. Her seniority of two years was trifling compared to Clara's six; she had made no prior commitments like the sisters Mary and Helen; she had been an honor student and Phi Beta Kappa at Drake and was at home in academic circles, unlike Sieur-Katherine; she had the refined sensibilities of a lady, unlike Christine; her writing and her speech were equally expressive, unlike schizoid Joyce; and she shared, as no other did, my Europhilia so far as France was concerned and I hoped to broaden it by introducing her to Germany and Italy.

*Ruth Jane Kirby before her marriage*

We dated that summer in the glass cage, my mother's electric brougham, or in the family Hudson when on picnics out of town. Ruth was not so sylph-like as my other loves. Her hips were slightly broader than her shoulders. At her height of five-seven, she weighed almost as much as I did at five-ten. She did not move lightly on the dance floor. One breast was slightly larger than the other. She had a sweet face but not what one could call beautiful. These defects would once have discouraged me. Now they seemed unimportant compared to her intelligent, cultivated mind and beautiful soul. She was also free of the puritanical hangups of many Iowa girls in those days.

The latter blessing facilitated our agreement to travel abroad together the following summer of 1930. Meanwhile we corresponded regularly in French, I in my recently refurbished knowledge of the language, shaky in syntax. Though we were both teaching that year, we wrote once or twice a week. Her letters shone with the clarity of an unblemished diamond—her *esprit clair* as I called it, so like the Voltaire of her favorite eighteenth century France. I regret now our decision of some years ago to destroy all our letters. Ruth, who carried this out, made an exception, I found recently in clearing the attic, of my letters during army service in 1942–45. And last week I found some of hers dating to 1938–39.

That summer of 1929 was my last prolonged stay in the family home. I left for the East a week or two before the beginning of the fall term at St. Lawrence. By arrangement with the Pages, I met them in Utica on their way from New York City in their car. As we drove the 130 miles north to Canton, near the Canadian border, I became aware of what John Updike, speaking of this country, recently called "a final thinning out," as if one were approaching "the end of the world." Accustomed to thinking of New York State as heavily populated, my astonishment grew as we proceeded northward. The North Country, as it is known, is bounded on the south by the Mohawk Valley, on the west by Lake Ontario, the north by the St. Lawrence River and Canadian border, and the east by Lake Champlain. As we left Utica the country became abruptly rural, a land of dairy farms, woodlots, and small, not "towns," as in the Midwest, but "hamlets" and "villages," after the parlance of the New England settlers. For nearly half the distance the modern road passed through the valley of the Black River, which drains the Adirondack uplift on one side and Tug Hill on the other.

Gene and Helen were good guides. Helen had relatives in the North Country, and Gene, with his quick grasp of realities new to him, was a fountain of differences, so to speak, for as an Iowan himself he knew what would strike me as novelties. Still, for all their interpretive skill, there remained one significant thing that I had to learn over the years by myself.

If you want to get in touch with America's past, I learned, so different from that of Europe, Horace Greeley's advice could just as well be turned around: "Go east, young man," as long as the reference is to the North Country. We assume that the original Thirteen Colonies were fully settled before the Revolution. This is not true of the North Country. The greater part of it, as large as the whole state of Vermont, consists of the Adirondack uplift, and of this geographer Thomas Pownall wrote in 1784: "This Country...called by the Indians Couchsachrage, which signifies the Dismal Wilderness or Habitation of Winter, is ...very little known to Europeans; and although a hunting Ground to the Indians, yet either not much known to them....I own I could never learn any Thing about it." Today the Adirondacks is the largest park in the nation outside Alaska, and forty-three percent of it is state forest preserve protected by a constitutional amendment that it shall be kept forever wild. Every year hunters and hikers get lost in the Adirondacks, and a few perish of exposure. Gilroy, a hiker I knew in the 1950s, set out one day in October to climb the Santanoni range. He never returned. An intensive search found no trace except his signature in a register on Santanoni Peak. Thirty years later a lone bushwhacker happened on Gilroy's remains. Accidents like that and the lessons to be learned from them are a regular annual feature of the Adirondack Mountain Club's periodical.

It took several years for me to learn that remnants of the old frontier still existed in populous New York State, and when I did, this thrilling knowledge was always with me. Some nameless writer for a Commission on Outdoor Recreation Resources in 1962 wrote with a passion uncommon in such reports: "When an American looks for the meaning of his past, he seeks it not in ancient ruins, but more likely in mountains and forests, by a river, or at the edge of the sea." The sea means little to me, but it was in the mountains and forests and on the rivers of the North Country that my Americanization slowly progressed.

Even the lowlands surrounding the Adirondack uplift on the west, 40–45 miles broad; on the north, 20–30 miles; on the east, 5–10 miles, were slow to be colonized. Migrants from New England began to move westward into northern New York after the Revolution, mostly in the first quarter of the nineteenth century. As late as 1803 Washington Irving, a young man of twenty, made the journey from Utica to Ogdensburg, nearly the same one I was making now with the Pages. The trip that took us three hours in Gene's car took Irving's party nine days. Irving fills his journal of that adventure with superlatives about the hardships of travel through an untamed wilderness over a wagon track littered with stumps and windfalls. Even today downstaters say of our lowland fringe at the top of the state that it lies "beyond the boondocks."

So, when St. Lawrence University was founded in Canton in 1856, it was said of the founders, with pardonable exaggeration, that they "have lit in the wilderness a candle which will never be extinguished." *Candle in the Wilderness* is the title of a centennial history of the University. Today Canton has little more than the population it had in 1860. Though other encroachments of civilization have come upon us, we have only to get in our cars and drive twenty minutes south to escape into the vast, continuous woods of the Adirondacks; into America's past.

"All the world knows," says Henry Adams, that European travel "unfits

Americans for America." If I had remained in Iowa or elsewhere in the Midwest, my Europhilia might have persisted and made me the misfit that Adams deplores. The move east was a stroke of luck. Though acclimatization was slow and faltering and not complete till a decade had passed, the North Country is to me now the dearest place in the world.

Location was not my only stroke of luck. St. Lawrence University itself is a bastion of liberalism. In my thirty-six years on the faculty I experienced no interference with my teaching such as I had known at Drake. The institution was founded by one of the most liberal of Christian sects, the Universalists, a church imbued with the Emersonian tradition of New England's renaissance. Two members of the Theological School faculty were among the most admirable men I have ever known: Dean John Murray Atwood, who put the search for truth above denominational doctrine, and Edson Miles, who returned as professor to his alma mater after a career as Shakespearian actor with the troupe of Sothern and Marlowe. Though a quarter of a century older than I, Edson became a close friend. Among other benefits he taught me the rudiments of gardening in the North Country in a plot we shared in the village.

In 1961 the Universalists merged with the Unitarians, and four years later the Theological School at St. Lawrence closed its doors permanently to a dwindling number of students. Today, in the Unitarian-Universalist Church in Canton, the minister Max Coots sustains the liberal tradition in the community by brilliant sermon-lectures on church history, government policy, and sociology. There are agnostics and atheists in the congregation.

Although St. Lawrence was founded primarily to train a well-educated ministry for the Universalist Church, the charter of 1856 also provided for a College of Letters and Science. The latter, according to the bylaws, was to remain an unsectarian foundation where the intellectual atmosphere was freedom of thought and freedom of teaching. Like the Theological School it was to be co-educational. The first woman student, Olympia Brown, was the first woman of record to be ordained in the Christian ministry in this country. She became chief assistant to Susan B. Anthony in the movement for equal rights for women.

From 1929 to 1942 student enrollment at St. Lawrence ranged between six and seven hundred excluding summer school. By the time I retired in 1965 enrollment had doubled to about 1,400, and in the 1980s it increased to over two thousand. Prior to World War II over half of the students came from northern New York. From 1946 on St. Lawrence became increasingly cosmopolitan, drawing students from all parts of the state, other states, and abroad. The quality of the student body improved steadily throughout my tenure as admission standards tightened.

During my first year I taught only the required freshman and sophomore courses. In the second I had an elective for upperclassmen in nineteenth century English literature. Soon after this course was split in two, Romantic and Victorian, each offered in alternate years. From 1930 to 1942 I was faculty adviser to the weekly student newspaper, the *Hill News*, which meant reading and correcting all copy and on rare occasions gingerly attempting to restrain provocative editorial writers without the appearance of censorship. I walked this tightrope without losing the confidence of any editor-in-chief, although on one occasion an associate editor vented some spleen.

For the two years before my marriage I rented a room in the home of Professor Hunt of the Education Department, the same house that Ruth and I were eventually to buy in 1955 when Professor Hunt retired. Harry Reiff, of the History-Government Department, also had a room at the Hunts'. Our relations with the family were cordial, and Harry and I saw much of each other at meals and on weekends. The Pages took me in hand socially and also introduced me to the Adirondacks. I had no car till 1932 and was dependent on them for trips out of town. They introduced me to climbs of nearby mountains and to Cranberry Lake, where Helen Page had the use of a camp owned by her aunt in Gouverneur. Once we took the mailboat tour of the lake, third largest body of water in the Adirondacks.

The greatest novelty of those first two years was the singles table at the Robinson House, where six or seven bachelors on the faculty and one single woman took meals. All of us were in our twenties or early thirties with high spirits unrestrained by family responsibilities. Table talk was lively; it was often dominated by my housemate, Harry Reiff, a Harvard Ph.D. We followed closely the events of that fatal fall of 1929—the stock market crash and the beginning of the Great Depression. By the winter of 1930 we convinced one another that the worst was over, and we began to nibble at common stocks, sure that the market was about to turn around. We took sharp losses before the lows of 1932, but at least we had jobs, having established ourselves on or before the eve of doomsday. Reading about the millions of unemployed was painful, but at that early stage of the depression, none of us was ready to question the market system.

## VIII  RUTH

IN EARLY JUNE, 1930, after Commencement at Drake and St. Lawrence, Ruth Kirby and I met in Montreal for our long-planned trip abroad. Six days later we landed at Cherbourg and took the boat train to Paris. I had made reservations for adjoining rooms at the Pension Parisiana, Rue Tournefort, near the Pantheon, where I had stayed briefly in 1928. Preoccupied with each other, neither Ruth nor I kept a journal that summer, so that I must depend on memory for times of stay and itinerary. I believe we spent two weeks in Paris, strolling or sitting in the Luxembourg Gardens, walking along the Seine, visiting the haunts of our separate discoveries on previous trips. In the dining room of the pension Ruth once overheard a remark of another guest aware of our separate registration and ad-joining rooms: *"Cèst très moderne."* We were flattered to be classed, even in Europe, with the avant-garde; significant progress for Iowans in that decade.

Paris in June was lovely, but the purpose of our trip was to introduce Ruth to Germany and Italy. So before the end of the month we entrained for Trier, just inside the German border. This is an ancient, historic city with celebrated Roman ruins, once the favorite residence of Constantine the Great. Of all this past Ruth and I were ignorant at the time. We had chosen this city as our first stop in Ger-many because of its location on the Mosel River (Moselle in France) at the head of a steamboat line. Lovers are likely to be quite arbitrary in their travels; to be impressed more by trifles than by monuments of the past. I vaguely recall archi-tectural splendors, but what Ruth and I took away from Trier was an item in the dinner menu at our hotel—*halbe Huhn mit Blumenkohl*, half a chicken with cau-liflower. The stark homeliness of this phrase aroused merriment in Ruth, so much in contrast was it with elegant French. For me this homeliness was engaging in the language I had learned to appreciate during my year abroad. At any rate, *halbe Huhn mit Blumenkohl* became one of those shared trifles lovers set store by, the phrase rolled on the tongue, serving as a kind of talisman for our travel in Ger-many, the item itself looked for on menus and ordered when found.

By the time we reached Trier, we were sufficiently in love to hanker for per-manence of some kind. There was a depth of understanding between us that I had never experienced with another girl. We had common backgrounds. Both Iowans, we had become critical of the puritanism and philistinism of our state. We were both academics with a similar range of interests; both, lovers of language. Physical attraction was also present. But we hadn't yet agreed on the kind of permanence. I still cherished the irresponsibility of bachelorhood. I had proposed to Ruth that we should continue teaching in our separate institutions during the school year and reunite each summer for a trip abroad, as we were doing now. This annual alternation of anticipation and realization seemed infinitely attractive to me. But Ruth was not impressed by my proposal. Yes, it might be *très moderne*, in the words of the Parisiana guest, but how would it play in straight-laced Des Moines and Drake, where she had to teach? She did not reject my proposal outright, but she was not enthusiastic.

It was the Mosel that brought us together. Moving water has a mellowing effect on me. And the Mosel is among the most enchanting of moving waters in the 118 miles between Trier and Coblenz. Winding, narrower and more intimate than the Rhine, it discloses some picturesque vista of castle, cliff, or vineyard around every bend. Availing ourselves of the privilege of a stopover and boarding next day's riverboat, we spent an afternoon and night in Alf, a small village tucked in a niche between the river and the hills. We walked on a country road to a hillside vineyard with a medieval castle on the crest. Trespassing, we climbed through the grapevines for a closer view of the castle with its modern appendage. Suddenly we confronted the owner and his wife taking the afternoon sun in a patio garden. They might well have resented our intrusion. Instead they welcomed us smilingly and invited us to sit and have a glass of wine. We conversed in their little English and my little German. For a quarter hour we enjoyed German *Gemütlichkeit*.

Warm feelings carried over into the evening as Ruth and I had a leisurely dinner at our inn in Alf with a bottle of white wine from the vineyard we had just visited—Arrasburger Schlossberg. It was ambrosia to us, who came from a country still under the pall of Prohibition and had few comparisons to go by. Sophisticated tasters doubtless knew of dry white wines superior to Arrasburger Schlossberg, but no other could equal it for us. (We looked for it in vain during the rest of our stay in Germany.) The mellowing effect of the wine, twice tasted that day, of our reception at the castle, and of the morning's float down the moving waters of the Mosel worked on me to overcome the pride and induration of bachelorhood, and I said to Ruth, "Will you marry me?"

We decided on Venice as the place for the ceremony. We knew nothing of marriage regulations in Italy but assumed that the American Consul could accommodate us on demand. Contingency intervened.

At Coblenz we boarded another riverboat, this time up the Rhine to Mainz. We stopped at Frankfurt and then went to Dresden, where we stayed a week. Dresden was a splendid baroque city before its destruction in World War II. We spent many hours in the galleries of the Zwinger Museum, visited a crowded Ratskeller for a variety show, and combed the jewelry stores for an engagement ring. Our final selection was a white gold band with a setting of two small diamonds on each side of a large amethyst. Ruth began wearing it at once.

Our next destination, after a stopover in Weimar, was one I had been planning long in advance for its association with the minnesingers of medieval Germany and with Wagner's *Tannhäuser*. It was the Wartburg, near the city of Eisenach. Inside the walled enclosure of the castle was a modern hotel, in which we engaged adjoining rooms for a week's stay. Our windows looked out over the hills and valleys of the Thuringian Forest, a groomed, immaculate German forest in which every stick that falls is soon spirited away for firewood and the forest floor is clean of debris except for a carpet of pine needles. Paths led down from the castle compound through this Hänsel and Gretel forest. Over the next three days Ruth and I followed several of them, in perfect agreement with a German tourist who spoke to us at one outlook site: *"Hier hat Man keine Langeweile."*

We were happy. Our future was settled, our present situation could hardly be improved on, and romantic legends of the past were all around us. Ever since, an etching of the Wartburg on its precipice, viewed through a wall of pines from another hilltop, has hung on the wall of my study as reminder of that three-day idyll, worthy of Faust's appeal, *"Verweile doch, du bist so schön."*

Then on the fourth day I fell desperately ill. I lay in bed most of that day, Ruth often at my side ignorant of the risk. On the fifth day my fever heightened. I called for a taxi to take me to a doctor in Eisenach. One look at my throat and he pronounced that I had diphtheria and would have to go at once to the Stadt Krankenhaus. First, however, I returned to the Wartburg to give the bad news to Ruth and check out of the hotel. We made hasty plans. She wanted to stay in Eisenach and wait out my hospitalization, but I insisted that she go to the Parisiana in Paris and wait for me there. We parted at the railroad station in the city.

Where and how had I picked up the infection? A possible explanation is the crowded Ratskeller in Dresden, where Ruth and I were obliged to sit at a table occupied by two others, one a man who, I recalled, between drafts of beer, sucked Sucrets from a tin in his pocket, the same pill I was provided with when I left the hospital and that was given to Ruth when she returned to Eisenach.

A heavy injection of antitoxin saved my life in the next thirty-six hours of delirium. The doctor told me that I had been near death because of the advanced stage of the infection. But I was soon able to sit up, write to Ruth, and read the novel I had purchased in Dresden, Thomas Mann's *Der Zauberberg*, with the aid of my German dictionary and, in tough spots, of my nurse, Schwester Margarete. This compendium of the best thought of the first quarter of the twentieth century, each *Weltanschauung* embodied in a living character, was the accidental but perfect reading for a convalescent provided that his time as patient was known to be numbered in days rather than the years of Hans Castorp's confinement on the Magic Mountain. It was the most absorbing German I had read thus far, better it seemed to me at the time than Goethe. And it helped me to converse with doctor and nurse, who had no English. Schwester Margarete knew French, and when my German failed, I could fall back on that. But by the time I left the Stadt Krankenhaus, I had enough facility to rely on a spoken German that conveyed understanding and amusement too, weighted as it was by chunks from Thomas Mann and larded with solecisms.

The burden of my talk was quick release from the hospital. Venice was already out of the question, and I would be in no state for marriage any time soon. The urgent objective now was the date of our boat reservations back to the States and the beginning of the fall term at our respective institutions. Three successive negative tests were the requirement for release of patients with infectious diseases. At the end of the second week I had had one negative test followed by a positive one. I felt sufficiently recovered to miss Ruth's company. That, at any rate, could be accommodated, the doctor assured me. Ruth would not be allowed in the contagious ward but could join me in the hospital garden if we agreed to refrain from hugs and kisses. I did agree, though the penalty seemed superfluous in view of Ruth's exemplary immune system. She had sat at the same table with me in the Ratskeller, exposed to the same aspirated germs; she had lain at my side in the Wartburg hotel while I was virulently contagious. And during the fifty-eight years of our marriage she not only resisted the infectious hepatitis I brought into the house but never spent a single night in hospital till the last one before her death of cardiac arrest.

So Ruth returned to Eisenach at my summons. At a small extra charge lunch was served to us at a table in the spacious gardens of the hospital. Other patients may have been a little resentful of this special privilege accorded to a convalescing foreigner. Conversing with Schwester Margarete in French, Ruth too became a friend of that gentle, affectionate, cultivated woman. Across an open field from the gardens the huge Graf Zeppelin was moored, symbol of a new assertive Germany after its defeat in World War I. During that summer of 1930 Nazism was surging all over Germany, but we were unaware of it. In later years I wondered which was the real Germany, the Germany of Goethe, Thomas Mann, the owners of Burg Arras on the Mosel, Schwester Margarete, or the Germany of Hitler.

By the end of my third week in the Krankenhaus two successive negative tests had come from a distant laboratory. That was enough for me. We had only one week left to meet our boat in Cherbourg. I pled with the doctor to release me. The next test would not come back for two or three days. Finally he agreed to let me go on condition that I would have another test as soon as I reached home. That test too was positive, and so, according to a letter from Schwester Margarete, was the one returned to the Krankenhaus after my departure.

Ruth returned to Des Moines for a last year of teaching at Drake, and I to Canton just as the fall term began. I could not meet my classes, however, or return to my room at the Hunts', who had a daughter of three and another, just born, of one month. I arranged for a room in the home of a practical nurse while awaiting the required number of negative tests. They were not forthcoming. In the second week I settled for the drastic remedy of a tonsillectomy. This was decisive. I could return to my room and relieve the instructors who had been meeting my classes.

In Des Moines, when they saw Ruth's engagement ring, the Ardent Sons, all but one, were pleased with their success in bringing us together. The dissenter, Hugh, was in love with her himself. He warned her of my self-sufficiency; I would bury myself in books and neglect her. The first part of this warning is true enough. I am self-sufficient when there is no better alternative. But Ruth was that better alternative. "When a person is completely in love," Freud remarks, "the object to some extent takes the place of the ego."

A warning of a different nature came from Marjorie Smith, who had known something of my past. I was unstable, she told Ruth; I would fall in love with someone else and desert her. Ruth braved both of these dire prophecies.

If I have anything to reproach myself for in our marriage, it is the initial arrangements. I considered only my own distaste for a family or church wedding. Ruth appeared to go along. But her ties to her father were deep. She had continued to live at home for several of her adult years after her two brothers had established themselves elsewhere. He was devoted to her; he at least should have had a part in our arrangements. But what I proposed was an elopement. We had graduated from family, I felt; I would be twenty-eight that summer of 1931 and Ruth thirty. I had things my way. After Commencement at Drake, Ruth came to Syracuse and we had a civil ceremony in the courthouse of that neutral city, where neither of us had relatives or friends.

Whatever else it lacked, our wedding had humor. When I met Ruth's train about noon on June 10, 1931, I was wearing dark glasses, for I had just come from an oculist who had applied drops as a relaxant before testing my eyes for new glasses. I was half blind for several hours. After procuring the license, we went to the courthouse and were introduced to a jovial Jewish judge. He called in from an adjoining office two clerks as witnesses, Frank and Joe. It was a hot day. They stood in shirt sleeves and open necks during the brief service. After congratulatory handshakes all around, Ruth steered me out of the courthouse in my state of semiblindness, and we checked into the bridal suite at the Onondaga Hotel. In the evening, my vision restored, we danced till midnight in the hotel ballroom, the orchestra obliging us with repetitions of our favorite dance tunes.

Although the Syracuse courthouse lacked the éclat of the Venice-that-was-to-have-been, at least the circumstances of our wedding served as a conversation piece in future years. And the week's honeymoon that followed at Lake Brantingham in the Adirondacks came closer to Venetian standards. There was no gondolier, and we were obliged to propel our canoe on the lake and its tributaries. But Ruth, who had never paddled a canoe before, won the approval of the hotel proprietor, who called her Pocahontas.

We were to have an aborted second honeymoon. Before I began teaching in the summer session to bring my year's salary into equivalence with Ruth's at Drake and soon after we moved into an apartment on Judson Street, two faculty wives, elegantly groomed and wearing white gloves, called to welcome the newlyweds to Canton. One, Barbara Priest, wife of the head of the Physics Department, offered us the use of a rustic camp on the Raquette River at the mouth of the Jordan, about twenty-five miles south of Canton inside the Adirondack Park. The Pages drove us there and were to come for us in three days. The first day was warm and sunny. We enjoyed drinking out of the pure, cold spring near the cabin, walking the path alongside the Jordan through a pungent conifer forest, and paddling a canoe on the Raquette. Nighttime was a different story. Having been closed since the previous summer, the camp was heavily colonized by mice. The presence of a fresh food supply excited them into high revelry. All night long they raced along the floor and the rafters. We could not sleep and Ruth, delicately nurtured in the city, was so appalled at the thought of another such Walpurgis night that we made a quick decision to decamp and leave the mice in possession. Early next morning I paddled across the Raquette to the old Hollywood Hotel and phoned the Pages to come for us that same day. There remained the embarrassment of thanking Mrs. Priest while at the same time explaining our sudden departure.

Looking back on Ruth's first two years in Canton, I wonder whether she was as happy as, at the time, projecting my own feelings, I assumed she was. A career woman accustomed to dining out with her father and having the services of a housekeeper, she now had to learn to cook and keep house in the four large rooms of our apartment in a big drafty house reputed to be the second one ever built in the village, back in the first quarter of nineteenth century. (It has since been de-molished and replaced by modern apartment buildings.) Canton must have seemed to her very primitive in those years of the Great Depression. As fall turned into an early winter, we discovered the worst feature of our apartment, its inadequate heat in spite of my frequent complaints to the live-in landlord's son. Our second winter there was decisive in driving us away. The winter of 1932–33 was one of the coldest on record in the North Country. Nighttime temperatures dipped into the thirties below zero and during the entire month of January the thermometer seldom got above zero during the day. The water main bringing spring water to Canton from Waterman Hill froze and sprang leaks. On Judson Street we were without running water for ten days. We had to melt snow for baths and transport drinking water from a farmer's well out of town. Ruth had a taste of life on the frontier that winter.

Social life leavened the austerity of those two years on Judson Street. As newlyweds we were in demand as chaperones at fraternity and sorority dances. We improved our bridge game under the tutelage of the Pages. We dined out once or twice a week at Nellie Rice's table with my old friends the singles on the faculty. In the summer of 1932 Ruth's father visited us and, observing how far we were from centers of population, bought us a new Chevy for the then great sum of $600. The car expanded opportunities for recreation. In fine weather we drove into the Adirondacks. Accompanied by friends, we visited Ottawa or Brockville in Ontario via the old Morristown or Ogdensburg ferries across the St. Lawrence. With Harry Reiff and his current girlfriend, a Wellesley graduate working in the Administration building, we danced at a night club strategically located just across the border in Quebec, the hamlet of Huntington, where liquors and wines were served to refugees from Prohibition in the States until the Roosevelt administration made them legal once more. As driver I had to exercise restraint, but Harry was under no such compulsion. On the return home he boomed out from the back seat some often repeated refrain in the polysyllabics he was addicted to, drunk or sober. One I happen to remember, an image from a dream, was "unconscionably hopping rabbits."

In 1932 Gene Page took a year's leave of absence to advance his studies toward a doctorate and then a second year, without leave, to complete them. He never returned to St. Lawrence but became head of the English Department at Albright College in Reading, Pennsylvania, and later at a college in the Midwest. We kept in touch through correspondence and widely spaced visits. Gene died in his sixties; Helen, remarried, now lives in Florida. Shortly after Gene departed Jack Douds, who had joined the English Department a year before I came, brought to Canton a bride he had known at graduate school in Cornell. Edith, from a professor's family in the South, became Ruth's best friend. She too was a student of foreign languages, especially French, and was besides a lively and witty girl of about Ruth's age. College faculties are volatile, however, and the Douds couple too left St. Lawrence in 1937.

In the depths of the depression, 1932, many colleges across the country cut salaries, some as much as thirty percent across the board. At St. Lawrence our cut was a modest ten percent. Thereafter, almost till our entrance into World War II, the earlier practice of annual increments was discontinued, and most salaries remained little changed from the 1932–33 rate. Faculties did not suffer so much during the depression as other segments of the economy but were slower to recover purchasing power in the second half of the 1930s. In 1935, however, I had a small inheritance from an aunt, and a few years later Ruth inherited a slightly larger sum after her father's death, so that we had a little income from investments and a nest egg to build on.

During our engagement in Germany Ruth and I had agreed that we did not want children. Having taught college French for seven years before our marriage, Ruth had tasted the rewards of a career and wanted some day to resume it. She doubted her strength to combine career and child raising. On visits to my family in Des Moines I joked that baby-sitting two sisters had satisfied my paternal instincts early on. The depression gave Ruth and me little encouragement to change our minds on this subject. The other members of the singles table at the Robinson House were not even venturing on marriage in the early thirties; I was the first to take this bold step. Besides, I have always felt inadequate to the role of father; I would have fallen into the same mistakes made with me or worse ones. Sartre indicts the whole institution of paternity in his memoir *Words*. "There is no good father, that's the rule. Don't lay the blame on men but on the bond of paternity, which is rotten. To beget children, nothing better; to *have* them, what iniquity!" This wisdom he garnered from his "family" of young disciples, blighted waifs fluttering to him as antidote for too much papa.

In the summer of 1933 we moved into a rented cottage on Lincoln Street, less than a block from the campus. It was a relief to be in control of heat during the ensuing winter. The only disadvantage of the location was that it left us open to visits at sometimes inconvenient hours. But the next four years in this cottage were happy ones for Ruth, occupied with furnishing and decorating our house and associations with congenial friends. During the two-week winter vacation we took the train (the Canton Creeper, as students called it till it was discontinued in the 1960s) or drove to New York City to see plays or operas and sometimes to attend meetings of the Modern Language Association. I had given up teaching in the summer session, and Ruth and I had the three summer months, a delightful season in the North Country, free for exploring the Adirondacks, swimming at our favorite beach at Higley Falls on the Raquette, picnicking, and visiting Canadian cities. As time went on and our attachment to the great woods deepened, we turned south more often into what used to be called up this way "South Woods," in contradistinction to the "North Woods" of downstaters. At the nearest entrance point to the Adirondack Park, Canton is only twelve miles; twenty miles at the one most frequently used, Route 56. Ruth's endurance on hiking trails was limited, but while I climbed a mountain she passed the time shopping or attending antique shows in Lake Placid or Saranac Lake.

One of the longest presidencies at St. Lawrence came to an end in 1935 when Dr. Richard Eddy Sykes retired. A generous-hearted, avuncular gentleman and ex-minister, he had presided over an era of good feeling and expansion of physical plant. He was succeeded by Laurens Hickok Seelye, who had taught philosophy and psychology at the American University of Beirut. Whereas Sykes had devoted himself primarily to raising funds for endowment and expansion, Seelye's main interest was the curriculum. He introduced a required course for freshmen called Civilization Discussion Groups, a watered-down Great Books course, in which students passed every three weeks to another instructor and a new book. Seelye himself took part and chaired the weekly meetings of instructors at his home. Representing the English Department, I was asked to take part along with instructors from five or six other departments. We were expected to be or become polymaths.

Much of that course seemed to me to consist of marking time on inferior books. Regardless of its position on the scale of greatness, each book was to be discussed over three weeks. Some were chosen simply because they were timely, such as *Growing Up in New Guinea* by Margaret Mead, the quality of whose research has since been questioned; and *Babbitt*, a novel so blatantly satiric as to need little interpretation. To squander nine class meetings on such a book seemed wasteful to me. I did not enjoy teaching that course and chose to drop out after one year.

## IX  LIMITED TENURE

I N THE SPRING OF 1936 President Seelye notified three of us junior
members of the English Department of limited tenure under a new system of
rotation meant to economize on salaries in hard times. English instructors
henceforth, and presumably instructors in other departments, were to be hired for
three-year terms so as to avoid promotions and increments for all but the senior
members of the department. Jack Douds was given two years, till 1938, to find a
post elsewhere; Lee Harlan, till 1939; and I, till 1940. We were promoted to assistant professorships, without increase in pay, to enhance our chances in the job
market.

Jack Douds, who had his doctorate, chose to go in 1937 when an opportunity
opened at Albright College, a post vacated by Gene Page. Lee and I, still short of
our doctorates, were in a less favorable position in those depressed times when
Ph.D.'s were readily available. The prospect of leaving St. Lawrence and Canton
was disheartening to me. I had the two electives I most liked teaching, and I did
not want to leave the North Country. My decision was to stay the full four years
and meanwhile to take a leave of absence for graduate study. Ruth would study
toward her doctorate at the same time, and we would go back to Columbia, where
we had taken our master's degrees.

During that year of leave, 1937–38, Ruth flourished in the French Department
and I languished in the English. I spent a nearly fruitless year investigating a
subject for a dissertation only to reject it in the end. I found little stimulus or profit
in the lectures I attended. Adding to my depressed spirits was a bear market in
securities. For living expenses in New York we were forced to sell common stock
for less than the purchase price. I considered leaving the teaching profession. I
visited a brokerage firm in lower Manhattan, but the ambience there was dis-
tasteful. All avenues seemed closed whether by my own disinclination or the realities of the depression. As good or ill fortune is doled out to us on a contingency
basis, I have been lucky on balance. But that was a year of stagnation, indecision,
and gloom.

Meanwhile Ruth was getting every encouragement from the Columbia faculty in French. After six years as housewife, she was happy to resume graduate studies. Her morale was high. I believe that she was determined to keep it so as evidence of the strength remaining in our partnership. All was courage and competence with her. By year's end she had chosen and received approval of a subject for a dissertation, a study of sensibility in the novels and plays of eighteenth-century Pierre de Marivaux. In the light of her progress, the job severance looming ahead of me came to seem less dire. We decided that she would return to Columbia the following year while I resumed teaching at St. Lawrence.

Our cottage on Lincoln Street had been sold. On returning to Canton during the summer, we took our furniture out of storage and moved into a small two-story, flimsily-built house (in local lore, a shingle slapped on a shadow) on College Court. The low rent was an advantage considering that I would have to support Ruth in New York during the forthcoming year. Actually the house proved to be quite comfortable during the next four years. The downstairs was adequately heated by one large hot-air register and the upstairs by an opening in the ceiling and the furnace pipe. One severe winter, it is true, shingle parted from shadow under a heavy accumulation of snow, and our roof partially caved in. But in the North Country we learn to cope with such emergencies. Now, fifty years later, that row of houses on College Court is still viable after much remodeling.

Ruth returned to Columbia in 1938–39 to complete her residence requirements for the doctorate. Her letters to me during that academic year and mine to her during army service in World War II are the only intimate ones which, for privacy's sake, have escaped the trash bin. Rereading them now brings Ruth back to me in the full flowering of her personality at age thirty-eight—her warmth, humor, gift for intimacy, playfulness, and two qualities that don't often go together, sensibility and clarity of mind and expression. I always knew what Ruth's feelings were and how to enhance or appease them.

Our reunions were frequent. During my vacations from teaching I joined her in New York at a friend's apartment, and she returned to Canton for long weekends at intervals of three or four weeks. Then we still had the Canton Creeper, a local train, one run of which stopped at every hamlet and several crossroads to pick up milk cans for the cities downstate. In the graduate French Department Columbia provided the ideal ambience for scholars that I had found lacking in the overcrowded English Department there. Ruth was happy in a renewal of scholarship. The following excerpts from her letters, six a week, limn her personality and also the nature of our marriage after seven years of apprenticeship.

I hope you keep your taste for Rubens and Titian women, honey. I'm certainly one of them, and I've never realized it more than I have in the last month. These slim people, both young and old, make me very conscious of my *"pleines cuisses,"* *comme dirait Rabelais.* I think I'm probably prettier naked. But my dresses don't look so nice. I shall really do something about it, afterwards. There is a scale upstairs in the infirmary, but it would be so dismal to know I'm fatter and be obliged to give up the ravishing desserts we have here. I prefer to remain in ignorance....

I have a good time here in Johnson [the graduate women's residence] now, so that I have all the distraction I can afford for the present. Last night we had our permanent table arrangements, to last till Feb. 1. We made up a group of six, and two more were put with us. I like them all very much. Two are librarians. One, a Mrs. Mason, is studying writing privately with Lafarge (?). She seems quite interesting and unconventional. And there is a nice girl from Ames, Iowa, who is a refreshing breeze from the cornfields. And another from Oberlin, whose father was a Methodist minister and who is trying to live it down. We had a circus last night. And I have another lovely friend here; her name is Ottoline Boissevain, but she calls herself Odile. She is completely bilingual, has a University Scholarship in French, and is taking the exam with me. Her father teaches at Rutgers and she is a graduate of Chicago. She is about twenty-five, awfully attractive, with thick blonde hair worn page-boy style and the loveliest willowy figure imaginable. She always seems to fly instead of walking. She studies for the exam by going to French movies, and I know she will get A's in everything. She comes in occasionally to borrow a book or to discuss Diderot. All the things I've had to learn were born in her....

You get only six letters a week, while I get seven. I suppose that isn't fair, but it does seem silly to write Sunday specials that are delivered in Canton on Monday. So I shall try to make your Saturday letters longer and nicer. But don't preserve these awful scrawls, darling. I usually sit in the middle of my bed and write them off at top speed. The sentiments are true and glowing, but the writing is awful. Yours are wonderful, darling—real love letters. I adore them, but I'm afraid they mean that you are pretty lonely....

Mr. Torrey [director of her studies in the eighteenth century] is awfully nice to me, and we have special things to talk about—not personal at all—that I wouldn't mention around Charlotte [another of her friends among candidates for the doctorate in French]. She says he likes me a lot better than he does her, and of course he does. I did good work for him, and there is just a little *intimité* of a special sort for that reason that I don't like to mix her up with. She asked me to join her in inviting Horatio [Smith, head of the graduate French faculty] to tea some day. I nearly fell dead. Charlotte said she had never heard such a fervent *no* in her life before. They are unusually nice professors—when I hear the troubles of the poor English students I realize it—but I prefer to keep them in their place and to keep mine. And you shouldn't be worried about Mr. Torrey. You know that I'm not the sort of woman who is a substitute for a burlesque show....

Mr. Torrey teased me the other day about being domestic, because I took such pleasure in fixing his tea, giving him sandwiches, etc. I told him it gave me exquisite pleasure to wait on a man again after these horrid weeks spent in libraries and classrooms. He's afraid I'm going to revert in a big way after the exam. I am, darling—I'm going to cook and cook for you, and fix my fingernails twice a day, and buy all the pretty things that are advertised in the papers. Why should I get all worked up over Montaigne or Corneille or the *"idées maîtresses"* of Pierre Bayle when I have a darling husband who matters more to me than all the ancients and moderns rolled together?...

Charlotte really is very clever and she does me lots of good. She encourages me just as you do by saying that you can't tell ahead of time just what you know but that all kinds of amazing things come to you at the moment [during an exam]. She says it is almost a religious experience, though she is really as much of a heathen as I am. Perhaps it will be a religious experience, with nice gods like Minerva and Mercury presiding over me. But at present I'm a little alarmed as to the kind of information that will come back to me. All I can seem to remember unexpectedly are naughty stories like the ones about Ninon de Lenclos or Mme du Châtelet's baby, the *"oeuvre mêlée."*...

On Saturday night when L. and A. [a married couple she had known in Canton] were walking home with me, I remarked that I hated weekends here because I was used to being played with and taken places on Friday, Saturday and Sunday. A. replied that she had never been played with at any time since her marriage. She said it quite frankly and bitterly, and L. hadn't a word to say....

Isn't Giraudoux nice! This is what he has Paris say when Hector is trying to persuade him to send Helen home and thus avoid the Trojan war. Hector reminds him that it wouldn't be the first time he has parted from a woman. *"Mon cher Hector, c'est vrai. Jusqu'ici, j'ai toujours accepté d'assez bon coeur les séparations.... Oui, tu as bien raison, l'amour comporte des moments vraiment exaltants, ce sont les ruptures.... Aussi ne me séparerai-je jamais d'Hélène, car j'ai l'impression d'avoir rompu avec toutes les autres femmes, et j'ai mille libertés et mille noblesses au lieu d'une."*

*Suis-je Hélène, chéri, ou une de ces autres femmes que Pâris est si content de quitter?...*

No, I certainly don't like it better in Johnson than with you, lover. That is a very silly question, for which you should be slapped gently and then kissed on the ears. I like not to have to cook—that is true—and I like the feeling of being halfway a professional woman. But I certainly do *not* like the constant company of females or life in a large group or any of the old-maid aspects of this existence. I want a job, an apartment, and my husband....

Charlotte is terribly embarrassed about a conversation she had with Horatio. The day after our tea with Mr. Torrey, she walked across the campus with Horatio. She told him about the tea, about our "lionizing" Mr. Torrey, etc. She said, "He was our lion. Won't you come sometime and be our unicorn?" He thanked her and said he would be glad to. Then in a minute he began to laugh and said something to her in French which she didn't understand. She pretended to, however, and laughed too. He said, "You know the unicorn out at the Cloisters in the tapestry is all covered with gore. Do you want that to happen to me?" And when he left her at Phil. Hall, he said in his best professorial manner, "I advise you, mademoiselle, to look up the history of unicorns before applying the name to me." When she told the story to me, however, I was able to enlighten her immediately. Of course Horatio was thinking of the unicorn who can be captured only by a virgin. He falls asleep in her lap and then the hunters stab him. And now she hasn't the nerve to face him. Doesn't she have an awful time with unicorns and professors?...

Henri Peyre told Jack last summer that Horatio Smith is a brilliant man and a fine head, but that *"entre nous"* he is a bit *"tapé"* on the subject of Ste-Beuve. Believe me, I'm up on the private life of Ste-Beuve. When he met his former mistress, Adèle Hugo, some ten years after their break, he wrote in his notebook, *"Elle n'a plus de coeur, elle n'a jamais eu d'esprit."* Isn't that dirty? Horatio would love to have me quote that....

Don't think I'm asking for too much freedom, lover, in wanting to have a career. Nothing matters to me but you, and yet I can be a much more attractive wife and also a much more devoted one if I have a professional life which will keep me alert and integrated....

I had a horrible dream about putting a recipe for chocolate bread pudding in my exam for Gerig. Charlotte made it up and served it to all the professors in oatmeal bowls! You see how demoralizing this double life of wife and scholar can turn out to be....

I'm so excited I can't write sensibly! Ottoline told me that all the grades were in. And when I reached the sec's office, who should be there but Horatio! Miss D. said, "You did very well, Mrs. Jamieson." Then she handed me a pencil and read them off. I was so pleased I nearly wept. Horatio looked up and said, "That's something to be proud of, to be sure." And he smiled his adorable smile....

I simply love what I am doing here, but also I simply hate to be away from you and have you all uncared for. *Méchant petit, je t'adore....*

I have examined very carefully my motive in wanting to wear the pink nightie for Paul Hazard. I know what it is and I have been fully rewarded. It was simply that I couldn't resist satisfying my curiosity about what you would do in the face of such a suggestion. You were magnificent, darling, a real *héros de roman*, who shoots his wife on the slightest suspicion of infidelity....

I'm trying to save some of the sparkle for you darling. I'm sure it will last, though I wish it would settle down just a little bit so that I could get into my thesis. I've been told that I scintillate so when I enter the dining room that people need dark glasses. But I'm not telling my grades, though one seeps out once in a while....

*Quelle idée!* To say that you have no vices except smoking! I could name dozens of them—you swear, you wear out the toes of your socks, you like everything that comes in bottles, you leer at women's legs, you unbutton their sweaters and slide their zippers, you read naughty French novels—I could go on and on, but I adore all these vices so much that it overexcites me just to enumerate them. But I've said enough to show that smoking would add very little to your wicked charm. Smoking makes a man all smelly like Harry Reiff. I am violently opposed to your going back to it. *Ariane te prie, petit, ne fume pas....*

I went to the Varney tea [Mme Varney was her professor in phonetics] with much fear and trembling, and I had a perfectly grand time. I dressed all up and really I looked quite nice in my blue dress and my hat with the veil, *comme tu sais, chéri.* Mme Varney was her sparkling self, and she introduced me as *"une brillante étudiant"* et *"qui a passé un merveilleux examen pour le doctorat."* Mme V put her arms around me and asked me to pour so that she could move about and chat. When we left, she came out in the hall and said to Mme Mariani, *"N'est-ce pas que j'ai des charmantes élèves?"* embracing me again....

I wish I could remember every word of my interview with Horatio this morning. He was charming and gracious as usual. I thanked him for the scholarship and he said that he and Professor Torrey had pressed it hard because they felt I was worthy of it. Then he adopted his usual line with women, "Don't work too hard." I said I didn't think women did overwork on scholarly things, that I envied men their ability to stay steadily by a job. He said he supposed it wasn't really overwork with women, but that they got themselves into such states! I said, "Yes, but we can always weep over it, Professor Smith." He beamed and said, "You don't know how lucky you are to have that resource. We men have to keep it all bottled up inside." He was just adorable at that moment, lover. He urged me to take walks and go to the movies. I said, "And visit my husband?" And he said, "By all means, visit your husband!"....

When we read in class, Mme Varney was most flattering to me. She said my reading showed *"beaucoup de goût, bien des choses fines et délicates"*; she praised me for having *"travaillé dure"* and for making *"beaucoup de progrès."*...

M. Muller has the department almost in hysterics over a presentation of the battle of Roncevaux, which he acted out in Philology class last Wednesday. He was in particularly fine form, and so was able to do Roland and the twelve peers plus the whole Saracen army all at the same time. His cheeks puffed out as he blew the horn, and he held his head when his skull cracked, as Roland's is supposed to do.

[ 84 ]

Then he began fighting—*il coupait la tête, tranchait le bras, perçait la chair jusqu'aux côtes*—in the meantime pulling off his coat, grabbing a ruler, throwing chalk, etc. The class nearly died, and Muller was so tickled that he did the whole scene all over again. *Malheureusement,* the poor man was so excited that he didn't get all his belongings gathered up properly. Sometime during class or shortly afterward, he lost his key ring, with both office and car keys. The hero of Roncevaux was obliged to abandon his car on the streets of New York and go home to Jersey on the ferry....

I wish you could have heard M. Muller at the Institut last night, darling. His *conférence* this year, *Paroles historiques,* was much better than the *Contes marseillais* that you heard last year. He was in wonderful form and the audience, a huge one, nearly had hysterics. He began with the baptism of Clovis at Rheims in 496, showing that the noble words spoken there represented more truly *"l'âme du peuple"* than do any of the great sayings of antiquity, such as *"Et tu, Brute"* and *"Delenda est Carthago."* He came on through the ages, quoting Charlemagne, Wm the Conqueror, Francis I at Pavia *("Tout est perdu, fors l'honneur"*—*le vrai esprit français!),* Henri IV (he debunked *"Paris vaut bien une messe"* but kept the tale about the white plume), Louis XIV *("l'état, c'est moi").* As a philologist he reveled in the wonderful consonantal bite of Voltaire's *"Ecrasez l'infâme"* and in the expressive accent tonique in such expressions as Sully's *"Labouráge et paturáge sont les deux mamelles de la France."* (The *"-ages"* could be heard all the way to Broadway.) After he had rounded things off with the World War, he closed with an epilogue that was truly Mullerian–*"paroles historique dans le drame."* He described a play called *Le Siège de Lyon,* in which an eyewitness, telling of the slaughter and pillage, speaks thus: *"On brulait les maisons, on tuait les enfants, et sur le sein de l'épouse on écrasait l'époux."* And he closed with the story of the counter revolutionaries of Vendée during the French Revolution. When the army was drawn up in battle array, the leader, Jacques Rougot (?), addressed them: *"Si j'avance, suivez-moi; si je recule, tuez-moi; et si je meurs, vengez-moi."* In a play *Les Vendéens,* with Rougot as hero, the actor who played the part was very jittery because a lot of his friends were in the audience ready to make fun of him. When he reached the historic words, he spoke them thus: *"Si j'avance, reculez-moi; si je recule, avancez-moi; et si je meurs, tuez-moi."* Cher M. Muller! On the way home Mlle Werner, her hand on her heart, pronounced the *parole historique, "Il n'y a que lui!"*...

Gaze long and hard at the enclosed stub because you'll probably never see another like it. Then put it in the little drawer of my desk so that I can save it to show the grandchildren. I went to the opera last night, love, and sat in the orchestra, first row on the side. It was an excellent seat, from which one could see every corner of the stage and hear absolutely everything and see most of the grease paint. The whole performance was one of the biggest surprises I've ever had. Miss Reiley got hold of ten tickets, four box and six orchestra, free, because it was a benefit performance for which rich people buy lots of seats and then give them away. She manages to get a number of tickets every year that way for Johnson Hall girls. The opera was the *Barber of Seville*, with Pons, J. C. Thomas, Martini, Pinza, etc. But of course Pons would be indisposed, so Bidu Sayao sang in her place. Will you look for a review in today's *Times*, lover? I thought it was grand, though the excitement of the orchestra circle probably had a lot to do with it. Thomas isn't such a good Figaro as Tibbett, by any means. But Martini was good and Pinza simply wonderful. I was disappointed not to hear Pons, though I like Bidu Sayao very much. The Rossini music is lovely....

M. d'H asked me to go out to dinner with him and then make whoopee during the evening. I told him I was too busy. He looked at me admiringly and said I always looked so brilliant and so healthy. He wanted to know whether I am an *"athlète"*! I told him no, that it was just *élan vital*, and he said yes and he envied me my quick mind and my fine memory....

Mme Varney almost sent me to the seventh heaven last night. She said I read beautifully, that the intonation is *"tout à fait juste,"* that it is an accomplishment extremely difficult for a foreigner to acquire and would be very valuable in college teaching....

Yesterday Nancy Osborne, a cute little girl here in Johnson, invited Mme Varney to lunch with her in Butler Hall. Nancy knew Mme V. in Paris before she came to Columbia. Nancy said she couldn't get five minutes connected conversation with Mme V., who was always interrupting to talk about me. She described me as *"une personne tout à fait sympathique, charmante, adorable,"* and all her pet adjectives....

Yes, the eighteenth century is adorable, darling. And do you know, I should never have been able to understand it properly without the long *apprentissage* with my love? You see much more in Chamfort than I did. I do adore my century and my subject. I have completely forgotten that there is some horrid philosophy in it that I can't understand....

Last night at dinner the girls were talking about Leslie Howard, whom they all admire, the esthetic type, you understand. One girl said she knew a man like that once, but unfortunately she let him slip away from her. I had all I could do to keep from telling them the measures I took to keep you from slipping away from me....

We are going to forget all about Europe now and concentrate on the arrival in Canton of Lotus and Magnolia, which will be much more splendid than Hitler's entry into Prague. The little things are all eager to come; I can hardly restrain them enough to settle down to Marivaux and Mme de Lambert. I just get in one good week's work after I come back, and then I begin to plan for the next visit. *Petit mari*, you are a very disturbing person. If only I had a more ordinary husband, I might really sometime become a *femme savante.*

Those letters seem as delightful to me now as they did then. True, there is a strain of narcissism in them. Childless, lacking an object on whom to externalize our pride, we encouraged narcissism in each other. It makes a contribution to happiness. And Ruth, in her scholarship and her independent career, escaped the fate of the generality of women-in-love as depicted by Simone de Beauvoir: "Byron well said:'Man's love is of man's life a thing apart; 'Tis woman's whole existence.'... [For men] the beloved woman is only one value among others; they wish to integrate her into their existence and not to squander it entirely on her. For woman, on the contrary, to love is to relinquish everything for the benefit of a master.... 'Without a master, she is a scattered bouquet.'" In our marriage I was not the master, nor was Ruth, for lack of a master, a scattered bouquet.

By 1938 the depression had generated a pocket of Marxism in the St. Lawrence faculty as elsewhere in academic circles. Apolitical at that time (I had yet to learn the leverage one has in a democracy like ours), I was slow to take an interest in this development. But friends finally persuaded me to read a handbook of Marxism. I was at first attracted by the idealism of the Communist Manifesto and the words of the young American observer in Russia just after the Revolution, John Reed: "I have seen the future, and it works." But in the thirties current events belied that idealism in the Stalinist dictatorship, the purges, the suppression of individualism and creativity, which to a humanist were unacceptable. I never became a communist sympathizer like a few of my colleagues, who did not abandon the faith till some years later.

I did, however, join a new labor union on campus, an affiliate of the American Federation of Teachers. The system of limited tenure for the English Department was the chief incentive for the formation of the union; members of other departments feared that rotating instructorships would soon be applied to them. There was a chapter of the American Association of University Professors at St. Lawrence, but the unionists held that it was not aggressive enough. By late 1939 over half of the faculty had joined the new union.

Ruth completed her residence requirements at Columbia in the spring of 1939. During the ensuing year she finished writing her dissertation here in Canton, with occasional trips to New York. She passed her orals and defended her dissertation successfully in the spring of 1940. Columbia required publication. *Marivaux: A Study in Sensibility* was published in a small edition by the King's Crown Press in 1941, and Ruth then received her doctorate. *Marivaux* was reprinted in 1969 by the Octagon Press.

The year 1939–40 at St. Lawrence was a stormy one that led to my reappointment and a change in administration. The following excerpts from the Watertown *Daily Times* and the campus weekly, *The Hill News*, tell the story. Coincidentally the Dairy Farmers' Union of St. Lawrence County was clamoring for higher milk prices. It and our campus union, representing quite different causes, worked in symbiosis. I remember spending evenings at the Locy farm near Canton—Eva Locy was secretary of the local Farmers' Union—plotting strategy. And of course this two-way strife was a bonanza for the Canton reporter of the Watertown *Times*. Most academic quarrels are zealously kept under cover. When one does erupt publicly, journalists are likely to reach for hyperbole. Thus the first article in the *Times*, dated January 16, 1940, confers a premature doctorate on me and a popularity more forensic than real. But events are reported accurately. I have inserted a letter from my father, an old hand at fighting unions, and a copy of a letter I addressed to the Pages in the midst of the fight.

*Watertown Daily* Times, *January 16, 1940.* Forty-eight members of the faculty of St. Lawrence University protested the dismissal of Prof. Paul F. Jamieson of the English department at a meeting held in the administration building yesterday afternoon. Dr. [sic] Jamieson was advised of his dismissal from the faculty this week. The dismissal will be effective at the end of the school year in June.

A resolution protesting the dismissal was passed unanimously with Dr. Laurens H. Seelye, president of the university, present. Dr. Seelye refused to discuss the meeting afterward, referring a reporter for the Watertown *Times* to Richard C. Ellsworth, secretary of the university.

Mr. Ellsworth declared that he was not at the meeting and knew nothing of what had occurred. He said: "The meeting was an informal one called by friends of Paul Jamieson and beyond that I know nothing."

Dr. Jamieson's dismissal was based on the rotating policy inaugurated in the English department by President Seelye four years ago and did not concern his academic competence, responsible administration sources declared today. At the time the policy was begun the younger members of the department, including Jamieson, were told that they should not regard their appointment as permanent. It was also pointed out that technically Dr. Jamieson is not being dismissed but rather not being reappointed for the coming school year.

Faculty members who called the meeting were reluctant to discuss it last night. From several sources it was learned, however, that between 15 and 20 members of the faculty had spoken during the meeting in support of Dr. Jamieson and that those present were unanimous in his support. Dr. Jamieson has been on the faculty for six [sic] years.

The meeting created wide discussion among faculty members last night. The discharge of the popular young professor has created a storm on the "hill" for the past week.... The meeting was jointly sponsored by the American Federation of Teachers' Union of St. Lawrence University and the American Association of University Professors.

On January 17, 1940, the *Hill News*, the student weekly, carried a front page news story nearly identical to the above-quoted one, a letter to the editor, and an editorial.

*To the Editor:* As students or former students of Mr. Paul Jamieson, we would like at this time to publicly protest the action of the Administration in failing to reappoint Mr. Jamieson.

We have the highest regard for Mr. Jamieson's qualities of scholarship and teaching ability. We admire him and respect him both as a man and as a teacher and we feel that the loss of a man of his caliber would be of great detriment to the University in general and the English Department in particular.

If the policy of "rotation" necessitates the dismissal of one of St. Lawrence's ablest professors, we should like to question the advisability of such a policy. As English majors we are also interested to know why the policy is in effect only in the English Department, when it is obvious that through such a policy some of the department's ablest professors cannot be reappointed. We hope that in the case of Mr. Jamieson the Administration will reconsider its decision.

> Betty List '40
> Carol Gilday '40
> Jerrie Posselt '41
> Beverly McCammon '41
> Betty Hatch '40
> Margaret Hannon '41
> Barbara Ramsdell '40
> Barbara Wakefield '41
> Caroline Meyer '40

*Editorial in the same issue:* As faculty adviser, Mr. Jamieson is closer to the Hill News than any of his colleagues. Nevertheless, he has not asked the staff for any publicity; rather, he has been strongly reluctant to have the facts of the situation, to say nothing of an editorial opinion, published in any newspaper. The Hill News, out of deference to Mr. Jamieson's wishes, probably would have ignored the case if one daily newspaper had not carried part of the story yesterday. But the story has been published, and the Hill News cannot close its eyes to the situation.

Members of the Hill News staff have attested to Mr. Jamieson's ability as a teacher, and a majority of the faculty have lauded his teaching ability, character and scholarship. It has been indicated by one member of the administration that neither Mr. Jamieson's teaching ability, character, nor scholarship is under fire. It has been pointed out that under the system of rotation Mr. Jamieson's time to leave St. Lawrence has arrived, and the administration regrets that it must sever relations with the professor.

Here indeed is a dilemma. Mr. Jamieson wishes to remain at St. Lawrence; the administration wishes he could remain; the faculty has petitioned the administration to retain him; students consulted would like him to stay; every group seems to agree that his retention would be fine. But a policy dictates that he must leave. The policy no doubt was adopted in the best interests of the university. Yet this policy has given rise to a situation in which mere theory has become a dogma that must not be violated. This is fantastic. Surely St. Lawrence is not a community chained to a formula.

The administration should reconsider Mr. Jamieson's case immediately; if the weight of right is on the side of Mr. Jamieson and we believe it is, then the policy should be abandoned. A policy does not approach the importance of a law. The constitution of the United States is the supreme law of the land; yet it has been amended by the people and interpreted in hundreds of ways by the supreme court. A democracy cannot falter when change appears necessary. The administration cannot be respected if it becomes a slave to theoretical conceptions.

*Resolution passed at a special meeting of the Thelomathesian Society, student governing organization:*

Whereas, we feel qualified to judge the teaching ability of our instructors and professors, and

Whereas, those of us who are students or former students of Mr. Paul F. Jamieson, assistant professor of English, believe in his excellence as a teacher, and

Whereas, a majority of the faculty lauded Mr. Jamieson's character, scholarship and teaching ability, and

Whereas, we believe the board of administration of St. Lawrence university would be grateful to be advised of our opinions, and

Whereas, the board of administration has seen fit not to reappoint Mr. Jamieson to the faculty for the college year 1940-41, and

Whereas Mr. Jamieson has requested the board of administration for reappointment,

Be it resolved, that we, the Thelomathesian society of St. Lawrence university, respectfully request the board of administration to reconsider its decision in regard to Mr. Jamieson and to reappoint Mr. Jamieson to the faculty for the college year 1940-41, and

Be it further resolved that the secretary of Thelomathesian society sign this resolution and forward it to the board of administration and forward a copy of the resolution to Mr. Jamieson.

Adopted January 19, 1940. Wallace St. Andrews, sec.

*Letter from my father in Des Moines, dated January 22, 1940:*

Dear Paul,

We received your letter and clippings Saturday. Of course I regret to hear of the controversy. A fight of that kind will do you no good even if you win. But now that you are in it I suppose you will have to go through with it.

You apparently have the Union fighting for you in New York. In Iowa I am still fighting the Union or perhaps the better way to put it would be to say the Union is still fighting me. They have been quite active the past three or four years. During the year when the sitdown strikes were popular they made their threats, but could not get a one of my employees to help them, so failed. They have tried every session of the legislature to have the state adopt legislation requiring the Union label on state work, but have failed. They are now trying to get the printing board to force some kind of action, but I hear the printing board refuses to do anything until the legislature acts. So what is next?

All that I have done is to refuse to sign, and to tell one of my employees who was being worked on, to ask the union representatives if they would guarantee him steady employment. They couldn't do it as half the union printers and binders in the city were out of work at the time. They are not bothering my employees now, but are trying in other ways to bring pressure on me.

I am writing the above simply to show you how stubborn an employer can be when he knows he was wronged at one time. That happened in 1919, almost twenty years ago. And perhaps the powers that are in control of the University may be just as stubborn as I have been. And suppose they should yield to the pressure of the Union, the professors and the student body, won't they always have it in for you having been forced to do something contrary to their desires?

You seem to think the publicity you are getting out of this will help you in landing another position in some other university. My opinion is that it will be harmful.

But please understand we are for you and are hoping that the University board will do away with the rotating system. We could never understand why it applied to the English Department and not to other departments.

With love and best wishes,

Yours, J. M. J.

Union busters die hard, and all my father had to say one month later was this: "Congratulations. We were all greatly pleased to hear the gratifying news. We hope you will get to stay in Canton as long as you desire to teach at St. Lawrence." He was not aware of the strength of the liberal tradition at St. Lawrence. My letter to

[  91  ]

Gene and Helen Page reflects some of that tradition in sidelights of the struggle that even the Watertown *Times* did not ferret out.

Canton, January 20, 1940

Dear Helen and Gene,

Things have exploded up here this week, and I am the ammunition. Once the firing got started, there was no controlling it, and it has gone far beyond what the union, the AAUP, or I had bargained for. Only Bill Houk and Charles Lightbody appear to have foreseen it all.

I hate a fight and would probably have gone meekly on to the June 1940 deadline if Bill had not managed to pump enough adrenaline into me last month to ask for reinstatement and, after it was refused, turn my case over to the union. The cases of Allen, Charles, and Ruth Willard had been handled in a quiet, underground way, and I supposed mine would be too. But after vacation the executive committees of the union and the AAUP hatched a scheme to call the faculty into session to protest my dismissal. I consented on condition that there would be no publicity, but someone not a member of either organization tipped off the Watertown *Times* reporter. To correct errors and secure a favorable press, the union officers then began to talk. The enclosed clippings tell the story of what has happened since. They do not tell, though, of the magnificent role played by Clarence,* who has had one conference after another with Slim (Seelye), spoke effectively at the Monday meeting, and at the regular Tuesday faculty meeting made and supported motions to appoint a committee to study a comprehensive tenure plan and to negotiate for faculty representation on the Board of Trustees. Both motions were passed unanimously, in spite of Slim's efforts to scuttle them. Dick [Gaines] says that his father is riding on top of the world.

Here are some byproducts: At the Monday meeting Warner rose to ask why the rotating plan should be applied to the English Department alone; why not to all departments; why not to the Administration, through to the president; and with that he cast the evil eye on Dr. Seelye and sat down.

The regular monthly faculty picnic on Monday evening was boycotted by all except two new faculty families and the Seelyes. Later Slim came over to the gym for a little company, but was so coldly received by the faculty volley ball players that he left after one game.

Demi Aguirre, dapper little Spanish instructor from Chile, is darting gleefully about from one group of intriguers to another. He says that he feels right at home; it is just like a Chilean revolution.

---

* Clarence Gaines, head of the English Department.

[ 92 ]

The Dean, Ellsworth, and Grace Lynde* (this is confidential) have been egging the union on. It was going too slow to suit them. When Doc Delmage** had a talk with the Dean early this week, the Dean rallied him: "Have you got any fight in you, Rutherford? You're a North Country boy. Got any fight in you? Your old father had." Our best guess is that it was Ellsworth who gave to the press the story of the Monday meeting. There is now a plan afoot to circulate a petition among the alumni to urge the Board to retain the Dean after he reaches the age of seventy this spring—in order to preserve and carry on the liberal traditions of St. Lawrence!

Jencks*** arrived Wednesday night and has been living in Dean-Eaton Hall ever since. He began his chapel talk on Thursday by saying that he had passed a very restful night in the dormitory, had had breakfast in bed according to the SLU tradition [a fabricated story in the New York *Times* about student life at SLU], and had found on his tray a copy of the Watertown *Times* and the *Hill News*. At this point everyone listened intently, but he went on to talk about the war in Europe. He just stays in his suite and receives one hothead after another.

My case happened to tap the climate of five years of gathering resentment in all quarters. All support of me is just vituperation of Seelye. The real issue is indicated by signs hung on the trees behind the Alpha House, which looks like the Forest of Arden, though the message is not so loving: "Back to Beirut."

After the student Thelomathesian meeting Doc Delmage, who always likes to dress the occasion up with his little speech—his coinages are current all over campus: "coolie labor," "academic sophistry" (Seelyeism), "a Machiavelli in skirts" (Dean of Women), "Slim moves in mysterious ways his blunders to perform"—shouted to a group of students, "You have saved the college! I would have resigned if this had not gone through!"

And all the while Jencks sits over there in Dean-Eaton looking like the Sphinx. Board meeting January 27. *Qui sait?*

Today I am fed up. This has been the longest week of my life. But if I am reappointed, I shall be glad, and for an utterly irrelevant reason. Last summer I discovered some lily pads, masses of white ones backed by the purple spikes of pickerelweed, all in full bloom, on the Saranac River under Mt. Ampersand. I think that is why I asked for reappointment, though Bill Houk and my scrappy colleagues, who want to scuttle the rotating plan, had something to do with it. If I am not reappointed I'm no worse off than before. The union is pure gold—a substitute for religion. Solidarity forever!

---

* Members of the Board of Administration.

** SLU graduate, my colleague and friend in the English Department and on into retirement.

*** Millard Jencks, chairman of the Board of Trustees and recently retired executive in the publishing firm Ginn & Company.

The Thelomathesian resolution viewed my case as a contest between policy and expediency. In this time of ferment another such issue arose as Dean Edwin Hulett approached the mandatory retirement age of seventy. In true Laurentian spirit it was expediency that prevailed. The issue was resolved as advocated in an open letter to the Board of Trustees. If I have ever known, today I do not know who wrote that letter; yet I have a strong suspicion that it was Doc Delmage, SLU '32, spokesman for Laurentian values during my time on the faculty.

*Open letter as quoted in the Watertown* Times *for January 20, 1940*: A rumor has recently spread about the campus that Dean Edwin L. Hulett might retire in June or September, 1940. In the uncertain state of relations which now prevails between the administration and the faculty of St. Lawrence university, nothing could be more unfortunate; nothing could be worse for the present and future good of our college. Dean Hulett enjoys the fullest confidence of all the students and faculty members at St. Lawrence. The dean is, moreover, beloved with the utmost warmth of affection and depth of loyalty by every living alumna and alumnus, as well as by every student and teacher on the hill. With Dean John Murray Atwood and Secretary Richard C. Ellsworth, he represents the living tradition of sportsmanship and justice and truth—the spirit which is St. Lawrence. He has always stood for scholarship, honesty and fair play.

According to trustee rulings, however, the dean, who this year will reach the age of 70, will automatically be retired, unless, of course, there is mass sentiment against this retirement. Because of present difficulties at the university, we believe there is such a mass sentiment in favor of the dean. We believe that he should at least be given the opportunity, as were those other two grand old Laurentians, Dr. Charles Kelsey Gaines and the late Dr. Robert Dale Ford, to retire or continue in service as long as he likes. A precedent has already been set; let the dean make his own choice.

If Dean Hulett is willing to continue as dean, we believe that he should be urged to do so by an acclamation which cannot fail to be unanimous. Upon him, Dean Atwood and Secretary Ellsworth, and upon them alone, depend and will depend the stability and continuity of instruction and fellowship which link the generation of Dr. Charles Kelsey Gaines with the generation of Dr. Ward Priest, and that with the generation now in college.

Let us not hesitate to visit the dean and express our complete and unqualified faith in him and in his progressive and democratic but at the same time sane and sober policies. Let us write letters to alumni and trustees in favor of his retention as dean after 1940. Above all, let us support him by an ovation from Thelomathesian. If Dean Hulett is willing, let us draft him for service for life, or at least until the time when the college is in no emergency and has no more need of him. He deserves a rest, but he has never been known to shirk the call of duty. Long live the old, the tried and true, the real St. Lawrence.

*Watertown* Times, *January 23, 1940:* A promise of "sympathetic" attention to the case of Prof. Paul Jamieson, dismissed English department instructor, was made by the board of administration of St. Lawrence university yesterday afternoon. The dismissal will be considered at the regular meeting of the board in February when appointments for the coming year are considered.

*Watertown* Times, *February 20, 1940:* Prof. Paul F. Jamieson of the English department has been offered appointment for the college year 1940-41, Richard C. Ellsworth, secretary of the university, announced today.

*Watertown* Times, *April 20, 1940:* Dr. Laurens H. Seelye will tender his resignation as president of St. Lawrence university at the board meeting here [Canton]. Announcement of the resignation was made in a press notice given out this morning by the secretary's office.

*Watertown* Times, *May 6, 1940:* Millard H. Jencks, Upper Montclair, N.J., chairman of the board of trustees of St. Lawrence university, will take over his duties as acting president of the university on September 1, it was announced today. Mr. Jencks was named acting president by the board on Saturday following the resignation of Dr. Laurens H. Seelye.

The rotation plan did not survive the Seelye presidency. But many years were to pass before faculty, administration, and trustees could agree on a comprehensive tenure plan. After World War II the union struggled to survive with dwindling membership but finally succumbed in the absence of any perceived injustice comparable to rotating instructorships. In initiating that plan in 1936 and applying it to one department only, President Seelye did not reckon with the strength of St. Lawrence's liberal tradition with its unwritten law of justice and fair play. When the *Antigone* of Sophocles came up for discussion in sophomore English class, it had a special impact on me. Seelye I associated with Creon, ruler of Thebes, who persisted in a fated course in spite of warnings that he was violating unwritten laws. Seelye had had time and intimations to change course: the erosion of support in faculty and student bodies, the defection of some fellow administrators, the growing strength of a militant union. When that union asked to take up my case, I agreed on condition that one last personal appeal be rejected. Seelye did reject it and held to that course amidst a Greek chorus of faculty, students, and the press.

## X  CALM WATERS

OR A MALE PROFESSOR one of the satisfactions of teaching is the quadrennial turnover of pretty girls. I was especially fortunate that year of 1939–40 when my job was in jeopardy. A half century later I can still visualize that class in the Romantic Movement. Pretty girls were generously distributed in it like water lilies on the Saranac River. I hardly knew in what direction to look for reactions to my best points about the romantic poets. Though I have no statistical proof, my impression over the years has been that the prettiest girls are also the brightest, whether by natural selection, the self-confidence that beauty engenders, or the unequal justice of the gods. So there is a double motive for fixing attention on these beauties. It gratifies the aesthetic sense and it is also a telltale register of the effectiveness of your remarks on qualified students. When the professor scores, eyes light up, mobile lips curl into smiles, and there is a flurry of note-taking. Your watchful glance is for her a dual tribute and for you a double gratification. Rapport blooms. Several members of that class were among the nine co-eds who signed a letter to the *Hill News* supporting my reinstatement.

Edward Blankman, Rutherford ("Doc") Delmage—both Laurentians—and John Bicknell joined the English Department in the 1930s. They became close friends of Ruth and me. John's wife, Evangeline, had a trained contralto voice, and almost every time we were together, I insisted that she sing for me that siren song *Mon coeur s'ouvre à ta voix* from *Samson et Dalila*, which in spite of its insincerity in the opera story, always moved me to tears. The Bicknells never returned after World War II, when John served in the Navy, but we have kept in touch. Ed Blankman and Doc Delmage have been lifelong associates and friends. Ed died suddenly a few years ago; Doc is enjoying a long retirement.

In the summer of 1940 Ed Blankman joined me in an eighty-five-mile, one-week canoe trip from Old Forge to Saranac Lake Village through the Fulton Chain of lakes, Raquette Lake, the Raquette River, Long Lake, and the Saranac River and chain lakes. We rented a wood-and-canvas canoe in Old Forge. At that time the Adirondack Division of the New York Central was still in operation, and rented boats were shipped back from Saranac Lake to the boat livery in Old Forge. The first four nights we slept in lean-tos or, when they were not available, under a tarp and an overturned canoe, the prey of blackflies and mosquitoes. One night we were drenched by a heavy rainstorm. It was a relief on the fifth night to take a room in an inn at Coreys, where we phoned Doc Delmage and John Bicknell to join us the next day. They drove up in John's car, and all four of us climbed Ampersand Mountain by the old trail, much of which was a rustic staircase constructed over the years by a former fire observer assigned to this fire-tower peak. After the climb we swam in Middle Saranac Lake and paddled across it to a piny island, where we camped on the sixth night. The last day Ed and I paddled down the Saranac River and through Lower Saranac Lake to the Ampersand dock, where John met us in his car for the drive back to Canton. That canoe trip intensified my love of the Adirondacks, already awakened by the mountaineering preceding it. The North Country was now home to me.

In the fall of 1940 Ruth was asked to fill a vacancy in French in the Modern Languages Department at St. Lawrence. She had satisfied requirements for the doctorate except publication of her dissertation, which followed in the spring of 1941. For the next twenty years she was to teach French at St. Lawrence first under Mlle. Plaisance then Mlle. Leliepvre and finally, in her last three years on the faculty, as acting head of the Modern Languages Department herself. She insisted on the title "acting head" because she hoped soon to be relieved of the burden of paperwork and hiring new instructors in an ever volatile department. But the Dean kept putting off the selection of a new chairman of the department, and finally, at the age of fifty-nine, Ruth took early retirement in 1960. Her teaching career, which also included secretaryship of the local chapter of Phi Beta Kappa, was deeply satisfying to her until those last three burdensome years, trying to her health.

In late May of 1941 I received word that my father was dying of a ruptured appendix and uremic poisoning. Classes were over for the year. I arrived in Des Moines just a few hours before he died at age sixty-nine to find him in an oxygen tent and a coma. My sister Ruth and her husband had arrived earlier and left soon after the funeral. Mary remained with Mother all summer. I stayed on for six weeks to settle the estate. Burdened by debt incurred in the collapse of market values in farm and ranch lands in the early 1920s, Father had finally worked his way clear but had not accumulated much capital. Assets consisted of equity in the house, one ranch on the plains of Canada, dubious shares in Texas oil fields, the bindery as a going business, a little cash, and the proceeds of insurance policies. Mother wanted to keep the house for the time being. My effort was to invest what capital I could raise in a manner to assure her of a living income and some protection against inflation.

The weeks dragged on before I found a buyer for the bindery. The war in Europe and the prospect of our getting involved made entrepreneurs cautious. Ads in the Des Moines *Register* brought no response. I could have sold the machinery and current contracts and liquidated the business. But this would have been unfair to employees who had worked in the plant most of their adult lives. I knew some of them well from my own work there as teenager. They implored me to sell the plant as a going concern. They had benefited from paternalistic management; it had been understood that my father would provide steady employment in bad as well as good times in return for their resistance to overtures of the union. A wily former business associate of my father waited out my predicament for some weeks before making a low bid to take over the plant as a continuing operation. The value of the machinery in the secondhand market was probably greater than his bid, but in the end I sold the plant to him, much to the relief of the employees.

My own investments in common stock had been piecemeal as savings accumulated; any congruity in the package was accidental. Now I had an opportunity to plan an entire portfolio for my mother at one time. The twelve issues I purchased worked out well in ensuing years. They assured her of a modest income and of appreciation in excess of the rate of inflation. Two years later she sold the house in Des Moines and moved to Los Angeles to be near my sister Mary. She was to have a widowhood of twenty-two years. As her health began to fail in her eighties, she liquidated most of her investments and purchased life care in a rest home in Hollywood. When I visited her there, I was impressed by the near-luxury and humaneness of her surroundings. At age eighty-seven she died peacefully in the hospital ward of the rest home.

In August, after my return to Canton that summer, an association began that was to last for the next thirty years. Stephen Slaughter, my Drake classmate and companion on the cattle boat, and his wife, Wilma, rented a cabin near Long Lake for the month of August in that and succeeding years. Ruth and I joined them for overnight stays or for day outings at some rendezvous point in the Adirondacks. Steve and I spent the days together climbing mountains while Ruth and Wilma amused themselves at the cabin or in shopping expeditions to Saranac Lake or Lake Placid. In late afternoon Steve and I joined our wives for a picnic at one of the lakeshore state campgrounds. A professional photographer with a portrait studio in Tarrytown, Steve took innumerable photos in black and white on our mountain hikes and of our picnics, sending us a selection each fall. Over the years Steve and I must have

*Paul and Stephen Slaughter returning from a three-day hiking and camping trip*

*Picnic at Meacham Lake from left, Ruth, Wilma Slaughter, Paul*

climbed nearly a hundred peaks, a few of them more than once. The initial essay in my *Adirondack Pilgrimage* is a sketch of Steve as the American Adam and a memoir of our adventures.

Doc Delmage fell in love with the prettiest of the pretty girls in my class in the Romantic Movement (also in his on Shakespeare) during that banner year for pulchritude on campus, 1939–40. She rejected his proposal of marriage. This was the love of his life. He has remained a bachelor. We all knew that Ed Blankman would eventually marry. He was not one to be boxed in by a one and only. When he joined the English Department, he was courting a girl in Gouverneur, a discreet distance from the campus. But in 1941–42 he fell in love with a co-ed in his freshman class, Ruth Costa, the daughter of an importer of Havana cigars and a concert singer and teacher of voice. Ruth inherited her olive complexion and classic bone structure from her Hispanic father. She did not at all resemble her mother, a woman of fair complexion, large girth, and conspicuously aggressive manner. As a visitor at their home in Scarsdale, I remember Mrs. Costa's graphic demonstration of how she elbowed her way through the crowds of Manhattan, jabbing victims to left and right on her imperial progress. Ed's attitude toward his mother-in-law was a mixture of affection and amusement. His pet name for her was Mater Battleaxa.

Love affairs between professor and student are fairly common throughout the land and are viewed indulgently. But Ed was inclined towards caution. To accommodate this quirk of his and share our warmth in the cozy little house on College Court during frigid winter nights, we offered him this haven on our nights out at the movies or bridge parties. This arrangement continued for months under the euphemism of baby-sitting. Ed and Ruth were married in 1943.

## XI  WORLD WAR II

P EARL HARBOR radically changed the lives of all of us. In the summer
of 1942 Doc and Ed were drafted into the Army. I turned thirty-nine that
summer, the uppermost age eligible for the draft. Exceptions were made for
men with dependents, especially older men. But Ruth and I were childless and
Ruth was employed. As the fall term approached and the Administration questioned me about my status, I asked the draft board in Potsdam about the likelihood
of my being called. I was told that the call would surely come, if not in September at least during peak induction later in the fall. Rather than begin teaching
classes I would soon have to abandon to some emergency replacement, I volunteered to go with the September contingent from St. Lawrence County. I told the
Administration of my decision so that they could find a replacement.

The next three years are the best documented of my life. Ruth kept my daily
letters from the Army as an exception to our decision to destroy all our letters to
each other. (I destroyed them after reviewing them for this chapter.) If I should
yield to the temptation to make use of that abundant material, the story of those
three years would extend to a length disproportionate to its place in the continuum.
Yet the Army was not an entire aberration in the life of a college professor. After
the first year of trial and trauma, I came to feel at home in the Army; even to find
positive compensations. It was my first experience in fraternal living.

Before leaving Canton I moved Ruth into a three-room apartment in one of the
best-built houses in town, known as the Robinson House after the family that had
occupied it since the 1890s; Marjorie Robinson, spinster, was still living in the
downstairs. Ruth had only a three-minute walk to her office and classroom. For
several months in the fall and early winter it was questionable whether she would
have a classroom to go to. Men students and faculty were being drained away.
Some thought that the college would have to close down rather than bear the cost
of operating far below capacity. But early in 1943 a Navy training program was
established at St. Lawrence to keep the college afloat during the remainder of the
war years. Ruth's job was not only saved but expanded. She was obliged to teach
Spanish as well as French and, more bizarrely, a course in the history of education

when a member of the Education Department was drafted to teach mathematics. That was not all. About the time the Navy V-12 unit was founded Dean Jane Louise Jones, the long-time dean of women, suffered a breakdown in health, and for the next several months Ruth served as acting dean of women while the Navy trainees were loosed on campus. Doc Delmage quipped that there had never been so many pregnancies as during Ruth's indulgent regime. But it was not all indulgence. On one of my furloughs she burst into tears following a phone controversy with President Jencks on some co-ed problem. I insisted that she demand release from that extra burden, and shortly after, the college engaged a full time dean of women.

Not only was Ruth burdened with a fifteen or eighteen hour schedule of teaching, but she also took on the role of morale booster to the U.S. Army by letters and packages. Besides her almost daily letters to me, she corresponded with other bored or disgruntled draftees from the faculty—Fred Parrott and Doc Delmage and even Ed Blankman, who had his own Ruth to write to but also appealed to mine for sympathy. Recently I found many of their letters mixed in with mine in boxes in the attic. In addition to monuments to the Unknown Soldier there should be a memorial to this forgotten heroine of the war effort.

Meanwhile I was shelling peas in a mess hall alongside a skiing instructor from Lake Placid and Claude Vandenbroeck, a former student, who marveled at the novelty of finding his English professor in that galley. KP duty at Camp Upton, Long Island, began at 4:30, when the victim was roused from his bunk, and stretched through the entire day till 7 p.m. The profligate expenditure of manpower in feeding an American army made me realize an advantage the Japanese had with their simplified diet of rice.

Luckily KP duty did not last long. Someone in the hierarchy must have read my personnel record, for I was soon transferred to the Testing Office, where the General Classification Test was administered to all inductees. The evident reasoning was that a college professor would know how to proctor a test. Most inductees left Upton in a few days and were assigned to training camps across the land. But those classified "limited service" because of age or other infirmities (age and near-sightedness in my case) were often assigned to several weeks or months of duty at the reception center. For the ambitious this was galling. No promotions were in store for the rookie till he completed basic training. I was held at Upton for more than four months.

It wasn't all wasted time. I got to know the natural man pretty well in barracks conversations such as this: "How do you find out about a girl at the USO? Just ask her if she fucks?" "Naw, you gotta be delicate. Dance nice with her at first and then begin feeling her up. If she don't object, just ask her if she lays. But say it polite." As a student of language, I thought that answer, in its precision and economy, a model of successful communication. Not so successful was an order given by our squad corporal "to pick up everything" in the picnic grounds of the camp. One nervous and over-zealous rookie filed past the corporal with a large mushroom in his hand. "What the hell are you doing with that mushroom?" A jittery voice replied, "You told us to pick up everything." Next morning the corporal amended his order to: "Pick up everything that don't grow."

The daily human comedy made barracks life endurable. I soon got to know all the men in my squad room, which began to feel a little like home. As "Jamy," I had a pleasant exchange of small talk with them whenever I returned from the Testing Office. At six in the morning Sergeant Cervone slapped me on that part of the anatomy that belongs to sergeants, "Up with you, professor." At roll call out in the cold one morning, after several men before me were either AWOL or answered in faint, sleep-laden voices, I emitted a loud "here." "That man is on the ball," declared Cervone. "A damned fine soldier, Jamieson." This was the greatest compliment I ever got in the Army. And so easily won too.

In November I had a weekend pass long enough to make possible a one-night rendezvous with Ruth in a Utica hotel, though not in Canton. Sometime during the night a thief stole into the room and lifted the first army pay I had just received. This episode exposed me to a ribbing in the barracks. "Was it worth it?" "What were you doing?" "A soldier should always be on alert."

My stint in the Testing Office coincided with the peak of induction. We worked in two shifts, day and night. And in emergencies when the IBM machine broke down, we had the task of scoring by hand. A few times my shift was obliged to work on into the next, up to fourteen or fifteen hours straight with only a break for a meager snack from the mess hall. At first the novelty of testing former students and colleagues from the North Country and checking their scores for eligibility for officers' training kept up my interest. Charles Lightbody, Rhodes scholar and colleague at St. Lawrence in the History Department, came in with a contingent at midnight, weary after an all-day trip on the bus. Charles, I noticed, played it shrewd by answering all the vocabulary questions first and then going back for as many of the arithmetic and mechanics as he had time for. Legendary on campus as an absent-minded polyhistor who bumped into trees and then backed off and apologized, Charles knew himself weak in mechanics and spatial relations. He contrived to finish with a pretty high score in spite of the 2:30 a.m. hour. Then there was the Jehovah's Witness who refused to take the test at all and next day refused absolutely to accept outfitting by the quartermaster. But the novelty wore off as the months passed. By January I was feeling the prick of ambition. I coveted a stripe or two on my shoulder. The war had settled down to a race between the defeat of Hitler and a corporal's stripes for me. I asked for transfer to Pine Camp (now Fort Drum), forty miles from Canton. I had not learned yet that the surest way of not getting what you want in the Army is to ask for it. It is better to rely on chance.

What I got, at the end of January, was shipment clear across the country to Fort Lewis, Washington, with fifty-eight limited service men destined for training in the Military Police. One was an editor with a leading publishing house in New York, two were teachers, another a buyer for a large city department store, a lawyer, and still another a concert violinist with the Coolidge String Quartet, which I had listened to on the NBC radio network on Sundays. I heard him whistling Mozart's G-Minor Symphony. As Easterners most of them were confused about geography in the rest of the country. Kansas was north of Nebraska, Colorado west of Utah, and Idaho ubiquitous. None could understand my excitement as our train passed through Iowa, no man's land to them. I reminded my seat companion, the editor, that Iowa had the highest rate of literacy in the nation. "Ah, yes," he replied, "but what of the state of culture?"

From Boise on the scenery was exhilarating enough to ween readers of the pulps and gamblers away from their pursuits. We persuaded the violinist to get out his fiddle. Surprisingly, the majority voted for classical over pop, and for nearly two hours, as the shimmering snow-covered peaks rolled by, we listened to one sonata after another.

At Fort Lewis we were first billeted at Tent City five to a tent, which was heated by a soft coal stove. It was the rainy season on the West Coat; drizzle almost every day mixed with an occasional light snow that quickly melted. My sharpest memory is of slogging through drizzle and mud to the latrine in early morning. Our training there was half-hearted under lazy noncoms inadequately supervised by a single commissioned officer. The hikes we were supposed to go on were usually aborted at half the distance specified, the noncom preferring a prolonged rest period. We had an introduction to the classic army tempo of hurry-up-and-wait.

After four weeks in Tent City we were moved to barracks in North Fort. Here intensive training for MP duty extended to several more weeks under qualified noncoms, who worked us over in the field, and several commissioned officers, who lectured us on military history, guard duty, and strike breaking. Having been a union member and beneficiary of union activity, I might now have to engage in breaking a strike at one of the Boeing plants. I asked Ruth not to mention this to my union friends back at St. Lawrence. Most of the lectures we heard were competent, but one unfortunate lieutenant, whose notes had probably been prepared by a noncom, tripped up one day when he sought answers to the question when the tank originated. Several hands went up; the first World War, of course. No, said the Lieutenant scornfully. 1912? No, long before. Napoleon? No. The first tank dates to 1496, four years after Columbus discovered America, the Lieutenant said triumphantly; it was invented by the same man that invented the submarine and the parachute, a Frenchman named Leonard de Vinc. Didn't he mean the

Italian Leonardo da Vinci? Absolutely not, his notes clearly read the Frenchman Vinc, and that was that.

In mid March 1943 I received a telegram announcing the death of my sister Ruth at age twenty-six. The cause was a ruptured appendix, of which my father had died two years earlier. If both had lived a few years longer, they could have been saved by the antibiotic penicillin. Ruth, married to a St. Louis man, had a daughter one year old. I applied to the Red Cross for an emergency leave and was granted one week plus travel time. I did not reach St. Louis before the funeral but spent about three days there with my mother and two more with her in Des Moines. Then I utilized the remaining two days of leave to rejoin my wife in Canton, my first visit home since induction.

Mourning the death of a sister, consoling Mother, and rejoining my wife after several months made that week an emotional one. War with its consequences of separation and reunion inundates us all in a grand wash of emotion. Doc, Ed, Fred, and I had led fairly rational lives before joining the Army. Now instinct and emotion held sway. An Ed Blankman new to me wrote of his first furlough: "My Ruth is unchanged, save for the lovelier. She and I are most happy for having each other; surely, surely has great love come to me at long last. And, Paul, our love goes out to you, old comrade."

Training was more arduous in North Fort than in Tent City. We crawled over rough ground under live fire. We graduated from the .22 rifle to the .30 caliber M1 with its disconcerting kick. We ran obstacle courses. One day, at horse and rider, I drew the heftiest man in the outfit, a Texan. When I asked his weight, he replied, "Wal, before I got in this here outfit I weighed two hundred pounds, but I reckon I've gained about ten since then." Jamieson, before he got in this here outfit, weighed 145, but I reckon he'd lost about ten since. After the push-ups, sit-ups, the burpee, the pull-ups, and the shuttle race came horse and rider, a hundred yards to run on the double with 210 pounds on my back. I had intimations of knees buckling and of breaking down at mid course. But all went well. Others bettered my time, but they did not have so much beef on their backs.

After being thoroughly briefed on the regulations and courtesies of guard duty, we had our first serious assignment at the ammunition dump of Fort Lewis. Blackest and loneliest vigil of the camp, it served to qualify one as a veteran sentry.

There was so much diversity of ethnic background and character among the army men I had thus far met that I could not longer accept as valid the representation of American conformity and uniformity in the novelists and satirists of the preceding twenty years. The world, it now seemed to me, was a gigantic trial-and-error experiment in differentiation, without any hypothesis to guide it. Here and there a lucky mutation threw off a genius strong and creative enough to impose a meaning on the whole show, but only for one generation or a little longer.

[ 105 ]

At last I saw Mt. Rainier. One day in late April the coastal fog lifted about four in the afternoon and suddenly the most majestic mountain in the lower states loomed up, seemingly quite near, the snow-covered peak shimmering in the late afternoon sun and a purple haze surrounding the lower slopes. It looked light and airy, like a floating island in the sky. But as our Adirondack Old Mountain Phelps remarked, it "ain't the kinder scenery you want ter hog down." Atmospherics saw to that. During the next two years I spent at Fort Lewis or environs, I saw it maybe forty times, so that the vision always seemed new and fresh.

About the middle of May Company D of the 778th MP Battalion moved into barracks ten miles from Seattle for a new assignment, guarding a new Boeing plant at Renton and policing soldiers on pass in Seattle. Most of the time for the next seven weeks my beat was the Boeing factory. In July relief from the monotony of guard duty finally came. Someone at Headquarters of the Northwest Sector of the Western Defense Command happened to turn over my personnel card and to call me back to Fort Lewis for an interview. There was an opening in the G-2 office, Army Intelligence. A few days later I was summoned to fill that post, still as a private. My only advancement thus far was a good-conduct rating and a sharpshooter's medal. But now at last I was attached to Headquarters Company, the top enlisted man's outfit north of the Presidio at San Francisco.

My job in G-2 was to keep abreast of happenings in all theaters of the war, write speeches for the Major, an Italian American from Brooklyn, and coach him in pronunciation and delivery during evening hours when we had the office to ourselves. He gave weekly briefings to the General Staff. A symbiosis developed between the Major and me. I did my best to improve his performance, and he showed his gratitude by finally getting me a promotion to private first class, the only opening in the G-2 office, and then reluctantly letting me go when there was promise of a further promotion in the Adjutant General's Office. The Major was a real gentleman in spite of his Brooklyn accent, and so was his superior in G-2, the Colonel.

I took to office work like the proverbial duck to water. And in Headquarters Company I had privileges undreamed of in the lower ranks. The Service Club with its library and music was nearby. American Lake, with swimming and boating, was only a fifteen minute walk. It was just two miles across the Fort and through the woods to Puget Sound. I could feed the tame deer, watch crabs crawling in the surf, and gaze at the snowy Olympic Mountains across the narrows of the Sound. There were women at the Service Club and elsewhere to soften the asperity of an army camp. On Saturday afternoon I could leave the Fort on a weekend pass till Monday morning. Once a month I was entitled to a three-day pass. On one of these I spent two nights at Paradise Inn high on Mt. Rainier and had a full day to climb above timberline as far as I could without a guide. Married men of whatever rank could live outside the Fort provided that they reported for calisthenics every morning at six. My wife was far away, but I still had strings to pull. I kept trying to requisition a bike till I finally succeeded, and this widened my range of exploration in that wonderfully scenic coastal area. Twice a year I had a two-week furlough plus travel time to visit Ruth in Canton.

*Ruth during Paul's summer furlough, 1943*

*Ruth, summer of 1943*

Daily life in the barracks was congenial among the handpicked men from various outfits of the sector command. Many in Headquarters Company were college graduates. I came to know them all well over the remaining twenty-two months of army service till the barracks seemed almost like home. With some of them—Temcov, Carr, Kalota—I continued to correspond after demobilization.

My four months in G-2 were a unique experience. Modesty retreated and egomania took over. In rank I was still the underling, a mere private at first, then with one stripe on my sleeve. Over me were three commissioned officers, colonel, major, and lieutenant; and two noncoms whose ratings I coveted but who showed no sign of budging. Yet in no time at all I was, in my own estimation, the kingpin in Intelligence, with an indispensable set of qualifications: a ghost-writing facility, aptitude in coaching the Major and the Lieutenant for their weekly speeches before the General Staff, a knowledge of geography in the European theater of the war from my travels abroad, and a flair for dressing my daily bulletins on the progress of the war with literary quotations. In office corridors and barracks it was soon "How's the war going today, Jamy?" I was big with power and influence as never before—or since.

The Major and I were soon on a first name basis; you don't address your pupil in English enunciation as "sir." Mike had the easy-going bonhomie that had so much attracted me in Italy. The Lieutenant, however, was shocked by this familiarity. One day he said of us three enlisted men in the office that we might be good civilians but, according to his lights, not good soldiers. We asked indignantly what he meant by that. "Discipline," he muttered weakly, a reply that played right into our hands. We said that the qualities that make Americans the best soldiers in the world are individualism, self-reliance, and a critical attitude toward their officers, who have to be good to survive the going over they get from us. In this new character I wrote to Ruth one day in September 1943.

The big news of the day is not that Italy surrendered but that Pvt. Jamieson became Pfc. Jamieson. The twin events are undoubtedly turning points in this war. A further congruity is that public announcement was delayed probably for strategic reasons: five days in the matter of the Italian armistice, forty in the matter of Jamieson's promotion. The company clerk's testimony notwithstanding, the promotion *was* a military secret rather than a clerical error. Unknown to me it had coincided with my birthday, August 1, a touching tribute but still a military secret.

When I first heard it today, my ego unfurled like the first Queen Elizabeth rose of spring in our garden. I put out three special bulletins today, signing them "Pfc. Jamieson." As the first person to hear over my private radio (we have only one radio in the building; they are restricted except for the official use of G-2) of the Italian surrender at 8:30 a.m., I closed my door against intruders, explaining that I had a scoop and they would have to wait for my news sheet. Under the heading *Flash* I typed a motto from *The Merry Wives of Windsor*, "Better three hours early than one minute too late" and followed it with the news. As copies rolled off the mimeograph machine, I opened my door and began distributing them to all offices. This created a sensation. They have been calling me Scoop Jamieson. The Colonel inquired about the source of my quotation. The rest of the morning my work was impeded by a file of brass through my office, hovering over the radio, curious as to the whereabouts of the Seventh Army and the terms of surrender.

So at eleven I brought out a second bulletin quoting a rumor spread by German reports that the Seventh Army was heading out of Palermo in two large convoys. This I headed with the motto: "In the case of news, we should always wait for the sacrament of confirmation—Voltaire" (for the Colonel's benefit).

My third bulletin, issued shortly after one, quoted a radio proclamation by Premier Badoglio and Admiral Cunningham's appeal to Italian sailors to put in at Allied ports; also some of the terms of surrender. This I headed "The ripest fruit falls first—Shakespeare." The two generals may have frowned on this frivolity, but my Colonel and Major were flattered to have a man of letters in G-2.

I told Mike that I intended to write a book about G-2 as soon as the war was over and I could tell all. He wondered how much I wanted in hush money. Since no such cash ever changed hands, I am free to tell about Mike's Swedish girlfriend and his portrait in oils of our Major General. Mike brought the portrait, finished and framed, into the office one day to receive our compliments. "Now tell me," he said, "don't you think it resembles a Rembrandt?" "No, Major, frankly," I replied, "it reminds me more of a Van Dyke. Just that ultimate touch of genius is lacking." But Mike was to have his glory. The General Staff adopted his portrait and presented it to the General's wife on her wedding anniversary.

The Lieutenant, a dog fancier, asked me to go to his quarters on the post and pick up a three-weeks-old pup he had just acquired. He thought it might be lonely. This request may have been his idea of discipline, but I refused on the ground that it was a personal favor rather than a military order. He fetched the pup himself. When he brought it into the office, Mike was on the phone to his Swedish girlfriend in Tacoma. He described the pup to her and then added, "The great Jamieson doesn't like it. He thinks it has no literary value."

For two or three weeks in October I divided time between the lively G-2 office and the sober G-1, the Adjutant General. About the first of November I was assigned permanently to G-1. The work of handling personnel records brought a reversion to my true character, the unassuming, plodding fellow best known to my friends. The reason for the change was that G-2 had no opening in higher rank but that G-1 had a vacant sergeancy. The incumbent, a product of St. John's Great Books and University of Chicago master's, got a medical discharge following a nervous breakdown. By mid November I was jumped over the rank of corporal, once my greatest ambition, to a three-striper. A week later I was shipped off to school at Washington and Jefferson College in Washington, Pennsylvania, for a six-week course in the fundamentals of personnel management. In January I returned to Fort Lewis, where for the last seventeen months of army service, I had charge of personnel records in the Northwest Sector. Shipment overseas had reduced troops at the Fort to about two thousand from the tens of thousands there when I first arrived in Tent City. In addition we still had under our command four coast artillery units.

*Paul, summer furlough 1944*

Office work was dull, but it was leavened by frequent travel around the Olympic Peninsula to inspect the records of the Coast Artillery at Forts Worden, Hayden, and Casey on Puget Sound and Fort Stevens in Oregon at the mouth of the Columbia River. I enjoyed periodic stays of several days to a week at each of these installations. The chow was excellent and the situations idyllic, in spite of big gun emplacements; a Shangri-la or a setting for *Midsummer Night's Dream*. All of the

*Paul and Helen Aitchison*

men had been converted to nature lovers and morale was high. Even isolated Fort Casey, on an island in Puget Sound, was a cherished post. Worden and Hayden were perched on mountain slopes at sea's edge on the north shore of the Olympic Peninsula, where the scenery was unparalleled. Vessels passed in and out through the Sound at all hours, and behind was the Olympic interior of mountain and rain forest with spongy moss and giant trunks. In late afternoons and on weekends I tramped into this primitive forest. One long weekend, from Port Angeles, I hiked into the interior to climb Mt. Angeles, a 6,500-foot peak culminating in an Alpine meadow and a knife edge overlooking the jagged, snow-capped peaks to the south. If I should ever leave Canton, I decided, my destination would have to be the town of Port Angeles on the north shore of the Olympics, a little pocket of dryness and sunshine just a few miles east of a zone with rainfall exceeding one hundred inches a year.

As the work load abated in the last nine months of the war and most of our soldiers at Fort Lewis had been shipped overseas, we enlisted men of Headquarters Company launched a mimeographed monthly magazine. Joe Kalota, master sergeant and the only regular army man in our company, and I were co-editors. Our first issue appeared in December, 1944. The reaction was mixed. Unknown to each other, Joe and I had prepared editorials for the January issue on the same subject—proposals for reform to meet criticism. He pulled rank on me, but I kept a copy of my editorial. The closing paragraph follows.

When we try to separate the reluctantly offered blame from the praise, we are confronted with the hint that our first issue was dull. We admit it. Like most beginners, we took ourselves too seriously. We are prepared to correct our mistake. Our sense of humor is no longer what it used to be many long years ago. This war has lasted too long. As rookies everything struck us as funny, even first sergeants. We went through basic training laughing from dewy reveille to dusky retreat. Though our Private Hargrave days are over and we have aged in the service, we still have some juice left in us. We are now about to undertake, like the great Milton, a thing "unattempted yet in prose or rhyme"—to entertain soldiers without resorting to smut. Smirt, perhaps, but not smut. So we appeal to the comic spirits of NWS. Give us a hand with the laughs, soldiers.

My editorials for the February 1945 issue were in rhyme. The two short jingles concern the two remaining units on the Fort under NWS command. "Calvary" was the popular term for the Cavalry outfit, deemed to be crucifying. The long Valentine is addressed to the enlisted men of Headquarters.

### Valentine Greetings

(An apology prefatorial
For riming our editorial
On St. Valentine's memorial
And sentiments amatorial.)

### The Ducky 115th

A Valentine to you, Lieutenant Zeus,
Whose moniker
Is similar
To a god's but rimes with choice.
To Sergeant Vivian and Captain Tiffany
We likewise raise our litany:
May they accept and share it
With all the men of merit
Both pres and abs (no AWOL's
And hardly any eightballs)
Of the ducky 115th.

### The Calvary

Amor, amor, amor—
We simply do adore
The lads of the Recon Troop or Calvary
Naught can stop our whoopin'
Our love for Corporate Toupin;
For Bighouse, Bloch and Coco
We are completely loco.
With Vilandre
Let's philander,
And when Cupid's darts we shoot, you catch 'em
Corporal Fish and Handy Latchum.
The same for all the recon crewmen,

Scouts and cooks and mortar crewmen
  Of the horseless Calvary—
    Amor, amor, amor
For the streamlined Calvary.


**Sundry Big Shots**

If you ask us whom we think a lotta
Well, it's our co-, Don Juan Kalota,
The wonder boy of his inamorata;
Plays boogie but loves a Bach sonata,
Does everything just like he ought 'a,
The model of a Sergeant Maja'.
For the mailman (né Kuchinsky), Kirby,
Our wish is, he soon may wear a derby.
Huzzah for Gibson, Gillette, and Lea, so
Too for one 405 named Kieso.
To think of Kane is to think of his Mrs.,
Blond bomber of Boeing's to whom we send kisses.
For a Valentine couple we give you the toitle-
Doves, cuddly Milt and his lovely Moitle.
For Bross and Farrant, Sabo and Fann,
Jankowski and Foley, we plunk with élan.
Our affection will flower for Hustak and Irby
When H follows through and Top wakes us less early.
For nifty cartoons and pin-ups, we vow it's
Walt Armstrong we love and Michael Wojtowitz.
These artists will give you a nude signorina
Such as, for his cooking, we wish to De Fina.
For Rotando, Fred Carr, and the cute twins O'Neal,
Sarge Johnston and Riddle, it's luv that we feel.
Two orchids to Temcov, nice guy, intellectual—
 In plans for the peace he'll inform and direct you all.
(To his wife, a dozen, a lady so charming
That our blood-pressure rises at rate quite alarming.)
To Sam Rosenthal, otherwise called Mother Rosie,
For conspicuous zeal in policing, a posy.
Welcome back and good speed in your project, Tursone,
Of resettling the gals hereabouts on your *own* knee.
Herb Horn has the look of a man marked to marry;
Our fond hope for him's that it may not miscarry.

What game cock of Brooklyn should we admire?
Why, whom but that master of gab, Jack McGuire?
Best regards of the season are certainly owin'
To Goodman and Hustad, Heubach and Bowen,
To Francis and Beaulieu, and, to go farther,
Montgomery, Patton, Nimitz, MacArthur,
Mr. Churchill, F.R., and a man who's named Stalin
But who, for our money, sure isn't stallin'.

P.S. We got no Valentines for Hirohito,
Hitler, Goebbels, Himmler and Benito.

My March editorial was a comment on a regular feature of the "mag," Sergeant Armstrong's drawings of nudes that possessed all the physical attributes soldiers most crave.

**The Problem of the Squeak-Easy**

A mounting volume of protest against our campaign to purify the soldier press causes us much anxiety. Not that we have lost faith in our purpose—far from it. But we see how difficult the task before us is, and sometimes our ill-success is discouraging. The taste for pin-up art rages unchecked. Though we have the support of inspecting officers in banning it from the walls of offices and barracks, a peek at the under lid of a fellow soldier's footlocker shows all too clearly that prohibition has only forced the evil under cover, into what we call the squeak-easy. Like the speak-easy of our fathers, the squeak-easy is imperfectly designed, considering squeaky hinges, to hide clandestine vice. Our campaign, announced in the last issue, of prevailing upon rampant models to stop posing for Sgt. Armstrong has failed. The editors found their interviews with these squeak-easy girls exhausting and hard to direct in proper channels. In order to preserve the dignity of our purpose, we had to give them up.

We resume our efforts with an attempt to clear up a misunderstanding. We are not, as has been charged, opposed to women. We do not condemn love, marriage, and allied pursuits. We find the bisexual order of things necessary, wise, and sometimes delightful. We have noted with interest that odd vibration in a field of force whenever boy meets girl. On those rare occasions when our military mission permits such meetings, we vibrate too. No subject is more absorbing to us than the difference between man and woman. *Vive la différence*, as a great Frenchman once said—yes, long let it live.

The difference between man and woman, however, is hardly as upsetting as that between woman in her natural state and the fantasies of pin-up artists. Nature's product is good enough for us. We do not demand an impossible perfection. We consider it dangerous to indulge in fancies of the ideal woman when it is, after all, with the real one we must live. At a conservative estimate there are three hundred billion cells in the body of a man and probably more in woman with her fancier construction. Since nature works in a haphazard way, it is folly to expect each and every one of those billions of cells to be perfect. Mathematicians among our readers may be interested in calculating the chances of one perfect woman emerging from three hundred billion possibilities of error. Solving this problem would probably win some enterprising soldier a diploma from the Armed Forces Institute. All we can say is that it staggers the imagination. Roughly speaking, the chances of an NWS soldier of meeting such a paragon in Olympia, Tacoma or Seattle, or even in Vancouver, Bali or Burma, are as slight as paying off the national debt, now on its way to three hundred billion, in our lifetime.

You may object that squeak-easy girls actually exist, that they are to be found in Sergeant Armstrong's studio. You must realize, however, that Sergeant Armstrong is an artist, not a photographer. He is motivated by a lust for perfection. To attain it, he flatters a line here, exaggerates another there. In this trick of deception the models aid and abet him, concealing their defects and thrusting their good points into prominence. We would wager our last dollar that this young lady of his latest drawing has a birthmark on her back, perhaps in a place where one would least desire to find it.

We members of the citizen army were deceived once. When our neighbors selected us, we went off with the airy delusion that this war would be over in a year, at most two. Many of us have suffered bitterly from that false hope. Let us not make the same mistake twice, men. Let us look reality bravely in the face. Let us learn to hanker after woman as she is, not as she ought to be. Burn that flossy display of pin-ups in your squeak-easy and replace it with candid photos of the girl back home. Return to her with a true, not a false, image in your mind's eye, and you will find her adequate, in spite of human imperfections, to comfort, console, and delight you.


The May issue of the *Sector Snoop* was the last one I edited. My editorial that month was on President Roosevelt's death.


We have lost our foremost soldier and the greatest American of our time.

The best qualities of the national character were combined in that personality that for twelve years guided our nation in peace and in war. In his statecraft were the courage and daring of the pioneers. Like the founders of our country, he was an experimentalist with vision, always confident that if something was wrong, a way could be found to fix it. As a politician, he had so great a degree of Yankee shrewdness and ingenuity that even his political enemies lamented, "You can't beat the Champ." This power he used wisely in the interests of the majority. His roots were in Jeffersonian democracy, with its belief in the dignity of the common man and its faith in progress. Like America, he was young in spirit, with the vigor and confidence of youth. With this went wisdom—the wisdom to plan a broad program of social reform, bitterly fought at the time but now substantially secure, and to plan and execute measures of national defense and preparedness that have saved many lives and shortened the war.

But the task for which the world mainly relied on his leadership—the shaping of a secure and just peace in the light of his Four Freedoms—he left incomplete. It was a task for which he was supremely well fitted, for he saw the world steadily and he saw it whole. That is why millions of GI's and the common men of all nations were inexpressibly shocked and saddened by his death. Men of good will everywhere looked to him for moral leadership in the difficult negotiations that lie ahead.

For a time it seemed as if the loss were irreparable, but now we know that it is not. The foundations he laid for an enduring peace are firm enough to survive and to guide the new administration, which has pledged itself to carry out his aims. He lived long enough to impress his vision of a free world on millions of Americans and men of all nations. We shall go forward in the confident spirit, so characteristic of him, that he expressed in the Jefferson Day message he was to broadcast the day after his death: "The only limit to our realization of tomorrow will be our doubts of today. Let us move forward with strong and active faith."

My spirits were high that spring, for an Army directive provided for the discharge of enlisted men of forty-two, an age I would reach on August first. I even broke my rule of refusing personal favors to officers when a Colonel asked me to write a love letter in French. The only limitation his wife imposed on his philandering, he said, was that his mistresses be at least as attractive as she was, a standard easily met. The notes he submitted to me seemed pretty silly. I converted them into sentiments elegant enough to conceal the crudity of my French.

Then the unexpected happened. Shortly after the German surrender on May 8—V-E Day—a new directive lowered the separation age to forty. I could expect release that very month.

There was time for one more duty-related trip to Fort Worden and one last weekend off-duty on the Olympic Peninsula. In the service club at Worden I talked with two noncoms recently returned from overseas campaigns with ribbons and points galore. Listening to these seasoned soldiers talk of their campaigns in North Africa, Sicily, Italy, and Southern France, I concluded that the war had turned the average GI into a man of the world, anecdotal, realistic, and self-possessed. As usual at Worden everyone was friendly. The cook, whose home was Olympia, advised me to try the Dosewallips River valley for my weekend hike, about thirty-five miles south of Worden along the coast. It is a chasm leading into ever taller mountains and innumerable rain-forest streams pouring over cliffs, so that one is never out of hearing of some waterfall. The rhododendrons were in full bloom.

In the Olympics as in the Adirondacks, characters from the outside world take refuge from failure, embitterment, and frustration or, more positively, follow some Holy Grail of their own creation. Returning from an all-day hike up the chasm, I stopped at tourist cabins to engage a room for the night and then walked on another mile toward the coast to a general store, where I inquired for a place to eat. No meals were served, but the old woman who tended store was preparing a meal in her home nearby. I asked whether I could have dinner with her. "Give me time to think about it," she said. "I don't give meals, but seein' as I'm cooking for one man I guess I can for two if they'll leave me be in the store."

Her husband came in. He was short, pot-bellied, shaggy but with an oddly intellectual air about him. He spoke with a strong accent, unlike his wife's native American. "We're having a soldier to dinner," she said. "*Ja wohl. Gut,*" he replied genially. "My name is Pape [the "e" pronounced], same family as Franz von Papen [German diplomat in the war years]. Back in the Thirty Years War the family split up, the Catholics remaining von Papens, the Lutherans changing the name to Pape."

It was an excellent T-bone dinner, but Herr von Pape was the *pièce de résistance.* He was a graduate of the University of Berlin in electrical engineering. During the First World War he was a technical expert on German submarines. He worked in Russia during the first five-year plan of the Soviets. Later he went to South America and Mexico, where he worked for General Electric. His political ideas were curious. He hated the Nazis but was cynical about bringing them to justice. Von Papen, Goering, and the rest would never be brought to trial because of what they might reveal. They were only pawns of international industrialists, who had bribed the Nazis to start the war. The Russians would never stop at the Elbe, and in a year or at most five we would be fighting them. Democracy, socialism, communism are words without meaning. The real rulers of the world are the industrialists. But here in the isolation of the Olympics Herr von Pape was content to live out his days, far from that world where things are not what they seem, opening oysters on the beach while his aging wife ran the store and tenderized his T-bone steaks.

On May 25, after a full day of physical exams, lectures, and consultations, I received my discharge papers and returned for one last night in the barracks for a leave-taking with friends in Headquarters Company. As the oldest among them I was the first to be discharged. Envy was mixed with their well-wishing. But their

FAREWELL TO ARMS

turn was not long in coming. It came for most of them shortly after V-J Day in August. The *Sector Snoop* continued through that month. The June issue, sent to me at home, contained a Sgt. Armstrong drawing of me, captioned "Farewell to Arms," on a loaded bike headed across the country to Canton, New York.

## XII  HOME AGAIN

A *NEW YORKER* STORY by Harriet Doerr describes a day in the life of an elderly widow and her state of mind at the end of it as "wrapped in the mists of her brief, uncertain future and the brilliant patchwork of her never-ending past." That saying is often in my mind as I write these memoirs in my eighty-seventh year. The past is indeed a patchwork of miscellaneous experience, like my two years and nine months in the Army. Yet I cherish the fraternalism of that time and the scenes amidst which it developed. Rereading some of the one thousand letters to my wife during those one thousand days lights up, and in that restricted sense makes brilliant, the Army part of the patchwork. The letters as well as my memory attest to a self-confidence I was not to know again in the same degree till my retirement. The state-side Army of World War II was a closed system in which you could operate to advantage once you knew the rules.

But like most servicemen (M/Sgt. Joe Kalota was an exception, remaining in the Regular Army to the ultimate retirement age), I was eager to return to civilian life with its wider freedoms linked to greater contingency and risk. And I had a wife to return to who overmatched André Maurois's definition of the happiest state of man: a mate with the intellect of a man and the body of a woman. Feminists of today would bristle at that chauvinistic remark. At any rate, Ruth had intellect equal to mine, the body of a woman, and besides sensibilities as fine-tuned as those of a Marivaux heroine, on whom she had written her doctor's dissertation.

Before returning home, I visited my mother and sister in Los Angeles for a few days. Mary was pregnant with her second daughter. My niece Penny, four years old, begged me to tell stories. Then she told them back to me with alterations she considered necessary for a topnotch story. Lewis Carroll would not have recognized her versions of *Alice*. Mother, having sold the family home in Des Moines and moved into a pleasant apartment in Hollywood some six miles from my sister, had apparently aged little since I last saw her. The only change I noted was that she was more talkative than ever. I told her that her talk reminded me of the ocean in that you never knew what never ceasing waves would wash up next on the beach.

That record of my visit to Los Angeles comes from the last surviving letter I ever wrote to Ruth. I must now rely on memory, an unsure prop, until 1954 when I began to keep a log of hikes and paddles in the Adirondacks and till the 1960s when I began keeping copies of letters seeking to influence administration and legislation concerning the park. Consequently the narrative of the next decade will be, in proportion to the last one, fairly short. I resumed my job in the English Department at St. Lawrence in the fall of 1945 just where I left off. In addition to the required freshman and sophomore courses, which we distributed equally among the staff, I had the same two electives, the Romantic Movement and the Victorian Age. One year I taught a course in Shakespeare's comedies and tragedies during a colleague's leave of absence. This experience aided me later when I was able to answer *The Winter's Tale* when asked, in the oral exam for my doctorate, to locate the stage direction "Exit, pursued by a bear" and to explain the circumstances in the plot.

Ruth and I arranged for an enlargement of the apartment she had occupied. We now had the entire second floor, six sizable rooms, with two fireplaces and a large, well-lighted front hall, where we kept the weaving loom we both used. The hall had a south-facing clear window and a west-facing stained glass one of the University seal, which has since been moved to the campus. Two generations of the Robinson family that had built the house had served as administrator or trustee of the University. Directly across from the campus library, it was one of the most desirable residences in Canton. I agreed to tend the coal furnace, mow the lawn, and shovel the walks in winter. We lived there for the next ten years until we bought a house of our own.

I looked forward to a leisurely summer before the beginning of the fall term, but soon Frank Crary, father of the Antarctic explorer Albert Crary, asked me to assist in the haying on his farm seven miles south of Canton. Manpower was short that summer preceding the wave of army discharges in late August. I agreed to work four or five days a week. Gas rationing was still in effect. I commuted on my bike, a fourteen mile round trip. What with the loading and lofting of hay and the biking, I was in better shape by the end of that summer than I had been after basic training in the Army.

The Japanese surrender came on August 14. Along with Helen Aitchison, our former student, Ruth and I celebrated the surrender at our favorite picnic and swimming site, Lampson Falls on the Grass River sixteen miles south of Canton. Aitchie, as she was known on campus, had kept up a correspondence with me during my army service. Our friendship has lasted for fifty years and embraces also her husband, Hank Ellison, since her marriage. Although they live in Connecticut, they return to Canton at least once a year. Aitchie has been an alumni trustee and maintains a close interest in University affairs.

Within a year of my return I realized that promotion beyond my assistant professorship would depend on getting the Ph.D. degree. I did not want to return to Columbia. Cornell had always appealed because of its location in the Finger Lakes. I enrolled there for the summer session in 1947 on a trial basis. Ruth and I rented a small house on the heights near the campus and sublet a room to another St. Lawrence faculty member working for his degree. I liked Cornell from the start. Candidates for the two advanced degrees in English were much less numerous than at Columbia and had easy access to the faculty. I decided to make use of the partial assistance provided by the GI Bill for two years of residence, 1948–50.

Whether by policy or contingency, the English faculty at Cornell usually consists of one stellar member of international reputation in a body of competent scholars. During my two years the reigning star was David Daiches. A Scottish Jew, he was the author of several critical works and a brilliant explicator of literary texts in the classroom. The idea for my dissertation originated from his books and lectures—that is, the symbiotic relationship between poet and audience. Daiches touched on that relationship mostly in the modern period, the age of Yeats and Eliot. My dissertation of over five hundred pages dealt with seven major Victorian poets and their relations to particular segments of audience—family, coterie, critics, mentors (Milton's "fit audience...though few"), and the common reader. *Poet and Audience in the Victorian Age* was comprehensive enough to be a valuable aid in my teaching.

Relaxed scholarship was the tone of my sojourn at Cornell. I had the advantage over younger candidates of several years of teaching and of language study abroad. I passed the qualifying and the French and German examinations with ease and felt confident about the two final oral examinations, the comprehensive and the one on my dissertation. While younger candidates were cramming for these hurdles, I enjoyed the freedom of self-directed study under the stimulus of a good faculty and pleasant surroundings. My feeling toward Cornell today is one of gratitude and affection.

While in residence, I had a room in a house owned by an elderly widow who, with her husband, had directed a preparatory school in Ithaca. She was a cultivated landlady. I escorted her to evening concerts and lectures on campus, just a ten-minute walk from her home. Frequent visits to Ruth in Canton were facilitated by another acquaintance, Mayfred Claflin, a high-school mathematics teacher in Ithaca with a permanent home at Langdon Corners near Canton. On weekends when Mayfred commuted to the North Country I was welcome to accompany her in her Packard as passenger and occasional driver. Instead of the semi-annual furloughs of army days, reunions with Ruth were at short intervals.

By May 1950 there were two Ph.D.'s in the family, mine garnered nine years after Ruth's, an interval during which one friend addressed letters to us as "Mr. and Dr. Paul Jamieson." To celebrate the occasion, Ruth and I went abroad that summer, our last visit to Europe.

After Ruth's death a year and a half ago, I discovered among her papers a diary she kept of that trip. Since her interests and some of her personality come through in those notes, I quote a selection from them here, from our arrival in Paris till our return there after a sojourn in the French Alps.

Wed. June 14. Arr. at 2 a.m. after horrible trip on boat train. No room at Récamier—*la patronne* had reserved a room for us at Hôtel Bonaparte. Napoleon would be ashamed of it. Nice breakfast—*croissants, beurre, café au lait.* Walked in Luxembourg Gardens—a great joy—*à la recherche du temps perdu.* Walked all day in quarter—on Rue Soufflot to Bl. Mich. At night down the Seine. Joy to be here again. Thurs. June 15. To American Express after moving to Récamier. Wonderful to be here. Atmosphere of Place St. Sulpice *"tranquille," comme dit Madame.* Lunch on Blvd. des Capucines. Tickets for Opéra Comique. Then to Louvre. Very touching to be back. Fri. June. 16. Quite sick in morning. In p.m. did churches in quarter—St. Severin (nicest), St. Julien le Pauvre, then Notre Dame. Saw S. Transcept again. Walked home along quais. Sat. June 17. Long afternoon in gardens by Medicis Fountain. Evening at Opéra Comique—*Pélleas et Mélisande,* a lovely performance. Almost every word could be understood. Came home on Metro—missed our station because we forgot that doors don't open automatically. Came home thru lovely dim streets, esp. Rue Cassette.

Sunday June 18. Lunch at Pommier Normand—wonderful *pâtisserie.* Sat long in Luxembourg Gardens. Never tire of watching children. Funny clothes, lovely faces. Much loved by parents. French women all have distinction—hard, firm figures, regular features. In this bourgeois quarter, they dress plainly but have an air of poise and charm. Women are more aggressive lovers—men are tolerant. Many students, many older couples. Some might be *académiciens.* Medicis fountain is nicest place. Visited Panthéon and St. Etienne du Mont, my favorite. Walked through narrow crooked streets of quarter....Later we walked thru Rue du Vieux Colombier, Blvd. Raspail, Rue d'Assas, & Rue Cassette. Quiet and lovely. Paris is the perfect city. Wish we were staying here all summer....

Mon. June 19. Visited the Ste Chapelle—beautiful in spite of cloudy skies—a little jewel box. Then strayed into the Palais de Justice, which fascinated Paul. The lawyers all looked like Daumiers—shifty and crooked. Strolled in the Salle des Pas Perdues & witnessed one court scene. We didn't understand it, but the crafty faces of the lawyers and unhappy people haunted me. Then a long walk thru the Ile de la Cité, with a stop for *glace* and *calvados*, to Ile St. Louis. Wonderful view of Notre Dame. Saw the Hôtel Lambert—stately and beautiful....Paul liked best the Palais de Justice—I, the Hôtel Lambert....Tuesday June 20. Gardens of the Petit Palais are beautiful. Pools have borders of blue and gold stones—are filled with red, pink, white, and yellow water lilies and gold fish. We sat on the porch a long time in the sunshine. Lovely setting for a museum. Later walked over to Ave Cours de la Reine, then back across Pont Alexandre III to Quai d'Orsay. Bright clear day. Had *glace* & Dubonnet at the Café de Flore on Blvd. St. Germain. Lots of Americans drinking coca-cola. Paul speaks of the continuity of French art. Virgins look very much like Fr. women of the blvds today. Ingres is the exception. Where did he get his models? Dinner at La Chaumière—a joy to watch Paul eating *yaourt* and *cerises*.

Wed. June 21. Lunch at Pommier Normand, *comme toujours*. Another trip by bus across quais to Musée du Jeu de Paume, where impressionist paintings, many formerly in Luxembourg, are grouped together. Charming exhibit. Several nice Degas—*Répétition d'un Ballet sur la Scène*—*Leçon de Ballet*—best of all is Monet's *Au Jardin*, full of light and grace. On the second floor many familiar things—Renoir, *Moulin de la Galette* and *La Balançoire*—Cézanne *Vase Bleu* and others—Van Gogh *Flowers in a Copper Vase*. Sense of happiness, of gaiety. Painter's life must have been happy in the late 19th century....Evening—dinner at Le Rallye. Then to Opéra Comique again—*Ariane à Naxos*. Strangest thing I've ever seen. Combination of Italian and Wagnerian styles. Much lovely music. Nice dances in first act. Ariane huge and red haired. Bacchus monumental—rose up in center of stage, standing on top of garden house, his ship shadowy in background. Trio of nymphs very lovely. Whole performance rather silly, but the audience went mad....

Thursday June 22. A wonderful day, in spite of rain. In evening we went to Théâtre Français—Salle Odéon, for Marivaux *Les Fausses Confidences*, an experience which must not be forgotten. Perfect setting—long yellow curtains— ivory chairs with yellow velours—*petit escritoire*. Lovely costumes—Araminte first in rose taffeta, with tight bodice and overskirt of white embroidered organdy. Later in white satin. Marthon in brown and red striped taffeta—tiny white apron bordered in red. French clear as a bell—perfect articulation, poised, sensitive acting—much style—assurance—completely perfect. Valets very spirited. Dorante handsome—language never seemed more beautiful. Followed by recitation of 19 Fables of La Fontaine by actors of the Comédie in 17th century costumes. Very good, especially the last two—*Les Animaux malades de la peste* and *La Veuve*. No other theatre in the world could put on such a performance with such style, such confidence. Dinner at a new restaurant on Rue de Tournon—Le Pascal. Walked later in artist quarter—Rue de Seine and Rue Bonaparte—to court of Ecole des Beaux Arts. Paris is never dull—always stimulating. Latin and Anglo-Saxon temperaments are at opposite poles....Saturday June 24. Last day in Paris. Lunch at Pascal, then to Place des Vosges and Maison de Sévigné. Rosy tint of old houses, uniform architecture very attractive. Souvenirs of d'Artagnan & Louis XIII. Bus home, via Blvd. St. Germain, which we have crossed so many times. I am always happy in Paris....

Monday June 26. First day at Sallanches—fine weather. Paul loves it here—he is happy in the mountains....Paul took a walk in the woods—came back happy, as usual. After dinner we walked up the hill above town. Beautiful view—moonlight on the way back....Tuesday June 27. Paul has gone out on a morning excursion. I am something of a liability. Wed. & Thurs. I certainly am! Was sick and spoiled the whole Italian trip. [Ruth's recurring dysentery, probably aggravated by the oily cuisine of French Savoie, forced a cancellation of the planned trip to northern Italy.] There is a wonderful doctor here, Dr. Georges Schlesinger, member of the faculty of the Univ. of Paris, former intern at Neuilly. He came twice, the second time simply because I was nervous and scared. He made me get up to *"chasser les papillons noire qui s'élevent dans la tête."* I have gradually gained strength and feel fine now. We decided to stay in Sallanches a few more days before returning to Paris. Paul made several trips on foot and loved them. In the evening we walked up the hill to see the sunset on Mt. Blanc and on the Aiguille de Warens, a huge, jagged peak directly in front of the hotel.... July 4. Last day in Sallanches. Long trip by bus & train—Megève, Le Fayet, Passy, Assy, Guébriand—back to Sallanches by train. Wonderful views of mountains. Mt. Blanc seemed very close.

July 5. Paris. Musée Carnavalet. Salle Mazarin, apt. of Mme de Sévigné. Much Napoleon memorabilia, Musset and brother as children, costumes of the period, slipper of Rachel, models of Bastille and of guillotine. Sat. night at Salle Luxembourg, *La Belle Aventure*, de Caillavet and de Flers. Very funny....Tuesday night at Salle Richelieu, *Le Jeu de l'amour et du hazard* [Marivaux] beautifully played, like seeing Watteau alive....14 Juillet 1950 [Bastille Day]. Rain, rain, rain. Parade on Champs Elysée out of the question. We stroll through the cathedral, which is swarming with tourists. Sit near the front and watch a service....Just make the Récamier before a terrific rain storm, which shuts us in the rest of the afternoon. About 9 p.m. we start for the Pont Neuf to see the fireworks. Dancing on Rue des Canettes, on St. Germain. Very amusing—students snarling up traffic. Mob at Pont is terrific. Fireworks very nice. St. Chapelle & Notre Dame, illuminated, look like frozen music. Long searchlights sweep the sky. Take Metro at St. Michel to Mt. Parnasse—crowds, but rather dull. Less spontaneous than St. Germain. Obviously designed for tourists taking the Paris-by-night tour. At La Coupole, band was playing and couples were dancing to Stars and Stripes Forever. At Rotonde crowd looked bored. Many Americans. Dome very quiet. This quarter has changed greatly since 1926. July 15. In Luxembourg after lunch, sitting near statue of Verlaine. Very peaceful. White urns among dark trees. Old women, children, dogs, statues. *"Dans le vieux parc solitaire et glacé...."* Soft breeze, soft sunlight. Gardens beautifully laid out. Around statue of Bacchus, in greenish bronze, is an oval bed, border pale green, inside banked with rose up to white marble base. Under Verlaine statue, petunias and marigolds with border of pink and green foliage plants. Nuns strolled through here, and professors, and whole family parties. The most charming park in the world.

Even in Paris, where food and drink were amenable to selection, Ruth was subject to attacks of dysentery that summer. It became apparent that nothing short of a return to the States would bring permanent relief. We arranged for early passage back, abandoning our original plan to spend the rest of the summer in Italy and the Pyrenees, and on calm seas and an American liner Ruth quickly recovered.

Before I left Cornell, Francis Mineka, then head of the English Department and the Victorian man under whom I had done my dissertation, offered me an assistant professorship at Cornell with the opportunity for promotion. The offer was tempting but not enough so to overbalance my distaste for the competitiveness of a large department and my motives for returning to St. Lawrence: my friends there, nearness to the Adirondacks, and the fact that both Ruth and I had places on the faculty.

In the spring of 1950 I received a contract reappointing me assistant professor of English at St. Lawrence for the ensuing academic year. In view of my forthcoming advanced degree, I had expected promotion to associate professor. In an interview on one of my trips to Canton, Dean Romoda rejected my request for promotion on that time-worn ground of administrators, the table of organization, an instrument as inflexible as the laws of Moses. There was no place for another associate professor in the English Department, the Dean said. Not satisfied with this, I made the mistake of asking whether my work was satisfactory. He replied that he had no opinion either way; nothing positive to say, nothing negative. This consigned me to limbo, that niche on the rim of Hell where Dante encounters "the wretched souls of those, who lived / Without or praise or blame."

Literature has a manic-depressive effect on me. An apt quotation heightens pleasure or deepens pain. Wordsworth sends me soaring ("free of mountain solitudes," "the sounding cataract / Haunted me like a passion," "Bliss was it in that dawn to be alive"). On the other hand, it was profoundly depressing to be linked to characters in Dante's Hell, especially those sad negative souls who are scorned "by both Mercy and Justice." Let us not speak of them, Virgil tells Dante, but pass them by.

That interview was chilling after a lovely, upbeat two years at Cornell. It soured my relations with Dean Romoda for the next fifteen years. I regretted the passing of Dean Hulett, who had been liberal with praise and encouragement. I rationalized a persona for his successor that ignored hints from colleagues that there might be more to the man than met my eye. We were opposites, I thought. He, who had been an athlete in his undergraduate days at St. Lawrence, was gung-ho for intercollegiate athletics. I was indifferent to them. He never saw me in the bleachers. Though I was pleased to hear of victories for our side, I had better things to do with my time than watching a boring game. Besides, the tempo is all wrong for me. Baseball is too slow. Ice hockey and basketball are too fast. Football is by turns too fast and too slow. Only tennis is just right, but it is better watched on TV. So when the Dean said that he judged a man by the cut of his jib, whatever that meant I was sure that it denigrated characters like me. Then, fifteen years too late, the miracle occurred. When I visited him on a matter related to my retirement at term's end, he said that he had just read and liked an article by me in his favorite magazine, the *Conservationist*. I was out of limbo at last.

## XIII  THE BEWKES YEARS

I N THE POSTWAR ADMINISTRATION I was not without friends. President Eugene Bewkes came to St. Lawrence in 1945 with the accolades of a scholar, among other qualifications. Having resolved that, if an advanced degree was not enough for promotion, I would go the other route favored by administrators, publications, I sent offprints to his office at the rate of one or two a year. He replied in flattering terms. And the promotion to associate professor came in 1952; to full professor in 1959.

Absorbed by the quotidian round, few of us faculty realized, during those eighteen years of the Bewkes administration, 1945–1963, how privileged we were in association with a rapidly improving institution. President Bewkes was not only an effective fund raiser but also a scholar persistent in his efforts to improve the quality of education at St. Lawrence. In his régime St. Lawrence progressed from a provincial college little known outside New York State to one of national reputation. The student body doubled in size over the pre-war years. The faculty more than doubled from a ratio of one to seventeen students to one in fourteen. The expected fall-off in enrollment as the wave of veterans subsided never in fact occurred. The growing reputation of St. Lawrence as one of the better small liberal arts colleges of the country brought more applicants than could be accommodated on campus. Admissions became selective while at the same time utilizing full capacity. The quality of the student body steadily improved. As temporary, prefabricated housing units were abandoned, new dormitories were built for both men and women. Temporary classroom buildings were replaced by permanent ones when the Agricultural and Technical Institute of Canton moved from its site on the St. Lawrence campus to another part of the village. "To lubricate the giving arm," as a consultant put it, funds were first raised for an ice hockey arena. Then a more ambitious campaign was started for a new library, opened in 1959. Participation in the annual alumni fund rose to seventy percent in 1963. The progress made in the Bewkes years was recognized in 1962 by the selection of St. Lawrence among twenty-one colleges to receive a challenge grant from the Ford Foundation of two million dollars to be matched by gifts from alumni and friends. Criteria for the grant were regional importance, strong support from alumni, strong presidential leadership, a tradition of scholarship, and a well-developed plan for educational improvement. The matching campaign was a success.

For the faculty the chief benefit of the Bewkes years was a better quality of students. Prior to World War II, the ultimate aim of our students, most of whom came from upstate New York, was a bachelor's degree in arts or sciences. After the war many planned to continue studies in graduate school and applied themselves in order to better their chances of admission to the large universities. In the 1950s and 1960s several of my students received Woodrow Wilson fellowships for up to three years of graduate study and have become professors of English in their turn. It has been a satisfaction to work with these bright, dedicated students.

In 1954 Professor Lee Hunt of the Education Department retired preparatory to moving to the southern tier of the state. His home, where I had lived as a bachelor during my first two years in Canton, came on the market. Ruth and I had long wanted a house of our own, and this one, as we looked about the village, was our second choice. Negotiations for the house of first choice failed; it was eventually purchased by the University as a home for present and future deans of the faculty. So in November 1954 we bought the Hunt house for cash. At 13 Jay Street, it is only a block and a half from the campus. We moved the first of January, 1955, and have lived here ever since. I have continued for the last thirty-five years to cultivate and expand the garden inherited from Professor Hunt. Now, a year and a half after Ruth's death, I am occupying the house alone except for my cat, Christopher, who, as cats' lives go, is about my age and showing it.

*Snowed in at 13 Jay Street, Canton*

Committee work occupied a good deal of my time in the 1950s. I was on the Concerts and Lectures Committee for several years. In 1952 I was appointed chairman of a faculty Committee on a New Library. Other members were William Mallam, history; Alfred Romer, physics; William Houk, biology; Andrew Peters, librarian; and various members of the library staff. After Andrew Peters' retirement in 1972, a series of tributes to him was printed in the library *Bulletin*. My contribution, "Andy's New Library," describes the work of that faculty committee.

We all had to learn the art of make-do in those depression years of the thirties when Andrew Peters first came to St. Lawrence as assistant librarian. When, after an absence of a few years, he returned in the forties as head librarian, things were not much changed. The great depression dragged on through the forties and early fifties in the nation's small private colleges. It did not relax its hold until someone discovered the magic formula of annual increases in tuition.

In those lean years Andy was better at making-do than anyone else. From his cramped quarters in Herring-Cole Library, outgrown a decade or two earlier, he operated on a grand scale with a series of annexations. The series began with the Catacombs. Here he kept hidden vigil with the cultural inheritance like the early Christians under Rome. Bumped heads and irritated sinuses led to the first strident demands for a new library. Just as Andy had planned, no doubt.

When every bit of crawl space in the Catacombs was crammed full of books and documents, Andy started to annex the rest of the campus. He became an authority on enclosed space. When vacuums were all used up, he began dispossessing users whose functions seemed to him marginal. He set up or expanded departmental libraries in Carnegie and Hepburn. But his big prize was the third floor of the Men's Residence (now Sykes Hall), formerly used by the faculty for handball courts and by the football team as dormitory during training periods. On a lower floor of the same building Andy established a browsing room. By this time the trustees were becoming alarmed. Were World War II and Korean veterans going to have to bunk between book stacks? Alarms were part of Andy's strategy.

A major fund campaign was finally started. Just as Andy had planned. In fact, he had already started one of his own, selling specially designed Wedgwood plates to alumni.

In 1952 President Bewkes appointed a faculty committee to plan for the new building, with Andy as secretary and me as chairman. The committee had plenty of time. Five years passed before the groundbreaking ceremony in June, 1957.

Those were good years for Andy. True, his book budget was still regularly exhausted by April, the cruelest month: no more rare books till the turn of the fiscal year in July. But the prospect of a new library buoyed his spirits. He kept us all in good humor. During the first two years the committee met weekly in one another's homes. At the first meeting we celebrated with cocktails; thereafter it was tea and cookies. This come-down was a lasting grievance to one member. But for Andy, practiced in making-do, tea was the cup that cheers.

He was an especially fine companion on trips. Our travel budget was meager, so that trips to inspect new college libraries were often made singly and with dual purpose, as when some committee member was attending a professional meeting or going on vacation. But Andy and I together visited the new Lamont Library at Harvard, and one spring vacation four of us visited Bucknell. Hearing that the shad were running in the Susquehanna, Andy squired us all into a restaurant in Williamsport for a memorable experience in dining on fresh shad and shad roe.

Our job was to specify the services and space requirements of a library ample for an enrollment of 1,300 and adequate for 1,500. The latter figure was to be the maximum future enrollment as determined by the Board of Trustees.

The book collection, counting everything in Herring-Cole and Andy's numerous annexes, reached 150,000 by the time the new library opened. We had been convinced by our visit to the Lamont Library and by talks with a consultant, Dr. Keyes Metcalf, director of libraries at Harvard, that an undergraduate college should put quality and turnover above the size of a collection. Obsolete or little used books should constantly be weeded out and sent to a regional depository, where they would be on call if needed. So we asked for shelf space for a maximum of 302,000: 280,000 in the stack core and 22,000 in special collections elsewhere in the building.

The rule of thumb then current for seating capacity in college libraries was a minimum of thirty percent of the student body. The author of a standard work on library planning suggested a maximum of fifty percent, saying that if the building was inviting enough, it would be fully occupied at certain times of day. We decided to ask for 530 seats for public use and 45 for staff....

Contractors' bids on this first set of plans exceeded available funds by a substantial amount. The committee wanted to wait while additional funds were raised. But it is an axiom with fund raisers that a campaign once closed cannot be opened again.

Further reductions were necessary. Seating, already at a minimum for 1,500 students, could not be reduced; nor could the capacity of the stacks in the south wing. The big reductions had to come in the central part of the building and in the north wing. Accordingly, the revised plans reduced up to twenty percent the size of the lobby, the general reading room, and working areas for the staff. A bibliography room and staff office were eliminated. Faculty studies were cut from ten to eight....

During the next decade strains developed in the new library as the book collection edged upward toward 250,000 and student body toward 2,000. Although an overflow science library was set up in Valentine Hall, gaps in the stacks relentlessly filled. And at times of peak use it became hard to find a seat where one wanted to be. But Andy was an old hand at making-do. Somehow he found ways of making a building work that was twenty percent smaller than it should have been for a student body three-quarters the size of the actual one of today.

On the first day of the first term that the library was open for use, in the fall of 1959, I walked past the building. There in the tall windows of the Josephine Young Browsing Room, all alone, sat a girl in an attitude of intent relaxation, a book in hand, shoes kicked off, and stockinged feet propped on another easy chair. After discounting the fact that a pretty girl reading a book is an object of natural attraction to a professor, I still took this picture in the window as augury of success for the new library.

In spite of its limitations in size and probably life span, the Owen D. Young Library has been successful, I think, largely thanks to Andy's humanism and good management. As stated in the faculty committee's report of October, 1954, "A college library is more than a storehouse of books and other materials. Besides this passive function, it has three active ones: to arouse interest in books, to encourage familiarity with them, and to give training in the art of using them." Andy presides over these three functions with a kind of princeliness.

The Metcalf policy of a core collection of limited size and rapid turnover has never taken hold at St. Lawrence. Here we have no backup library available such as the Widener at Harvard. Our library serves the community as well as the students and to some extent the research needs of the faculty. So the book collection has continued to grow, and so has the student body, to a maximum of 2,300. In 1979, under the administration of President Frank Piskor, a large, handsome addition to the Owen D. Young Library was completed. Now users enjoy the luxury of uncrowded space, dispersed, semi-private seating areas, an electronic on-line cataloging system, and other state-of-the-art inducements to scholarship. But already, as the book collection has reached 400,000, the floor-level shelves in the stacks are filling up, much to the distress of aging knee joints. It is only a question of time.

I finally began writing in earnest in my sixth decade. At sixteen I wanted to become a writer. With a portable typewriter, I could roam the world, I thought, in complete freedom, just as then, having paddled across a lake in northern Wisconsin to escape the family and summer resort neighbors, I was seated under a Norway pine, typewriter on my knees, trying to think of something to write about. I dreamed of the success of a first novel. It would solve the problem of a livelihood till I turned out the next one.

I learned that things seldom work out that way. Certainly they do not if you have no subject that demands outlet with the urgency of congestion, something as compelling as the confrontation of two cultures, American and European, that took possession of Henry James early in life and never relaxed its hold on his imagination. I had no such subject. If I had chosen journalism as a career, as some successful writers do, a subject might have turned up. In the teaching profession this is less likely. The academic world is a hermetic one. And teaching tends to develop the critical faculty at the expense of the creative. When I first turned to writing, it was as a critic writing articles for professional journals. The motive was promotion in rank to associate professor and then full professor, though the subjects of the articles were absorbing enough at the time.

Those articles, the first in 1952, broke a barrier. Some were favorably noticed by other scholars in the English and comparative literature fields. When finally a subject derived from personal experience became manifest, the transition from one kind of writing to another came easily. But it came late. For over half a lifetime my imaginal faculty was undernourished. The weakness in my writing today is dearth of imagery. I envy John Updike's image-making fertility: the clarifying or connotative power, the occasional explosive power, of metonymy, simile, metaphor. Aware of this weakness, in partial compensation I aim for an accessible style that avoids the recherché, seeks transparency of thought and feeling, and maintains forward momentum by rhythmic flow within the paragraph. Often these qualities are not attained till the third or fourth revision.

## XIV  GOING IN

T HE SUBJECT FOR WRITING that became compelling by my sixth
decade was the Adirondack Park. My interest in it had begun in 1929, the
year I first settled in Canton. A quarter century is little enough time to explore and comprehend so large a region, the largest of all state and national parks
outside Alaska, larger than any one of six Eastern states and of the three smallest
ones combined. Canton lies just off the northwestern corner of the park, twelve
miles by the nearest of our three common entrances, the Clare Road; twenty-one
miles by State Route 56 in the Raquette River valley; and twenty-eight miles by
way of Hopkinton and St. Regis Falls. To an Iowan, fresh from the cornfields and
the flatlands, the luxury of uneven ground, mystery of wild forest, intricacy of
waterways, lure of mountaintops just a little way south of Canton were an immediate fascination and seemed to invite a lifetime of exploration. As I say in the
preface to *Adirondack Pilgrimage*, "Going in is no ordinary event. It is a rite of
passage into a different order of space and time. Space is no longer parceled out
in village streets and dairy farms; it is the great continuous woods. Time is no
longer linear and exigent; it is relaxed and cyclical, in gyres of day and night, the
seasons, old growth and new growth feeding on decay....An inner ceremony of
adjustment begins at wood's edge, where holstein gives way to whitetail country."

What the woods offers us is another chance, an escape, however brief, from the
dominance of linear time. In ordinary life we have only one go at time. But space
allows us a return visit. And in returning to the woods, we are caught up in the
cyclical spin of night and day, the seasons, growth and decay; in a brief remission
of linear time.

My first published article on an Adirondack subject, in 1954, was simply a review of a book that has remained a touchstone of regional literature in the twentieth century, William Chapman White's *Adirondack Country*. Its last sixty
pages, describing the changes that each month brings in the woods, is a paean to
the "playful spin" of the seasons in the Adirondack year.

Since that review of *Adirondack Country* thirty-six years ago, writing has been
a second career. I have published approximately one hundred articles, essays, re-

views, and chapters or introductions in the books of others; served as consultant and editor to four publishers of Adirondack books; and produced three books of my own that are still in print. I have also written innumerable letters seeking to influence policy or legislation on Adirondack issues. In a democracy such as ours the individual is not powerless. If he is courteous and persistent and has a good case, he can influence the way things are managed and get legislation passed, at least at the state level.

My first book was an anthology, *The Adirondack Reader*. It was published by the Macmillan Company in 1964, the year before my retirement from St. Lawrence. For several years I had been reading widely in Adirondack literature of the nineteenth and twentieth centuries. When Warder Cadbury, an Adirondack historian with whom I corresponded in the 1950s and 1960s, casually remarked that the time might be ripe for an anthology, the idea struck fire with me. Adirondack letters are extensive. As Roderick Nash remarks in *Wilderness and the American Mind*, "By the 1880s more had been written about the Adirondack country than any other wilderness area of the United States." That flow of writing has continued and vindicates T. Morris Longstreth's 1917 prediction that the Adirondacks would become of increasing value to American writers.

The reading, selecting process, and writing of preface, sectional introductions, and author notes for the anthology were my education for this second career. The *Reader* had less value for Macmillan. Although I was satisfied with sales figures for a book of regional interest, the publisher was not. At the end of the third year, without notifying me, Macmillan followed the practice of many commercial publishers of remaindering a book of slow sales figures. When I learned indirectly that some fifteen hundred copies of an original five thousand had been sold to a remainder house, I called attention to a clause in my contract that provided for prior notification to the writer of such an intention. All I got was an apology. Meanwhile the Adirondack Museum at Blue Mountain Lake, which had bought the entire lot from the remainder dealer, was profiting from sales in its book store. William Verner offered to sell me copies at the price the Museum had paid for them. I accepted this offer for a certain number of copies, which in turn were sold to people who applied directly to me.

In less than two years both I and the Museum disposed of the remaining copies of the *Reader*. In the 1970s it became a sought-after item in secondhand book stores, where prices soon reached the original list and then went higher. There is a body of dedicated Adirondackers, renewed with each generation, that likes to read about the area as well as experience it directly. I received fan mail urging a new edition. Another incentive for a revised edition was the discovery of a few writers I had overlooked and the appearance of new writing in the following two decades, especially works of fiction by three novelists of national reputation.

[ 133 ]

Resolved this time to shun large commercial publishing houses with their practice of remaindering, I obtained release of rights from Macmillan and turned to a regional publisher, the Adirondack Mountain Club. The intention of the original founders of the Club was that it would in future publish not only guidebooks to the park but also books of a more general nature. The *Reader* was such a work. The Club's response was favorable. I felt I could count on it to keep the book in print for the foreseeable future, with revisions at about twenty year intervals under new co-editors. Annual sales in the last eight years have been modest but steady. Published in both cloth and paper bindings, the second edition, copyrighted 1982, appeared early in 1983 and sold 1,880 copies that year, 1,000 the following, and since then from 700 to 800 annually.

Critics have had diverse but favorable opinions of the *Reader*. One reviewer thought it amounted to an informal history of the Adirondacks; another, that it led into the main stream of American letters. A French reader returned to Paris after residing for several years in New York State called it a book of nostalgia. A lifelong summer resident of the Adirondacks said that it makes a fine Christmas gift. A reviewer in a Connecticut newspaper remarked that by attesting to the beauty and grandeur of the park, the *Reader* is a powerful appeal for preservational measures. Paul Oehser in a review in the Wilderness Society quarterly wrote: "To lovers of wilderness this book will be sheer delight." For Neal Burdick, editor of *Adirondac*, the *Reader* is "my all-time, number one favorite Adirondack book…a banquet of matters Adirondack." My purpose, especially in the second edition, was to make the book a mirror of the cultural heritage of the park as visitors, summer residents, and natives have contributed to it and a reflection also of our national heritage of wilderness experience from colonial times to the present.

During the 1950s and early 1960s before retirement, writing absorbed only a part of the three summer months free from professional duties. Recreation accounted for the other half, and recreation came to mean, first of all, exploration of South Woods, as the Adirondacks used to be called here at the top of the state. Forest recreation is the birthright of every American. For some it means the fall hunt and spring trout fishing. For me it has always meant tramping through the woods and up the mountains or paddling the waters for what is there and not for the taking. So in 1952 I joined an organization that promotes this kind of recreation, along with conservation consistent with it, the Adirondack Mountain Club. Maintaining membership now for forty years, I have made valued associations with other members, served a three-year term on the Board of Governors, written for the Club's periodical, the *Adirondac*, and am now wedded to the Club as publisher of my three books. Until 1970 I was a member at large; thereafter a founding member of the Laurentian Chapter of St. Lawrence County.

By 1954, realizing that I had climbed twenty of the so-called High Peaks in the northeast sector of the park, I decided to climb all forty-six of four thousand feet or higher. That summer was one of the rainiest in many a year. Resort keepers complained about their losses as would-be vacationers remained in the cities. William Chapman White, in his column in the *Herald Tribune*, called that season in the Adirondacks one of the worst since 1816, the year without a summer. Yet I climbed, sometimes drenched, fifteen peaks that year, seven of which were my first ascents of over four-thousand footers.

On one of the rare sunny days that summer, Fred Clark and I climbed Whiteface from the Wilmington side and also its twin peak, Esther. Esther was without a trail, but the traverse from a shoulder of Whiteface was not difficult. On the summit we found the tablet commemorating the first recorded ascent in 1839 by Esther McComb, a neighborhood girl of fifteen. The mountain is named for her. According to the plaque, she came to it for "the sheer joy of climbing." While we idled on the summit, a boy of seventeen and two sisters appeared. We had met them earlier on Whiteface and had told them how to reach Esther. They were from nearby Chazy, they said. The older girl, just fourteen, spoke with poise and enthusiasm of her previous climbs of six of the High Peaks. Her loveliness set us dreaming. Her name was Donna, but for us she was Esther McComb, more than a century later, here to remind us that the joy of climbing is a timeless emotion.

That summer of 1954 was exceptional not only for its foul weather but for an escaped cop killer. Returning one day from a climb of Gothics, Saddleback, and Basin, we were stopped several times by state troopers trying to run down a fugitive who had killed a Lake Placid policeman, wounded two other officers, and had probably stolen jewelry worth over one hundred thousand dollars from the Lake Placid Club. Ordinarily the Adirondacks are pretty free of crime, but when it does occur, the opportunities for escape are very real in dense forests. Traces of the fugitive in this case were reported in various parts of the woods over the next two months. His German Luger pistol was found, along with a copy of the *Rubaiyat*, in a summer cabin in the Tupper Lake area. He was finally arrested on another charge of burglary in Reno, Nevada. His fingerprints matched those found at the scene where he had killed the Lake Placid policeman. In his possession in Reno was a newspaper clipping about the Lake Placid shooting and manhunt, which had involved five hundred troopers and volunteers. He was an air force major absent without leave, named James Call.

In an Elizabethtown jail Call told the story of his two-and-a-half month, three-hundred-mile flight from one part of the Adirondacks to another. He had sprinkled pepper along his trail to throw bloodhounds off the scent. For one four-day period he was without food except for the blueberries he found in open areas of the woods. His narrowest escape came at the cabin near Tupper Lake when he saw the owner approach and fled out the back door. It was there that he left his belongings, including a sleeping bag, the German pistol, and the copy of the *Rubaiyat*.

Knowing how to survive in the woods, Call made good his escape only to be apprehended on another charge. Those who lack survival skills and become disoriented may perish of exposure, like the young boy who wandered off into the woods from his family's summer camp and was never found, though his wealthy parents paid the costs of an extensive year-long search. An aspiring Forty-Sixer whom I used to meet at Adirondak Loj, Howard Gilroy, never returned from an October hike on the Santanoni Range in 1958. He had signed the register on Santanoni Peak and then had probably attempted to reach trail-less Panther across a heavily blowndown ridge in the same range. Forty troopers, forest rangers, and others made an intensive search during the next month but found no trace except for the signature. The woods were so dense and so laced with deadfalls that bloodhounds were useless in the search. For several years we climbers of the trail-less peaks looked for Gilroy's remains on that savage ridge leading to Panther. But it was not till thirty years later that a hiker, apparently off course in trekking between the two summits, happened on remains believed to be those of the hapless Gilroy, who had sought recognition as a Forty-Sixer to compensate for a failed life.

Remembering Gilroy, I usually refrained from going alone on the trail-less peaks and other bushwhacking excursions. But failing to find a companion in a few instances, and gaining confidence in orienteering, I made solo climbs of Tabletop, Gray, Panther, and a few lesser peaks in the western Adirondacks, conscious of the risk and deliberate in planting the next step over broken ground in blowdown areas. Ironically, my only broken ankle occurred in a fall from a stepladder in my backyard.

For the most part it was easy to find companions on the St. Lawrence faculty or simply in chance encounters at Adirondak Loj. By 1956 I became acquainted with several other hikers on the way to becoming Forty-Sixers. We arranged joint hikes and traded information about the best routes to follow to avoid the worst blowdown from the hurricanes of the early 1950s. In 1956, the year the hermit, Noah John Rondeau, weakened by old age, finally left the woods after thirty years as Mayor of Cold River Flow (population one), the void left by his absence was filled, for me, by other forest wildings, such as the wife and children of Paul Schaefer. I used to meet them singly or in family groups, all imbued with their father's deep love of the Adirondacks and his preservationist philosophy. Caroline, the mother, Mary and Monica qualified as Forty-Sixers that year. Monica was just ten years old, then the youngest to become a Forty-Sixer, though that age record has been bettered since. Mary, aged twenty, stays in my memory as a wood nymph, a little disheveled, a smudge on one cheek, lithe, lean, eager to talk about her adventures on and off trail. Brief encounters in the woods strike a spark of sympathy and understanding. The matrix of the woods confers on them a lasting aura. Normally people's interest in one another is rather small. But the woods creates an instant bond.

In essays collected in *Adirondack Pilgrimage* I have written of some of my hiking companions of those years leading up to my qualification as Forty-Sixer in 1958 and will not duplicate their stories here. Richard Babcock, father of Larry, the subject of the essay "A State of Mind, Brisbane," died in the year of this writing. The following piece is a memorial I wrote for *Adirondac*.

Richard Babcock, recently deceased, was a cherished companion of the woods and waters. Though he lived in Montpelier in easy reach of the Green Mountains and the Whites, he preferred the Adirondacks for their wildness. When I first met him at Johns Brook Lodge in the summer of 1956, he had climbed thirty-eight of the High Peaks. By September of the same year he, his son, Larry, and his daughter, Barbara, all became Forty-Sixers. Dick's wife, Dorothy, responsible for commissary and logistics, was retarded a bit and finished a couple of years later, as number 161.

There was something special about every outing I had with Dick. It began with our ascent of Mt. Seward through the blowdown of the year 1957. Aside from the fact that it was my birthday and my first ascent of Seward (Dick's second), the occasion was special in that Dick had been chosen to mount a new, durable Forty-Sixer canister on the summit to replace the former tin can. This he accomplished with much ceremony, and our party of five became the first signers in the new register.

Having acquired a nineteen-foot Grumman canoe, Dick decided he wanted to explore Follensby Pond with it, the site of Philosophers' Camp in 1858 but now in a private preserve. Dick considered it a defect in that famous camping trip of the Boston-Cambridge-Concord pundits that his favorite author, Thoreau, was not among them, but he would settle for Emerson and Lowell. So one day in early May when the Raquette spread over its floodplains with snow melt and spring rains, we paddled through brush and trees to cut out the bends (bushwhacking by canoe we called it) and then up the outlet of Follensby and through its entire length, look-ing for the probable site of the century-old camp. The remarkable thing about that trip was the bald eagle that soared majestically overhead as we were returning through the lake. In that DDT contaminated year prior to the alarm sounded by Rachel Carson, our eagle was probably the only one in all the Adirondacks. We did not have long to admire it. A motorboat raced out of a cove and chased us to the outlet, possibly the caretaker. Thanks to Dick's powerful strokes of the paddle, we scraped over the spillway at the foot of the lake and made good our escape.

Like father, like son. Larry, not knowing how but resolved to learn by doing, built an Adirondack guideboat. The three of us christened it on a cruise from Long

Lake village to Tupper Lake. It conveyed us with safety and style.

Some years later, after Larry had built his second, improved guideboat, he and Dick hatched the scheme of christening it on Duck Hole. Why, I asked, not some more accessible water? No, it had to be Duck Hole. Even if we were to have the luck of crossing the private waters of Henderson Lake and the Preston Ponds without being ticketed for trespass, there would still be a formidable uphill carry of two miles with a ninety-pound Grumman canoe, a seventy-pound guideboat, and packs for two nights in a lean-to for five people, including Dorothy and Larry's bride, Virginia. Dick and I took turns carrying the Grumman. Everything about this Babcockian scheme worked as planned. I for one finished the trip with a sense of accomplishment for the two-hour muscle-straining hike in and the ten-minute paddle on Duck Hole. Besides, there was all that magnificent scenery.

In July of 1958 my sister Mary visited us from Los Angeles. Her visits were rare in those years while she was still raising a family of three children. I introduced her to the Adirondacks in a three-day camping and hiking trip with a climb of Mt. Marcy from Lake Colden, where we camped two nights in Cedar Point Lean-to. The breeze off the lake discouraged insects but also obliged us to draw our sleeping bags close for body warmth at night. Mary was then thirty-nine and would turn forty the next month, but as ever she looked ten years younger than her age.

Mary was a good companion on the trail; she had energy and a quick comeback after exertion. She was cheerful, always smiling, observant, and rewarding to look

*Mary Carlson, Paul's sister, on a camping trip in the Adirondack High Peaks, 1958.*

at with her blond curls, taut figure in jeans, and California tan. On the summit of Marcy a group from a boys' camp flocked around her as she spread smiles among them and exclaimed over the view and the tiny Alpine flowers amidst the rocks.

On the trail by Feldspar Brook and the Opalescent coming down, she picked up scores of red spruce and hemlock cones, filling her day pack with them. They were small enough, she said, to make wonderful ornaments for Christmas packages; in the Sierras all the cones are too large. Like our mother, Mary is a "picker-up of unconsidered trifles." The following Christmas the packages Ruth and I received from California were elaborately decorated with linked spruce and hemlock cones from the Marcy trail. Mary included also a photographic record of her visit.

*Mary and Paul on the summit of Mt. Marcy, 1958*

In mid August, 1958, Larry Babcock handed me a Forty-Sixer shoulder patch on the peak of East Dix. Having now climbed all of the High Peaks as number 146 in the sequence, I was free to explore the rest of the Adirondacks. Westerners scoff at our Eastern so-called mountains and at the term "High Peaks" of the Adirondacks. Yet so far as vertical elevation ascended by the climber, there is not a great deal of difference between East and West. Roads through mountain passes in the Rockies and the Sierras reach elevations of ten to twelve thousand feet. The climber begins his ascent from those passes to summits of at most 14,500 feet. He who climbs Mt. Marcy from the Keene Valley side by the Phelps Trail parks his car at the Gardens, elevation 1,523, and hikes nine miles to the summit at 5,344 feet, a vertical ascent of 3,821. Missing of course are the effects of high altitudes on the lungs and the spirits and the vast open spaces above timberline. The compensating factor is the woods, a forest of endless variety close up and shading off into mystery at its depths.

Of the nearly three hundred peaks I have ascended in New York and the three northern New England states, my prime favorites, excluding the High Peaks of the Adirondacks, are Katahdin in Maine and in the Adirondacks, St. Regis, Jay, Catamount, Baldface (twin of Debar Mountain near Duane), and Long Pond Mountain in the St. Regis Canoe Area. The last two are trail-less. One of several Catamounts, the peak I first discovered in 1959 is in the southwest corner of Clinton County, six miles north of Whiteface. The mountain is more distinctive than its name. Though its bare 3,168 feet of elevation may be scorned by aspiring Forty-Sixers, it is a fine mountain for the unambitious to explore. I have climbed it by various routes at least a dozen times, alone or with companions qualified to appreciate its architectural intricacies.

*Catamount Mtn. from the west*

Catamount was once stripped of its woods to feed the charcoal kilns in the Little Black Brook valley beneath it. The charcoal in turn was used to smelt iron ore in numerous veins in the vicinity. The mines have been idle for a century now, and new woods are finding a foothold in the deepening humus of the central ravine and in crevices of rock elsewhere. But much of the bedrock structure is still exposed, and it is as handsome as many a medieval cathedral.

The approach from the east through the hamlet of Black Brook, by what used to be called the Port Kent–Hopkinton Turnpike, winds through a narrow valley between the Wilmington Range and the three-mile long southern flank of Catamount. It gives an unfolding acquaintance with the mountain, which grows in height, bulk, cragginess, and steepness as one ascends the valley. But I prefer the western approach from Bloomingdale and Franklin Falls in the valley of the Saranac. The view from the west is sudden, spectacular, unforgettable. Here Catamount is the "picture" mountain of the Adirondacks as Chocorua is of the Whites. Rising abruptly from a plateau, massive and isolated, the west face is a broad-based pyramid with slightly irregular flanks. Half way up the north ridge is a nubble, and two-thirds of the way up the south ridge, a prominent shoulder separated from the rocky summit cone by the headwall of a ravine. Turned slightly southward, the west face receives the sun most of the day. It presents a variegated pattern of sunlight and shadow, open rock and young, struggling forest, evergreen and hardwood foliage. The evergreens have the look of an invading army on steep

*Paul at the chimney on Catamount Mtn. (Photo Duncan Cutter)*

ramparts. This western face with its mixture of strain and repose has an irresistible appeal to the climber.

The trail, not by the shortest way up, obligingly introduces one to the mountain's intricacies of structure, first up the central ravine, then over a broad terrace of the southern shoulder, up its steep south ridge through a chimney, over its crest to the headwall of the ravine, and finally up a giant staircase of open ledges, with blueberries in the crevices, to an open summit. Views open in all directions. To the south, six miles away, is noble Whiteface. Close by on the north are Taylor Pond and Silver Lake. The peaks of the northern Adirondacks form a ring beyond the Saranac River valley. On the east are Lake Champlain at its widest and the Mt. Mansfield region of the Green Mountains. Catamount is a refuge out of the world for a day.

Noblesse oblige is a moral imperative among Forty-Sixers. Once you have qualified you must become an informal guide on the trail-less peaks to those on the way up. Few are more fortunate than I in their charges. The following letter from Herbert McAneny began a warm friendship that has lasted to this day. The salutation is a reference to the title "A State of Mind, Brisbane," of my article about Larry Babcock, reprinted in *Adirondack Pilgrimage*.

Princeton, N.J.
November 27, 1958

Dear "Brisbane,"

After reading your piece in the September-October *Ad-i-ron-dac* I thought to myself, This is one of the most delightful things I have ever read in this magazine. Now I have just reread it to make sure, and it still is.

It's a gem of a character sketch—of two people. Young Natty is especially vivid. I can remember when the highest virtue to me seemed to be to be able to walk through woods without stepping on a single dry twig, and how hard I tried to emulate Hawkeye in this. Another quality which I tried to follow—or rather, followed without trying—was the Indians' habit of laughing silently. I still feel a bit superior whenever I hear anyone break out in a loud guffaw.

[ 141 ]

Anyway, I wanted to tell you that I enjoyed what you wrote. The part that made me determine to write you was the sentence, "At fifty-five one is not washed up." I am 55, and that sentence sounded wonderful. I too have spent too many years in low country, and this summer in one glorious week alone raised my tally from 24 to 30. Now for the first time I really want to finish the 46. My ulterior motive in writing you is to express the indefinite but real hope that, if you are loose in the Adirondacks next summer, perhaps you might be willing to take me on as a pre-cardiac companion and mosey up a few of the trail-less ones with me.

Anyway, I enjoyed "A State of Mind."

Subsequently I learned that Herbert taught English at the Princeton Country Day School. For an interval he was headmaster. One of his most gifted students was Adam Hochschild, now a writer. Herbert grew up in New York City, where his father was Manhattan Borough president and later president of the Board of Aldermen. He and his brother Arnold attended the private Riverdale School and spent summers during their youth at the Riverdale Camp at the foot of Long Lake, where they began exploring Adirondack woods and waters. Herbert graduated from Williams College and then spent two years at Oxford reading English literature. While abroad he met his future wife, Marguerite Loud, who, having graduated *summa cum laude* from Barnard, was then a student at the Sorbonne. After her marriage Marguerite became curator of the theater collections of the Firestone Library and manager of the theater of Princeton University. Shortly after her death in 1989 Herbert and his daughter published a volume of Marguerite's letters to her family from Paris while she was a graduate student there on a fellowship. To me this collection, *An Elegant Time*, seemed the essence of youth at its best—cultivated, witty, effervescent. Paris in 1923–24 was a festival to her, a realization of the model she had adopted from Epictetus: "Try to enjoy the great festival of life with other men." Since I too was student at the Sorbonne four years later, that volume of letters is one of the books I have most enjoyed in old age. It revived my Europhilia.

The following narrative recounts my second or third climbs and Herbert's firsts of thirteen of the trail-less peaks during the next four years. Herbert completed his round of the forty-six in 1962 as number 231. This was forty-five years after his first climb of Mt. Marcy in 1917 with a group of boys from the Riverdale Camp.

January 15, 1983

Dear Herbert:

When your daughter Leslie asked me for a contribution to a scrapbook-biography in celebration of your eightieth birthday, I picked up volume four of my Adirondack logs and began reliving the adventures of two aging mountaineers on thirteen of the trail-less peaks. The entries are in my usual redundant style, much in need of pruning. I'll touch simply on the highlights.

Our first trip to the Dix Range was on August 20–21, 1959. We were both fifty-six, you the older by five months, which didn't seem to make much difference in our evenly matched pace and endurance and temperament. Arnold accompanied us on that trip.

On the way in to our campsite at the base of Macomb, we kept passing about a score of stragglers of a New Jersey hiking club. They were returning, much the worse for wear, from a day's hike, to Elk Lake Lodge. Oddballs they certainly were; we kept hearing the word "charcoal," their password for the day. The notable thing about this trip to the Dix Range, at the height of the summer hiking season, was its human encounters. Everyone seemed to be in the woods those two days.

After climbing Macomb by the slide, we went on to South Dix over the col. Arnold, not an aspiring forty-sixer, waited for us there while we pushed on to the summit of East Dix, where we met our second party. Three distinguished looking gentlemen from Philadelphia had climbed the peak from the opposite direction. The most magisterial of the group, a gentleman with sandy hair and mustache, introduced himself as James Charlesworth, professor at the University of Pennsylvania and president of the Academy of Political Science. In a fifteen minute chat you and he discovered common friends and interests, and he handed you his card.

Returning to South Dix, we rejoined Arnold and began the descent to our campsite on the Elk Lake trail. On the way down through untracked woods we heard the muffled voices of another party, and shortly after reaching our camp, a party of six hove into sight—Lint Stone, Clint Miller, the Hohmans (Peggy had been a student at St. Lawrence) and their two teenage children. Clint Miller had just finished his forty-sixth peak that day, and the party celebrated with a bottle of warm champagne. My log comments, "If one wants to meet everybody, the way to do it is to climb a trail-less peak late in August. The aspiring forty-sixers are rampant."

The day's three peaks were for you numbers 31, 32, and 33. You and Arnold spent the night in the clearing. As I drove home in what seemed a veritable cloudburst, I wondered how you were faring under that flimsy tarpaulin slung over a rope as ridgepole. In a letter a few days later you said, in a classic understatement, that you and Arnold had "kept pretty dry" and had a "leisurely drying out" next morning over breakfast.

Our next two-day trip was more solitary, July 11–12 of the following year. The first day we climbed to Scott Pond. Coming down the gorge of the outlet, you took some fine photos of the ravine and of the MacIntyre Range. After camping in Scotts Clearing that night, we set out early next morning for Marshall. Approaching from the west was a new route for me, and I led us astray on the ascent so that we lost a good hour in beating our way up an intermediate ridge of blowdown. We took a more direct route on the descent, but all in all it was a tiring day for both of us. Marshall was your 34th. I hope you will put into the scrapbook the good photo of you beside the canister on Marshall's summit.

On a camping trip a week later, July 19–21, we climbed Cliff, Redfield, and Gray, numbers 35, 36, and 37 for you. We speculated that perhaps you would have the distinction of taking the longest time to complete the course, since you had climbed the first of the High Peaks in your early teens while at the Riverdale School camp on Long Lake. The whole story of this third trip was wetness—wet wood, wet foliage, wet clothing, wet feet, swollen brook crossings. "A camping trip such as this," says my log, "is a mixture of the pleasant and the disagreeable. There are moments that make up for the discomfort and aching muscles."

Our next trip, June 23, 1961, was at the height of the bug season. It netted two more trail-less peaks, Nye and Street, in a one-day hike from Adirondak Loj. It was a fine clear day and our orienteering was pretty accurate, though we did get into some pretty bad blowdown. Between our last hike and this, you had climbed Sawteeth, so that Nye and Street were your 39th and 40th. And during the rest of the hiking season that year, you must have climbed your 41st and 42nd.

Our next trip together was on May 25–26, 1962. We climbed remote Allen, your 43rd, which has lately become hard to reach since Finch, Pruyn closed its lands to hikers. We met at Tahawus late in the afternoon and had dinner at the Coffee Shop. It is worth remembering that our dinner, complete with milk shake, cost just $1.45 and our austere but adequate private rooms in the mining community just $3 apiece.

The witchhobble was in full bloom on that May day all along the intricate route we took to the mountain. On the summit we were the first to sign the register that year. Nowadays there would have been a number of signatures right through the winter. With only day packs to carry on the Allen trip, we came through fresher than on most of our trail-less hikes. Allen has remained one of my favorite peaks.

Our next trip, June 28–30 of the same year, was on the Seward Range. Maitland DeSormo accompanied us, having volunteered to be quartermaster for the three-day trip. He carried in an appalling amount of impedimenta, including an extensive larder of freeze-dried foods. We dined sumptuously the first night in the Ward Brook Lean-to. The second night, after a sixteen hour hike over the range, we were all too tired to eat anything more than soup and tea. Mait had to carry out most of what he had lugged in. But then, I have made the same mistake myself.

On the second day, because of some poor orienteering on my part (in spite of a gentle reminder from you that I might be off course), we missed Seward itself, the first peak in the range. This didn't matter too much because all three of us had climbed it before. Once we had gained the ridge between Seward and Donaldson, after fighting terrific blowdown, we were faced with the prospect of several miles of cripplebrush, the tough dwarf balsam fir laced with a network of hidden deadfalls to bark the shins. With every step it was push, push, push. Mait, impatient where the going was rough, lunged into the cripplebrush. It was a hot, sultry day. We were short of water, with only two canteens among us. Mait, sweating like a trooper, needed most of it. With our slower, steadier pace we could have kept going, but he called frequent halts to rest. By the time we had signed the register on Donaldson and were on the way to Emmons, we were a sorry looking group. Mait's shirt and knapsack were ripped. One of your pant legs was torn from waist to cuff, your bare leg accumulating numerous scratches in the waist-high balsam. I had a bloody nose from a snapping branch. I have heard that, since our traverse of that savage ridge, hundreds of aspiring forty-sixers have beaten out a kind of herd path through the cripplebrush. Less honor to them.

Donaldson and Emmons were your 44th and 45th. We began the descent from Emmons to the Northville–Lake Placid trail at 4:30 and reached a clearing near the trail at 6:45. We all three sprawled in the grass for a much needed rest before the seven-mile hike in gathering darkness back to the lean-to. It was a relief to find the going easy now, and you and I loitered behind while Mait raced ahead. He was in such a hurry that he bypassed the lean-to in the dark and did not discover his mistake till he bumped into the gate of Rockefeller Park. Turning back, he finally reached the lean-to at 10:45, about a quarter hour after we had lighted a fire to guide him. That walk back on the trail in gathering dusk and then darkness is a pleasant memory for me, and possibly for you, in spite of an aching hip. An owl hooted at us. In all, it was a sixteen hour day for us—not bad for a couple of fifty-nine year olds.

One more to go, remote Couchsachraga, often the last to be attempted. Again we spent two nights in a lean-to, August 16–18, because of the long pack in to the Cold River and out again. Of the two lean-tos at Cold River, we chose the upper one and were alone the first night. When we returned late the next day, we found that Don Dickinson and his son had occupied the lower lean-to. As darkness fell, their lean-to across the way looked like a stage setting in its pale glimmer and dim figures moving about the fireplace.

On the seventeenth we followed the many angled but easy route that Larry Babcock had discovered to the base of the mountain. Though the day's hike was a long one of twelve hours, it was wholly pleasant. Larry's route led us to a logging bridge over the Cold River that had been left by a lumber company after fairly recent operations before that corridor along the river had finally been sold to the state. (The whole valley between the Sewards and the Santanonis is now solid Forest Preserve.) In addition to the bridge, we passed through the remains of a logging camp. An extensive clearing there had been taken over by the first stage

*Herbert McAneny, summit of Mt. Marshall, 1960*

of successive revegetation, a flourishing raspberry patch now at its peak of ripeness. Even more engaging than the raspberries was the view from the bridge of that solemn, silent, spacious mountain valley, ringed by high peaks shutting out the world. You too, Herbert, must remember that stop on the bridge, going and returning, as the essence of the Adirondack experience, of Adirondack wilderness.

On the peak of Couchie, your forty-sixth and last, we lacked the traditional bottle of champagne, but I had a Forty-Sixer patch to give to you.

So ends the story of two gentle, aging mountaineers on the trail-less peaks. But it was not the end of our shared adventures in the woods and on the waters of the Adirondacks. That would make another story.

In the 1950s my goings-in extended to the winter season. Skiing was not then so universally popular as it is now, and it was still possible to find companions ready for a slow plod through winter woods on webfeet. Bearpaw snowshoes seemed fitting for the dense woods and mountain slopes where I wanted to go. Until my retirement such trips were limited, except during vacations, to Sundays only, for St. Lawrence was still on a six-day schedule of classes. After retirement winter hikes became more frequent till I turned eighty and they began to taper off.

Seasonal variations are extreme in the northern latitude of the Adirondacks. Forest

*Herbert and Paul on Catamount Mtn.*

recreation changes radically with the calendar. In 1988 I tried to describe some of these changes in a script designed for the show Fred Brink prepared for the new Interpretive Centers at Paul Smiths and Newcomb. In the end the show he produced was very different from my understanding of what he was after, and my pieces on the four seasons were never used. I see now that they were inappropriate. They are too long and too studied for the brief, popular show we now see at the two centers. They are also too personal, even too idiosyncratic, a response to Adirondack seasons, but just for that reason they may be quoted in the willful context of autobiography.

*Winter.* Snowshoeing is not a sport in itself, like skiing or snowmobiling, but a means of enjoying the winter woods at leisure and without disturbing the silence. Silence is an almost physical presence in snowy woods. It is palpable in the twilight fastnesses of evergreens draped with snow or, as you emerge from these tunnels, in the serene open brilliance of a snow-covered lake or beaver meadow. When the silence is broken by the hammering of a woodpecker, the scream of a blue jay warning of your approach, or the excited welcome of a chickadee (*dee-dee-dee*) following your steps, your ears spring to awareness as if to a fire alarm in your home.

The winter woods are tidy and parklike. The blanket of snow hides debris on the forest floor and smooths out uneven ground into gentle dips and swells. Under a slanting winter sun the long shadows of hardwood trunks paint abstracts across this undulant surface.

There is less life in winter than in summer, but what there is you are more likely to see, now that the hardwoods are bare and long vistas are open. In the intervals between sightings of a treed porcupine, a deer in blue coat, a coyote, you can study their tracks. The prints of the white-tailed deer are common in the runways of wintering yards and on lone forages in outlying hardwood stands. Oval depressions, melted to the ground by body heat, mark deer beds. Bare spots mark the places where they have nuzzled for greenery or beechnuts. Also common are tracks of the snowshoe hare, a miniature version of your own. That trough with a waddle to it is the mark of a porcupine's slow progress. A nearly straight line of prints, as if all four legs were arranged on the same plane, suggests a red fox; or was it a gray fox? A runway between spruce trees means a red squirrel. A half circle of five toe marks sparks an argument: was it a weasel, mink, marten, or fisher? You may be still hoping to find the tracks of the moose, now returning to the Adirondacks in small numbers after more than a century of extinction.

You may see signs of a struggle between predator and prey to remind you of a grim alternative in winter woods, eat or starve, eat or be eaten. But the play instinct survives even the harshest winter. To see it at its most engaging, you skirt the ravine of a tumbling river, where otters are most likely to be fishing through holes in the ice. Slides on the embankments or a frozen waterfall mark playtime after a satisfying meal. You may be lucky enough, hidden in evergreen foliage, to see two or three otters at play, climbing the embankment by turns and sliding down with evident glee, like kids trying out a new sled at Christmas.

Your own outsized webfeet may become the object of curiosity or alarm. Returning once through the woods on our outgoing tracks, we noticed the fresh prints of a deer approaching ours at a right angle, stopping a foot or two away, and then abruptly reversing direction at a fast pace. What had changed its mind about nibbling the tender twigs of the witchhobble on the other side? Perhaps our big feet suggested the Abominable Snowman, too dangerous to mess with.

*Spring.* Spring comes gingerly up this way. It bows prematurely one day in late March when the breeze shifts to the south. But there is no commitment in it. For the next seven or eight weeks winter and spring seesaw. Look upward and it is winter on the snowy mountains. Walk along the river valley, and it is spring you hear in the brawling water. One day winter sweeps down from the mountains. The next, spring struggles upward into the hills.

April is mud season, not good for much, say most of the natives. But others break the spell of cabin fever by going trout fishing. And from the cities die-hard skiers, reluctant to give up a winter's sport, still come to the slopes as long as snow, natural or man-made, lingers. Others come with kayaks and rafts, wet suits, helmets, life preservers, and rescue equipment to run the raging rivers. For them April is the best month of the year as they sample the whitewater of the Hudson, "the grandest of all whitewater runs in the East," says John Kauffmann; or the Moose, Ausable, St. Regis, Saranac, or horrendous Boreas, so narrow that you have little choice of left, right, middle. Thrill seekers without the kayaker's skills join rafting parties. And the flatwater canoeist finds novelty in April when rivers sprawl over floodplains and you can bushwhack by water through lanes of swamp maples and half-drowned undergrowth to the accompaniment of the bittern's agonized *ong-ka-chonk.* Water, water everywhere.

In early May the grays, browns, and dark greens of winter give way to delicate pastel shades of pink, rose, lilac, yellow, and green as catkins unfurl and leaf and flower buds begin to open on hardwood hills. This is the time to tour secondary roads or cruise the rivers and gaze at the symphony of pale color on the slopes.

As May advances, the last wave of summer birds, the warblers, return, and there is a flutter of mate-finding and nest-building in woods and river corridors. Loons nest on the ground on lake shores and guard two precious eggs with menacing attitudes and harsh clamor against hungry raccoons.

Gradually the pastels give way to numerous deeper shades of green. The real spring comes in the last two weeks of May. For those who can tolerate the blackflies that come with it, this is a good time. It is ushered in by the wistful song of the white-throated sparrow, spirit of the North Woods. Hikers now take to the trails, bushwhackers to the open woods, free of snow at last except at the highest elevations. And they are greeted by one of the loveliest manifestations of an Adirondack spring, witchhobble bloom. This variety of viburnum shrub won its popular name because of its spiteful way of tripping or entangling the legs of trampers. For most of the year witchhobble is unlovely and unloved. But once a year, as in folktales, this witch of the forest turns into a fairy queen gowned in white lace and holding out beckoning arms. Where it grows in profusion, the woods are filled with airy white figures frozen in the postures of a dance.

*Summer.* You have entered the Adirondack Park by one of the roads that wind through thirty river valleys on the perimeter. As the woods close in, you may experience an inner adjustment, triggered perhaps by a landmark such as Sunday Rock in the Raquette River valley. This glacial erratic is poised between the last farm and the foothills. It is called Sunday Rock because it stands for all the restraints of civilization. As you pass it, or some similar landmark, you are released from schedules and obligations. You escape into the space and liberty of the woods. There is no Sunday here, or any workday either; just the easy cycles of day and night and of the seasons.

Since you are now deep in the interior, you have had a chance to gather some general impressions of the park: its great size, the diversity of landforms, the abundance of water, and the omnipresence of the woods.

Few parks in the nation have so much water as the Adirondacks. There are over twenty-eight hundred lakes and ponds, thousands of miles of rivers radiating out from the axes of elevation, cross-grained interconnections, and countless mountain brooks, each a rock garden in itself. In the last century the Adirondacks was the nation's favorite region for small-boat travel. "What luxury it is," wrote W. H. H. Murray in *Adventures in the Wilderness*, "to course along the shores of these secluded lakes and glide down the winding reaches of these rivers overhung with outlying pines and fringed by water lilies." Now in the late twentieth century paddlers of canoes and kayaks are rediscovering this boater's paradise.

As you drive along the highways, miles of unbroken woods may begin to seem monotonous. This is the macro-vision. But leave your car and enter the Forest Preserve on foot or by canoe and the perspective changes to micro-vision. The woods throw a mantle of mystery over the broken land that invites exploration. Henry Abbott, a city businessman, said of his thirty years of backpacking hikes in the Adirondacks: "Repeated excursions in the shade of this wilderness serve only to increase the pulling power....The chief charm of exploration lies in the uncertainty of always finding what one starts out to find, and in the equal certainty that one may find something else." It doesn't matter what the discovery is. A thick bed of bunchberry bloom giving an immaculate look to the forest floor, a colony of lady's slippers, a deer nuzzling on the ground for beechnuts, a huge white pine, a spruce seedling growing out of the humus of a decaying stump, new life battening on the dead—any one of these will do as well as an unmapped esker or a lost pond.

[ 149 ]

You spend the night in a lean-to. As you wake in the morning with the birds and animals, a red squirrel that has slept in the bushy top of a big pine makes a head-long dash down the branchless trunk emitting a lusty squeal. This performance is stunning. For all its small size, the red squirrel has a lot of personality. You interpret the cry as a celebration of life, liberty, and pursuit of happiness in the ancient woods.

A split has long existed between the people of the waterways and the mountain people. The former have tended to prefer the Lake George–Lake Champlain valley and the central and western areas of the park where lakes are more numerous and rivers more likely to be navigable all summer. The mountain people tend to favor the northeast sector of the park, where all of the so-called High Peaks are located. But besides the High Peaks, culminating in Marcy's 5,344 feet, there are hundreds of lesser ones which offer remoteness and solitude. The greatest attraction is probably the forest that all of these mountains bear on their backs. The interest of a ramble through the woods is heightened on mountain slopes, where in two hours one passes through three zones of vegetation. In the view from the summit the forest is again dominant, dropping away and spreading out over the horizon in green-blue billows accented by shining lakes and outcroppings of gray rock.

*Autumn.* The incentive to explore is heightened in autumn by the tapestry of color on the hills. Color is richest where some disturbance—fire, logging, windfall—has occurred. Aspen, paper birch, red maple, ash, and cherry move in to occupy the site. They are followed by sugar maple, yellow birch, and beech. Simultaneously a scattering of conifers appears to give the woods a dark green accent year round. The result is the complex, colorful forest of approximately half of the Adirondack Park. Natural and man-made disturbances are common enough to insure that the many-hued hardwoods will continue to paint highway and water corridors during the brilliant euthanasia of the year.

Color reaches its variegated height in late September or early October on the plateau. The mountaineer or paddler may consider this the best time of the year if he is not job bound and is free to seize the good days of a changeable season. Most of the tourist traffic is confined to the highways and secondary roads, where leafwatchers cruise from one motel to another, exclaiming over the painted hillsides. This army of the retired is reluctant to take to the trails and waters: most are content with what they can see from car windows. So on trail or waterway the lucky few enjoy a solitude that in summer only the bushwhacker can be assured of.

The forest is now a gallery of oil paintings, Titians and Tintorettos, in sharp contrast to the watercolors of spring, as you climb the Brothers Trail with its succession of lookouts across the Johns Brook valley to the Great Range. Or, if you are more ambitious, you take the east trail to Giant Mountain over a series of

*Paul in his Old Town canoe, Middle Branch of the Oswegatchie.*

progressively higher summits—Blueberry Cobbles, Mason Mountain, Bald Peak, Rocky Peak, and Rocky Peak Ridge, a vertical ascent of 4,810 feet. Spread out below are all the colors of a dying forest canopy, most vivid, unlike human life, in senescence.

The paddler in this season is no less fortunate. Color lingers in the valleys, in the yellows and golds of aspen, birch, and tamarack, weeks after it disappears on the heights. Lakes, ponds, and flatwater streams are best suited to the mood of the season, for they allow leisure for a roving eye. As early as 1860 Alfred Street praised the "liquid vistas" of Tupper Lake and its changing lights and colors. So when the proper paradisal day comes during the first two weeks of October, you drop everything and drive to Tupper Lake with your girlfriend at your side and your canoe on the cartop. The day must be still and sunny. The breeze, if any, must be from the south. You paddle to the south end of the lake, where Bog River Falls makes its dramatic entrance and mainland shores are lined with birches and aspens at their peak of color. A slight haze throws a purplish wash over sky and mountain. Illusory horizontal lines of white light gleam where island shores meet water; far islands seem to float in air like hovercraft. You turn back in late afternoon, the sun now at your back. The purple tints are deeper, the birches more golden, and the glassier water repeats a slightly wavering image of the birches. Paddling lazily within this golden rim under an empurpled sky, you wish that such a day would never end.

The season offers one more interval of color. In late October and early November the tamaracks in the floodplains turn a dusty gold before shedding all their foliage, the only Adirondack conifer to do so. Reluctant to end a season on the waters, you launch your canoe on the upper Chubb, where tamaracks grow in profusion on the borders of a great marsh and flaunt their antique gold amidst a ring of somber mountainsides. Or you select an even narrower stream, the outlet of Massawepie Lake, and meander through a royal corridor of tamaracks accented at stream side by the red berries of winterberry holly.

I used to join in the almost universal lament in Canton over the shortening days of summer and autumn and the inevitable approach of a severe northern winter. But snowshoeing reconciled me to winter. All seasons have their uses in the woods. I still have favorite times—the last two weeks in May, August for its lower humidity favorable to all day tramps, the first halves of October and February—but some of my best snowshoe trips have been in January or March; canoeing in April, June, and November; hiking and camping in July and September. Adaptability is the key to enjoyment of the seasons' "playful spin" and to sustaining the illusion that human life is congruous with the cyclical time of nature and the cosmos. Illusion it is, for the day comes when you can no longer go to the winter woods on webfeet. But meanwhile, the serenity of retirement allows you to live by the illusion that life, like the spinning seasons, is a top that need not waver and fall.

After 1965 Ruth and I were free to travel out of state in the two seasons we found most rewarding, two weeks in early spring in the Southeast and two weeks during the height of fall color in New England. The fall trips alternated between the northern and the southern tiers of Vermont and New Hampshire into coastal or inland Maine or Cape Cod. The spring trips alternated between a coastal route south to Charleston and an Appalachian route into the Great Smokies by way of the Skyline Drive. Seeing Ruth settled in some rural motel with a book or a sketch pad—she had taken up drawing and watercoloring—I sometimes contrived to climb a mountain in other ranges besides the Adirondacks. One fall as we were staying in the Crawford House in the White Mountains, I ascended five peaks in one long day with a chance acquaintance—Mt. Washington, Monroe, Franklin, Pleasant, and Clinton. Ruth and I sought out the best of New England inns in our fall trips—cooking in the South was less congenial—always contriving to spend a night in the tiny hamlet of Newfane, Vermont, for the sake of its two excellent inns. In late March and early April we met the spring on its slow progress north, first with flowering forsythia and redbud and dogwood, then deeper in the South with azaleas and rhododendron.

These trips continued from 1965 to 1976. After returning from our fall trip in 1973, we acquired a three-weeks old male kitten, of Himalayan breed, beige with orange points, who turned out a poor traveler. For the next three years we deposited Christopher in a kennel during our twice yearly trips. But the kennel was just as traumatic to him as traveling by car for any distance over ten miles. So after our fall trip in 1976 we decided we had seen enough of New England and the Southeast and were ready to substitute the year-round pleasure derived from our cat. He tolerated day-long absences from home. And thus our travels came to be bounded by the Blue Line of the Adirondacks or Ottawa, which was rapidly turning from a provincial to a cosmopolitan city, one of the most beautiful in North America.

Ruth did not have the strength to share in my hiking and canoeing, but she loved drives into the mountains and was content to shop in Lake Placid or attend antique shows and visit Greta Chase's shop in Saranac Lake while I took to trail or paddle. For several years we spent two or three days over Christmas at the Mirror Lake Inn in Lake Placid, where the proprietor at that time knew how to make his Christmas guests happy.

As a memorial to those twenty good years before the onset of her Alzheimer's disease, Ruth left a page in a notebook headed *Good Things*. It is simply a list: "Paul's retirement—the Fowlers—Clayton's pictures (*Bridge at Piercefield, Yellow Trees, Island at Waddington*)—Hatteras in April—Monticello—Great Smokies—Our garden—Our porch, always!—Painting and drawing—Mrs. Chase at the China Cat—Beautiful house—Cape Cod—The ocean—Antiques group—Trips to the mountains with Paul—Ottawa, beautiful city, art galleries, concerts, restaurants—Picnics with the Slaughters, especially at Meacham Lake."

I N THE YEARS shortly before and after my retirement we had a small circle of congenial friends in Canton with whom we dined at restaurants or played bridge. Evenings at bridge were fairly frequent with Frank Curtin, chairman of my department, and his wife, Mary, before they too retired and moved to Pittsburgh. Dinner exchanges usually were with our neighbors Fred and Idella Warner or with Clayton and Helen Fowler. Fred was in the Mathematics Department at St. Lawrence, and Clayton in Fine Arts, where he taught art history. Ruth and I admired his paintings and acquired several of them over the years. On the occasion of his retrospective exhibit on campus in the winter of 1978, I was asked to write a profile for the St. Lawrence *Bulletin*. What follows is my original piece, which had to be shortened by a third because of space limitations.

Art and uxoriousness brought us together. It was in late summer of 1964, before Clayton Fowler began his first year of teaching at St. Lawrence. He and Dick Holladay were inspecting some oils newly acquired for the Fine Arts collection.

*Ruth Jamieson, c. 1975*

As I happened by, Dick introduced us. Clayton commented on the new paintings in masterful detail. As one who had always taken little more than instinct into a gallery, I was dazzled by how much could be said about a painting and how revelatory it was on being said.

When the conversation shifted to personal grounds, Clayton and I discovered a similarity in our marital relations. Neither of our wives likes to cook; both enjoy dining out. The rest of the equation went unspoken, but one uxorious husband recognizes another on sight.

A decade or two earlier it would have been unthinkable to invite cherished friends out to a restaurant dinner. The North Country was then a gastronomic wasteland. Restaurants knew but one art of cooking—disguise-in-breading and fry-to-a-crisp-in-yesterday's-oil. But there was a slow evolution toward better things after World War II. And today there are a half dozen restaurants within easy driving of Canton where one can, barring a crisis in the kitchen, enjoy the ambiance of civilized cuisine.

So, partly to curry favor with our wives and partly to take advantage of this flowering of civilization in the North Country, Clayton and I began exchanging dinner invitations shortly after that first meeting. We could tell any young person coming into the country all he needs to know about area restaurants, for we have been dining out at regular intervals for thirteen years.

"Regular" is not a bad adjective to describe Clayton's outward way of life. It seems governed by rule and convention. To be seen in his company is good for the ego. People look twice when he enters a dining room. He might pass for a top executive of Alcoa or Corning Glass, just as, any day of the week, he would win the approval of fashion designers as the best-dressed man on campus in any competition excluding Vilas Hall.

This regularity is more than skin deep. He is inclined toward the conservative side in politics. He is a baseball and football fan. Watches all the big games on TV. Holds his own with any red-blooded, cigar-smoking citizen of the republic.

Don't misunderstand. He has the volatile temperament, the restlessness, the creativity of the artist. But he also has a secret yearning for respectability. Thomas Mann, one of his favorite authors, makes much of the dichotomy between artist and bourgeois. It leads to serious problems in *Buddenbrooks* and other novels. Clayton resolves this conflict by combining both opposites in a new synthesis.

Clayton's hobby is the Civil War. A fast reader, he manages to keep up with most of the fat volumes published on that subject. Generals of both North and South are the intimate companions of his mind. He broods over their strategy and chides them when they fall short of what he would have done.

At bridge he impersonates his favorite generals. His bidding is a desperate gamble like Sherman's march to the sea. He never makes an honor count. He is fond of the close-out—three no-trumps or five diamonds on his initial bid. He counts on the trumps and honors his partner surely must hold if there is any justice. Sometimes he takes spectacular losses. But more often he snatches victory from almost certain defeat. Once he has won the bid, his tactics suddenly change. His play is cautious, devious, cunning. To everyone's surprise he makes a clean sweep of the last six tricks. If the North or the South had had the benefit of his strategy, the Civil War would not have taken four years to bring to conclusion.

A complex personality can't be pinned down in a bridge game. What else? He likes to startle his company by elaborate arguments reaching bizarre conclusions. He enjoys playful spats with his wife, ending with a tap on the wrist. He is loyal to old ties in the places he has left behind. He still corresponds with the ninety-one year old emeritus professor of art under whom he studied at the University of Michigan. He likes ceremony. On New Year's Eve, promptly at 11:30, he stops the bridge game and tunes in on the doings at Times Square and the Waldorf Astoria

(Guy Lombardo's passing he took as a personal affront). At 12 sharp he initiates a series of toasts in champagne.

As subjects for his landscapes he prefers the rural north part of St. Lawrence County to the wild forests of the south; holstein to whitetail country. He says he can't paint wilderness. The only two Adirondack watercolors among his *oeuvre* that I am aware of are *Piercefield Flow I* and *Piercefield Flow II*. Both are among the seven Fowlers that Ruth and I are pleased to own.

A clue to his dominant trait is the statue at the fountain in the square of his native Wolcott. It is the graceful nude figure of a girl approaching maturity, a subject you might expect to see in the fountains of Brussels, Paris, or Rome, but not in a village of western New York. According to Clayton, all the urchins of Wolcott were in awe of it. They respected it too much to deface it, and there it stood, year after year, a virgin still among those young barbarians.

From then till now Clayton has kept intact his reverence for works of art. It has informed his career as teacher, art historian, and practicing artist. It has taken him on pilgrimages to most of the principal shrines and museums of North America, Western Europe, Greece, Egypt, Taiwan, and Japan. He has communicated it to his students, who, long after graduation, write letters of appreciation for the doors he has opened to them. It was evident to all of us recently in the rich display of colors and forms in his Retrospective—painting stretching back from the late 1970s to 1925, when he was a boy of thirteen playing around the fountain in the square.

Clayton died several years ago, not long after his retirement. Helen and I occasionally meet at dinner for old time's sake. Recently at the Warners' we both discovered that we had forgotten how to play bridge.

Among my companions of the woods have been several students and faculty members of St. Lawrence. William Frenette, of Tupper Lake, I did not know while he was a student here, but we have gravitated together since because of mutual interests. Bill is a dedicated Adirondacker as recreationist and, somewhat exceptionally for a native, as preservationist too. Bill and I served simultaneous terms as trustees of the Adirondack Committee of the Nature Conservancy; he is passionate about preserving the wilds. We have paddled the Raquette below Piercefield, the East Branch of the Ausable below Keene, and the Boquet. The following piece is the story of a mountain climb. A slightly different version appeared in the *St. Lawrence Bulletin*.


### Awash in the Colden Dike

There are two trails on Mt. Colden, but the sporting way to climb is by the trap dike and the rock slides of the west face above Avalanche Lake. I had climbed by the trails only. In one's seventh decade the undone begins to irritate the conscience. As newly retired, I needed some evidence of not being washed up. Another prompter was a letter from a Peace Corps worker in Togo, West Africa. Scott Manuel, SLU '64, wrote that he had climbed the dike several times as guide to the boys of a Lake George camp. Why should scouting be a monopoly of the young? Having squandered my own youth in the lowlands, I determined to recover a piece of it in the Colden dike.

I proposed the trip to Bill Frenette, SLU '51, of Tupper Lake. By avocation Bill is a bush rover and mountaineer and whitewater paddler. For the Audubon Society census he keeps track of the distribution and mating activities of the bald and golden eagles and the osprey. He is a Forty-Sixer. He had ascended the Colden dike in winter, using crampons, pitons, and rope. As a volunteer rescuer of the lost and disaster-ridden, he was a member of the squad that first reached the wreckage of an Air Force B-47 bomber on the summit of Wright Peak in January, 1962. This summer [1965] he had found and helped carry an exhausted old man out of the woods north of Horseshoe. But the old man had been in there alone for several hours. Unpleasantness like this might be averted, I told my wife, by taking the rescuer along. Bill is not only a good companion but a pillar of strength to one's wife at home. Thirty years ago mine began insisting that I was too old to rough it.

Bill arranged a party with five other good companions, including two more Laurentians. Victor Sacco, once my student, Bill's classmate, and now a teacher at the Peddie School, helps run Forestcraft in summer, a boys' camp on Upper Saranac. Victor's mountaineering began ten years ago. He has received and given training in climbing techniques and is a Forty-Sixer. His wife, "Scotie" MacLaren, SLU '51, also climbs but on this occasion was absent with a bad knee.

Bill's wife Ginny (Virginia Stanton, SLU '49) and her friend Theresa were to climb Colden by the Lake Arnold trail for a rendezvous with us on the summit. Ginny, like Bill, started skiing under Otto Schniebs and is now active in the ski patrol on Big Tupper. She has climbed eleven of the High Peaks since her marriage, as many as she could work in while giving birth to one son and seven daughters, all actual or potential mountaineers. Theresa, who was visiting her home in Tupper Lake, works for the U.S. Army in Korea and thinks she may soon be transferred to Vietnam. Climbing a mountain would be good training, she thought. It was—with a monsoon storm thrown in.

Louie Simmons joined us for the tramp in. As editor of the Tupper Lake *Free Press and Herald* he dutifully reports births, marriages, and deaths, but puts his heart into keeping abreast of Tupper Lake's past, its heroic age of trappers, guides, river drivers, and lumber kings. Louie shares John Ruskin's view that mountains are best appreciated from the bottom looking up.

Last, there was Charlie Frenette, SLU '73 if he can ever be induced to leave the woods for four school years. He had climbed ten of the High Peaks but not Colden, and he was excited over the prospect of ascending by the dike and open slide, where his father had slipped on the way down two winters before and had been held by the rope close to the edge where the west face drops away like a house wall.

As I left Canton at six in the morning, there was a heavy overcast. Two days of thunderstorms had broken a drought, but the forecast for this Sunday was favorable—warm and sunny with possible thunderstorms toward evening. Exactly the reverse occurred. The rain began about eight and lasted most of the day.

The sight of Bill's curly-headed, pearl-and-rosy cheeked daughters at the Frenette breakfast table was enough to brighten a dull day, however. Though Bill insists that the strain is Irish and German rather than French, these little girls are straight out of a canvas by Renoir and make plausible the Frenchiness of Frenette.

Bill rounded up the rest of the party in his bus and drove to Heart Lake. It was raining hard there. Louie waterproofed his sketching material as well as possible, and we all set out in ponchos on the trail to Avalanche Pass.

It was still raining at Marcy Dam, the two-mile mark. The mountains were truncated by low clouds, and there was no sketching there for Louie. More rain as we reached the two Avalanche lean-tos. Ginny and Theresa now left us to take the Lake Arnold trail to Colden. It rained up Heartbreak Hill, where the first steep grade brought protests from Louie. The parts our ponchos had kept dry now became bathed in sweat. A drink from the cold waterfall at the height of the pass was both a necessity and a ritual as we straddled the ridgepole where the waters divide, splashing north into the St. Lawrence watershed and south to the Hudson. It rained through Misery Mile as we squirmed through, under, and over the ruins of two broken mountains in the narrow pass. Across the head of Avalanche Lake the towering slabs of Colden were scored by a dozen waterfalls—a beautiful but disquieting sight. We came to Hitch-up-Matilda, the log bridge that spans two places where the cliff of Avalanche Mountain drops sheer into the lake. In days before the bridge was built guides used to wade, carrying city folk pickaback. The place got its name when a modest lady slipped too far down the back of Bill Nye and the rest of the party chortled "Hitch up, Matilda!" We needed the humor of this recollection to brace us for the full-face view of the trap dike across the lake.

I have heard many explanations of the Colden dike by amateur and professional geologists. Since Bob Bloomer's condescension is easier to take than his derision, my explanation will necessarily be a Simple-Simon one. The dike is a cleft running up the west face from Avalanche Lake. Wide and deep at the bottom, it tapers in both dimensions toward the top. It results, so they say, from the differential weathering of a pocket of softer rock (gabbro?) in the hard stuff (anorthosite?) the rest of the mountain is made of. Anyway, from Hitch-up-Matilda the dike looks like a giant's staircase. The steps are separated by leg-stretching pitches approaching the vertical.

But I had never seen it like this before. Drainage is fast on the bald west face of Colden, and on most midsummer days there is only a trickle in the dike, enough to cool it a little and provide drinking water. Climbing it on such days is strenuous but presents no problems to anyone used to heights.

But now, after two days of thunderstorms and on a third of heavy rainfall, the dike was all awash. It had turned into a flume. A torrent shot out over the steps in a spectacular series of waterfalls. In narrow places there seemed to be no space for passage between the sheet of water and the sidewalls.

If we had been dry, we would probably have given up at that point and tried another day. But after hiking five miles in the rain, we were used to the element and less easily discouraged by a concentration of it. We decided to try at least. So we left the trail at the foot of the lake, passed the site of the old Caribou Lean-to destroyed in the avalanche of 1942, slogged through a narrow marsh, and scrambled up the talus at the mouth of the dike.

It was still raining, but we took off our ponchos and stuffed them in our packs. They would be an encumbrance now. Vic volunteered to try the first steep pitch. Soon he emerged from the scrub eighty feet above on the verge of a waterfall and signaled a go. It was useless to shout in the gully. The girls said later that in going up by trail, they were frightened by thunder and lightning. In the dike the noisy waters drowned out the thunder, and with our eyes trained on the slope in front of us we were unaware of the lightning. Several times we waited while Vic scouted a way to the next ledge. Rain and splash blurring my glasses, I had to rely on Bill to interpret the signals from above.

Fording and refording the torrent where the going appeared better on the other side, we slowly moved upward. A little probing uncovered cracks in the rock for toe and handholds and roots or trunks of dwarf balsam firs secure enough to take our weight. In two or three places the way up looked impossible, while the way down over slippery rock was unthinkable. I gained confidence by watching Charlie and occasionally giving him a boost over pitches where his reach fell short. His eyes shone with excitement. This was an adventure to him. He was unafraid yet cautious—a fine mountaineer. His father had trained him well.

We came to a place in the dike that even Vic admitted was no go. The gully narrowed to a chute, and the side walls were too steep and smooth to afford footing around the trough of brawling water. Bill and Vic believed that this pitch was the final one over the steepest part of the mountain, and that we ought to ascend it before exposing ourselves on the open slide. But we had no choice. We took advantage of a chimney in the right-hand wall and climbed out of the dike to finish the ascent on the slide.

Climbers often leave the dike too soon or too late. We saw immediately what leaving too soon means. We were below a ridge line on the west face where the grade tapers off. We gingerly tested the slope. Dry, it would have given little trouble. But rain was still falling, and patches of soggy lichen broke loose from the smooth slab when stepped on. Vic reminded us what to do in case of a slip: take a spread-eagle posture, belly down, to make as much friction as possible. This advice gave less comfort, though, than the one-hundred foot nylon rope Bill had brought along.

Taking advantage of lips and cracks in the rock, Vic moved up cautiously, found a stance about ninety feet above, wrapped the rope around his body, and threw the loose end down. Bill held it while Charlie and I walked up, feet flat on the surface and hand over hand on the rope. Bill then advanced. Two or three such belays put us over the steep slope, and we walked the rest of the way to the top without difficulty.

Long before we could see the two girls through the clouds, we heard answering calls from the summit. Finally two figures in ponchos, looking larger than life in the mist, appeared in the shelter of a boulder. They had been waiting, and shivering, for over an hour. It had taken us three hours and a half to climb the dike, and it was now mid-afternoon.

The rain had finally stopped, but we had no view for our pains. Clouds blanketed the peak and limited vision to a hundred yards. Over lunch we swapped adventures. The girls had had a wet climb through the woods, the trail having turned into a brook complete with waterfalls and pools. Theresa said she was now ready for the rice paddies and rain forests of Vietnam.


The publication of *The Adirondack Reader* on the eve of my retirement had two consequences in my later life. First, it gave me the reputation of an authority on Adirondack letters. Publishers and other writers began to consult me on manuscripts and to ask for jacket blurbs, introductions, or reviews. I was asked to edit book manuscripts for several publishers, sometimes for pay, sometimes not. Among these are Dan Brenan's *Adirondack Letters of George Washington Sears* (Nessmuk), Albert Fowler's *Cranberry Lake from Wilderness to Adirondack Park*, Mildred Phelps Stokes Hooker's *Camp Chronicles*, Herbert Keith's *Man of the Woods*, Lewis Fisher's *Old Hollywood*, eight volumes of the transcripts of St. Lawrence University's annual conferences on the Adirondacks, and G. Atwood Manley's *Rushton and His Times in American Canoeing*. In the last instance I was assistant writer as well as editor. For some of these books and for Nathan Farb's book of color photographs, *The Adirondacks*, I wrote the introductions.

The second consequence was the *Reader*'s influence as a catalyst in widening my circle of friends and acquaintances. I value the associations that have sprung from my writing and editing, some casual, some close; associations with Bruce Inverarity, former director, Bill Verner, curator, and Harold Hochschild, founder, of the Adirondack Museum; Kenneth Durant, descendant of a family famous in Adirondack history and himself an anthologist and writer; his wife, Helen Van Dongen Durant; Paul Schaefer, defender of the Forest Preserve; Herbert Keith and his wife, Mimi; and Winifred La Rose, Richard Lawrence, Arthur Savage, Wayne Byrne, Tim Barnett, George Davis, Gary Randorf, Greenleaf Chase, Clarence Petty, Eleanor Brown, Maitland De Sormo, successive presidents of the Adirondack Mountain Club, and several commissioners of the Department of Environmental Conservation.

My association with Kenneth Durant antedated publication of the *Reader* and continued till his death in 1972. He first wrote about an article of mine in the *Adirondac*. We quickly discovered that we were both preparing anthologies, his *Guide-Boat Days and Ways* and my *Reader*. This led to exchanging tips. We also exchanged visits. After his death I wrote a memorial essay for *Adirondack Life*, reprinted in *Adirondack Pilgrimage* as "Eden Without Snakes." The fact that this essay quotes extensively from Durant's incisive comments about Adirondack matters led the Adirondack Museum to request the originals of our correspondence. Helen Durant, his widow, and I exchanged copies for our files and then turned the originals over to the Museum for its archives. I continued to correspond with Helen after Kenneth's death, and when she completed the work he had brought forward, *The Adirondack Guide-Boat*, I wrote a review of it.

Paul Schaefer is the most lasting fan of the *Reader*. Every now and then, out of the blue, I get a note of appreciation from him as he picks up the book in his library at St. David's Lane in Schenectady. He complained when the first edition went out of print, saying that he had given away copy after copy and now had none left of his own. I sent him one from my dwindling stock. Whenever I met him in ensuing years, he urged me to bring out a new edition. When it finally appeared he wrote: "It seems but yesterday that you and I discussed the possible reprinting of your *Adirondack Reader* at the North Woods Club. I expressed the hope that nothing would interfere with your noble work. And thank the good Lord, nothing did." In the second edition, considerably revised, I included a passage from Paul's own writings, entitled "Discovery 1960." He was pleased with this choice, saying that he valued that particular piece as best expressing his feelings toward the Adirondacks and that to appear in the *Reader* was "as great an honor as I can conceive." This was in March 1983. In July came another missive out of the blue: "Just a note to tell you again what a treasure your *Adirondack Reader* is; how often I pick it up to get new inspiration from the priceless collection you have put together."

In 1989 Paul Schaefer, through the Syracuse University Press, published his own book about a lifetime spent in defending the "forever-wild" principle of preservation in the Forest Preserve. The Press sent me the manuscript for an evaluation. I hope that my enthusiastic endorsement had some influence on the decision to publish this fine book.

My association with Harold Hochschild began while he was preparing several offshoots from his monumental history of the central Adirondacks, *Township 34*. Some of the manuscripts were sent to me for a check of accuracy. I corrected a very few errors of fact, for which he sent me a note of thanks. Then in 1963, when he received an honorary degree of Doctor of Laws from St. Lawrence University, I wrote the citation. At the luncheon following the Commencement ceremony I was introduced to him and his wife, Mary Marquand Hochschild. She was among the first to express appreciation when the *Reader* appeared in the following year. And in the summer of 1965 Ruth and I were invited to lunch at Eagle Nest, the family camp occupied at all seasons of the year in Harold's semi-retirement, on Eagle Lake. There were other guests. When I remarked that Herbert McAneny, my hiking companion, had called their son, Adam, the most brilliant student and best writer he had ever had in class at the Princeton Country Day School, Mrs. Hochschild turned to Harold with some such comment as "You see, Harold." I sensed then that they had differences about Adam's emerging career as a left-wing journalist in California. This hunch gained credibility when I read Adam's book, after his father's death, *Half the Way Home*, about his uneasy relations with his father till something like a reconciliation took place at Harold's death bed.

Harold Hochschild was to crown his services to the Adirondacks in his chairmanship of the Governor's Temporary Study Commission on the Future of the Adirondack Park, which made its epochal report in 1970. In October of the following year Ruth and I were again invited to lunch at Eagle Nest. The guest list was larger this time. There were some of his metallurgical associates and of her associates among artists and art historians (her father had founded the art department at Princeton). There were also friends they had in common. One of these was Hector Prud'homme, a house guest, who had had a varied career in engineering, banking, diplomacy, and college administration, throughout which his favorite recreation was canoeing. I had had some correspondence with him prior to the luncheon in connection with my project of preparing a canoeing guide to the Adirondacks. After cocktails a buffet luncheon was served of two soups, tongue and chicken, cheese, and fruits. Except for the larger number of guests, the occasion was much as before. Conversation in the lounge followed lunch and then a motorboat tour of the lake for all who wished it. Debarkation at the dock was a hint that guests were expected to take their leave.

I have heard since that the pattern of these luncheons was ritualistic. But regularity did not diminish the geniality of the hosts. I admired Hochschild greatly as a man and for his services to the Adirondacks. He was unique among large land-owners in that he permitted public navigation on Eagle Lake, which he owned in entirety. The lake is part of a popular canoe route, the Eckford Chain, including the Marion River. Other owners of private parks in the Adirondacks, for the last one hundred years, have contravened common-law rights of navigation on rivers and lakes by posting or by erecting barriers.

A cherished friendship with Eleanor Brown originated in the 1960s while she was editor of the *Adirondac*. We have corresponded for over twenty years and have met fairly often at organizations we both belong to, as well as once or twice for canoeing trips. She visited Canton from her home in Schenectady for the autograph party at the village library on publication of the second edition of the *Reader*. Her membership on the Publications Committee of the Adirondack Mountain Club has smoothed the way for publication of my three books by that Club. Eleanor and I are in agreement on conservation issues and have joined forces to bring about re-forms in the management of the Forest Preserve. The first of our efforts began in 1969. Eleanor sent me a copy of her letter to Commissioner Stewart Kilbourne of the Conservation Department urging the discontinuance of permanent tent platform permits on state land. I had long resented this special privilege of the few at the expense of the temporary camper and decided to support Eleanor's initiative. I made an on-site inspection of a row of such camps on Follensby Clear Pond and addressed the following letter to Commissioner Kilbourne, with a copy going to the Study Commission on the Future of the Park, which at that time was preparing its report. (District 7 is now known as Region 6, and District 9 as Region 5.)

November 19, 1969

Dear Commissioner Kilbourne:

I should like to call attention to a striking difference in the way the Forest Pre-serve areas of two districts I am familiar with, 7 and 9, are administered. In District 7 a successful effort has been made to eliminate all permanent state permit camps. Partly for this reason, it is possible to experience in southern St. Lawrence County a sense of being in a real wilderness. Scores of good sites for overnight camping are available on the shores of Cranberry Lake, the banks of the Oswegatchie above Inlet, and the backwoods ponds. Here the purpose of the act of 1892 creating the Adirondack Park is fully realized: "Forever reserved, maintained and cared for as ground open for the use of all the people for their health and pleasure."

In District 9, however, and especially in the lake region of Franklin County, many of the best sites are reserved for the health and pleasure of a few of the people—the holders of state camping permits. Tent tops are only a camouflage for permanent private camps—furnishcd, provisioncd, and padlocked, though for most of the year unoccupied.

The 150 lakes and ponds of the St. Regis quadrangle, most of them in state land, are ideal country for the canoeist and hiker to explore. But if he wants to camp overnight, he is often out of luck. He finds that the best sites on many of these ponds are monopolized by permit holders. The same situation exists on Lower Saranac Lake, on Moose Pond in the McKenzie wilderness area, and to a lesser extent on the rivers in District 9.

These permanent camps are not only inequitable; they are eyesores. To test this general impression, I revisited Follensby Clear Pond and looked at a row of permit camps both from canoe and by a trail behind them. Follensby Clear is a major link in one of the circular tours described in the CD folder "Adirondack Canoe Routes." As nature endowed it, it is a most attractive pond, with islands, irregular shores, good natural beaches, and tall white and red pines and hemlocks on its fringes. But it is now disfigured by eroded banks and ugly tent-platform structures.

Though state permit camps surround the pond, I inspected only those on the south-facing shore of the easternmost bay. On this stretch of about seven-tenths of a mile are eighteen housekeeping units on raised tent platforms, all furnished and all padlocked. On November 12, the day of my visit, none was occupied. I found only twelve permit shingles. Four of the largest clearings (trees and shrubs have at one time been removed against state law) have two housekeeping units of approximately equal size but a permit shingle on only one. One other double camp has no permit number in sight.

Besides having outdoor fireplaces, these camps are equipped for indoor heating and cooking, and from two to seven propane gas containers lie about each clearing. No. 1457, however, uses coal, to judge by a three-foot high pile of coal ashes behind the tent. Rusty bedsprings and oil drums, broken furniture, old lumber, pieces of canvas and plastic tarp, cans and bottles litter the edges of the clearings and the fine hemlock forest behind them. The rotted canvas of at least half the units is topped by a variety of overthrows, from translucent white to opaque black. The wood sidings are painted in a variety of fading colors or unfinished.

The view from the water is equally unattractive. On the sand beaches and eroded banks are pieces of lumber, boats in disrepair, rusty oil drums, gasoline cans, jerry-built floats, pieces of tarp, and weather-beaten chairs and tables. In addition to the four permissible structures named in Recreation Circular 2, a majority of the camps have ramshackle docks. No. 986 has a board walk to the dock; 1384, a totem pole; 965, a rustic fence on the bank and log steps; 770, a flag pole on the dock; 1368, stairs up the bank. Only one, 1123, the outermost, seems both neat and clean and in conformity with regulations. The rest of this shore is a camping slum.

As nearly as I can tell, the permit camps remain unoccupied most of the year. Theoretically, outsiders can secure permission to use them when they are not occupied. But the red tape is formidable. Getting the district ranger's permission is not enough; the key must be secured from the "owner," along with his blessing and consent to use his personal possessions. In actual fact, the tenure of the holder is as exclusive and presumptive as that of the squatters who plagued the state during the first thirty years of the Forest Preserve, and who were not finally ousted till the administration of Commissioner George Pratt, 1915–1921.

The most innovative of all commissioners in promoting recreational use of the Forest Preserve by all people, George Pratt introduced the first recreational circulars, built the first lean-tos with state funds and labor, erected the first fireplaces on lakeshores, which developed into the public campgrounds of today, and started a system of trail making. But Commissioner Pratt made one mistake. To give a quick nudge to camping, he started the system of state permit camps, probably not intending or foreseeing that the tent platforms would become permanent and exclusive holdings.

There is no justification today for continuing these special privileges. The Preserve is no longer under used as it was in 1915. There is no shortage of campers. What is in short supply at times of peak use is desirable lake shore sites for overnight camping.

I remember reading, three or four years ago, a statement that the Conservation Department had determined to issue no more permits and to allow no more transfers of existing ones to relatives of the present holders. These measures do not seem adequate. Phasing out the camps would take forty years or more. As the number dwindled, the privileges enjoyed by holders would come to seem increasingly special and exclusive. Public resentment would grow over the inequity of denying all new applicants and yet allowing present holders to enjoy occupancy for a lifetime.

There must be a better way, fair both to the public and to the permit holders who have invested labor and money in their camps. Since no new permits have been granted in the last three or four years, all permit camps could be phased out in six or seven years. People who have held permits for long periods could be given one or two years' notice.

It is high time to retrieve Commissioner Pratt's one mistake, just as he got rid of the squatters' summer cottages and hotels. District 7 has already eliminated permanent tent platforms, and the satisfactions of a wilderness environment are apparent to anyone who uses the Preserve areas of southern St. Lawrence County. Achieving the same results in District 9, the most varied and scenic part of the Adirondacks, would be a considerable public benefit.

In its report of the following year, 1970, the Temporary Study Commission recommended that all permits for tent platforms in areas of the Forest Preserve classified as wilderness and primitive be rescinded within one year, and that permits in wild forest areas be rescinded within a period of five years. The time frame suggested in my letter came closer to the mark than the Study Commission's recommendations. Getting rid of all the camps proved formidable, and it was 1978 before they were all razed and the clearings around them cleaned up.

I don't know how much influence, if any, my letter had in bringing about this favorable end, but at any rate I determined to act in future as if the individual in our system does have influence if he has a good cause and is persistent. Since then I have taken an active role in championing measures bearing on recreation, conservation, and preservation in the park. More often than not these initiatives, usually with the help of others, have proved successful, and I have become a firm believer in American democracy.

Friends closer to home than those I have mentioned above were more accessible companions in the woods. Some of them, notably Lewis and Betty Weeks and Duncan and Lois Cutter, attend the Unitarian-Universalist Church in Canton, where I first met them. Unitarians have a special affinity for the woods, perhaps as a substitute place of worship. I had been drawn to the local church by Ruth. Her affiliation in Canton was originally with the Episcopalians. In the 1950s the rector here was a rare bird, an Oxonian who had married a woman of means (she had been left a fortune by a wealthy widow whom she had served as companion). Both husband and wife were cultivated, witty people. I believe that the hierarchy in the church was resigned to letting Father Fraser languish in a small parish because of his unconventional, if not to say subversive, views. To him the American Revolution was a catastrophe. We in America would be better off today under British rule and British culture. The last American he could enthusiastically embrace was eighteenth-century Sir William Johnson, ever loyal to the Crown. These views were not popular in America, and in Canton Father Fraser was wise enough to let them be known only to trustworthy parishioners. Ruth liked his sermons on Anglican history and the moderately high-church services he conducted. But when he retired and moved to Johnstown, where Sir William had held sway over Loyalists and Indians, and was replaced by a young priest of a quality commensurate with the size of the parish, Ruth switched to the Unitarian-Universalist Church, and I switched with her.

Instead of loving sermons on Anglican history, we now listened to brilliant ones on sociology by Max Coots. Ruth, to whom tradition and aesthetics counted heavily, was less satisfied with the new church than I was. I liked Max's sermons for their liberalism, humor, and occasional poetic quality. This church was linked with the liberalism of St. Lawrence University, founded by Universalists a century before their merger with the Unitarians. I was happy to support a church responsible for that strong liberal tradition and hospitable to agnostics and atheists as well as theists. When Jehovah's Witnesses knock at the door in their well-groomed pairs of young folk with pamphlets and unction, I have only to announce myself a Unitarian to frighten them off. They realize that there is no possible convert in this house.

George Santayana, bred in the Roman Catholic Church but turned agnostic in maturity, was amused by the Unitarians of Boston when a Harvard friend enticed him into church. "It seemed a little ridiculous," he writes in *Persons and Places*, "all those good people in their Sunday clothes, so demure, so conscious of one another, not needing in the least to pray or to be prayed for, nor inclined to sing, but liking to flock together once a week" and hear a sermon that flattered their bourgeois virtues as harbingers of a better world. So Boston, so Canton. Our congregation is like that except that it seems to enjoy singing. Unlike Santayana, nostalgic for the religious spirit even in his agnosticism, I feel comfortable with such people and do not find them ridiculous. And are there not hints, in this decade of the 1990s, that other nations are beginning to yearn for those bourgeois virtues and values?

Since Ruth's death I go less often to this church, for my hearing is no longer a match for Max's voice. But I retain my friends among the good bourgeois who love the woods as their primary shrine of devotion.

## XVI CHRISTA

IN THE EARLY 1960s a camp came on the market that appealed to Ruth and me. It was in a part of the central Adirondacks we liked, near what was later designated as the St. Regis Canoe Area. It was just the right size for a retired couple, with an extra bedroom for guests. Attractive and solidly built, it was on a knoll above a pond, its clearing surrounded by tall red pines. We went so far as to price it. It was within our means, for this was before the great inflation triggered by the Vietnam War and Lyndon Johnson's formula of guns and butter. I have not been so strongly tempted before or since to become, like many others, consumers of space. But on reflection we decided against buying it. We concluded that what gave us greatest pleasure was going to the woods, not living in them. In just a fifteen or twenty minute drive from the northwest corner of the park, we could follow any momentary whim. There were ceremony and anticipation in the going-in. We had our choice of returning to a favored corner of the woods or exploring a new one, for the park is vast enough always to leave a margin of the unknown. If, on the other hand, we owned a camp, we would have the care of maintaining it, and life in the woods would settle into a routine. The camp owners of our acquaintance settled down in one place and knew little of the Adirondacks at large. They sat on their docks and watched the boats go by. Or if they were more energetic, like Harold Hochschild they took a morning swim around Eagle Lake, entertained guests at lunch, and in the afternoon gave them a motorboat tour of the same lake.

Besides, if we bought an existing camp, someone else would build a new one on some other lakeshore. Eventually the remaining private land within the Blue

Line would become overdeveloped before the state could enlarge its holdings of forever-wild Forest Preserve through successive bond acts. And my hope for the future was that the Adirondacks would always be a refuge where Americans could recover a bit of our national heritage of a virgin continent. We have abused that heritage by greedy consumption of material goods, including space. The middle class must have its second home, the wealthy three or four homes in the most desirable parts of the country. The continent is large, but there are still limits to open space.

The first ingredient of a happy retirement was for me this freedom of going-in. The second was a fit companion to share the woods with. As the student body expanded during the Bewkes administration, so did the number of new young instructors in the English Department. Most of them were good companions on hiking and canoeing trips. In 1964, the year before my retirement, two newcomers, Roger Goodson and Don Makosky, joined me for two nights of camping in the High Peaks, during which we climbed Marcy and Haystack from the Keene Valley side. Don happened to remark that his wife, Christa, liked the woods and mountains. So later that summer I invited him and Christa on a trip to the Cranberry Lake area. We drove first to Wanakena for a short hike on the south side of the Inlet to a grove of virgin white pines. I had brought a tape measure to try on No. 1, as the nearby Ranger School had marked it—reputedly the biggest pine in the state. It is branchless for about ninety feet from its base and by our measurement, waist high, fourteen feet three inches in circumference. As we were gazing up at the canopy, Christa spotted a pileated woodpecker in a nearby tree. When we approached closer, the big bird flew off in a flash of red and with a squawk like a hen's. Afterwards we drove through Cranberry Lake village and climbed Bear Mountain to the lookout crag on the far side.

Christa liked our wild, unmanicured woods, so different from those of her native Germany, and I liked Christa. As I found out later, she was just thirty, the best age in a woman's life according to Balzac. Don had met her while he was a Fulbright scholar in Germany at the University of Kiel. She had a degree in chemistry but also, as I was to discover, a humanistic culture. She spoke English fluently with a slight, charming accent. Tall, slender, and lithe, she was an energetic hiker. Though our walk that day was short, I judged correctly that she was capable of all-day tramps.

For the next six years, until her death at thirty-six, Christa was my preferred companion on winter and summer hikes and canoe trips. I learned the story of her life gradually. As World War II began, her family of three was living in Berlin. Her father, who worked for the German National Railroad, was killed on the last day of the war as the Russians entered Berlin. Meanwhile, as Berlin came under heavy bombing attack, Christa and her mother were evacuated to a ruined castle in central Germany, where they remained for five years, 1943 to 1948. The ages of nine to fourteen are crucial in one's education. While, along with many of her generation, Christa's formal education was interrupted, she was taught by her mother and a friend, both educators; subsequently she became a university graduate with a master's degree. She also had, during those years in the castle, an education in means of survival. Besides cultivating a small vegetable plot offered them by a peasant farmer, she and her mother combed the woods for edible plants and firewood. The castle was in the midst of a forest. Perhaps this training explains the sharpness of her senses. As it became clear that Germany would be defeated, Hitler ordered that the women be issued vials of cyanide as the better alternative to rape by invading armies of "inferior" race.

My imagination played over that personal history: over the terror of bombs falling around her home in Berlin; over the young girl in the castle ruins foraging for food in a forest storied in German fairy tale, legend, and opera; over the draft of poison held close against the worst eventuality. In America we know little of this. The oceans protect our country against invasion. No hostile bombs have fallen on it. We lack ancient ruins to put us in mind of "old, unhappy, far-off things / And battles long ago." We are not forced to scrounge for food in the wilds. Our forests are almost unstoried. We have no Siegfried to slay the dragon and talk with the birds, no Brunhilde to be rescued from a ring of fire, no Tannhäuser as thrall in the cave of Venus, no witch in the gingerbread house to threaten the broom-maker's children. How lucky it is, from one point of view, to be born an American and have a go at a clean slate, at innocence, at making new stories of our lives free from compelling prototypes. But from another point of view, how diminishing it is to lack a long past and a tragic view of life. That past and its accompanying apprehension clung to Christa even in America. Her gaiety with friends disguised a persistent unease. But in the woods she seemed able to shake off the past in a clean exchange of the supernatural German forest for a naturalistic American one. On our outings she was the naturalist. Being in the woods with her, I once said, was like a walk with Thoreau.

Christa was usually aware of the minute, secretive life of the woods before I was. On the summit of Coney Mountain one spring day she found the den of a deer mouse and its tiny scats in a trough of vegetation where it had nibbled off grass ends as winter food. In deep snow she spotted a tuft of hair and uncovered the carcass of a fawn killed by exposure and starvation. The ground nest of an ovenbird or a hermit thrush was not well enough camouflaged to escape her notice. She would then draw us away lest the five eggs be untended too long, a note of tenderness in her voice. In frozen bogs with a light snow cover she would look for the red cups of pitcher plants, half full of frozen liquid. One day in March as we were snowshoeing along the shore of a pond, she pointed to a dirty-looking circle in the snow, as if pepper had been sprinkled there. Then she noticed that the pepper was engaged in a zany dance. It was only then that I recalled a passage in Colvin's reports remarking on what a wonderful country this is where there are landforms such as eskers (not knowing their origin he called them sand dunes) and where snow fleas dance in winter. Lacking her keen observation, I would have missed that dance, which I have noticed several times since always with a thought of Christa.

In two different locations in winter woods Christa was able to lure colonies of chickadees onto our hands, shoulders, heads, and shoes with crumbs from our sandwiches or, on return visits to those places, with sunflower seeds we had purposely brought. The pressure of their delicate feet on our finger tips as they fed from our palms was incredibly light and endearing. Another winter day, as Don and I pushed ahead up Baldface Mountain, Christa, a pace or two behind, watched four balls of fur emerging from under a log we had stepped on. They raced up an aspen tree. Four pairs of round black eyes blinked down at us. They were flying squirrels, the first I had ever seen since their habits in summer are nocturnal. As we kicked the trunk, they soared through the air on widespread membranes that served as gliders, to alight at the foot of another tree and race to its top. Seldom without her camera, Christa photographed the squirrels in the branches above us. She seldom passed a beech tree without looking for the claw marks, in patterns of five, where a bear had climbed for mast, and again her camera came into play when she found a good specimen. With a lens adapter she photographed the succession of spring, summer and fall wildflowers, assuming contorted postures on the ground to do so. She learned the popular names of all the common vascular plants of the Adirondacks.

Christa liked the woods in all seasons but had a special fondness for the silence and solitude of our winter tramps on snowshoes. In the 1960s there were fewer snowmobiles than in more recent decades. We could cross a large frozen lake without hearing a motor or meeting another human being in the central and western Adirondacks. She often made comparisons with Europe, where in the Black Forest and the Alps the slopes were alive with skiers and one could seldom escape the crowds. Here on a frozen lake the unbroken solitude, the purity of fresh snow, the ring of hills and mountains formed a world apart, unpeopled and solemn. The following is a description in my log of one of our late winter excursions.

March 19, 1967. A wonderful day following a cold spell. Overnight the wind shifted from NW to SW, and during the day temperatures rose to just below freezing under flawless blue skies. We drove to Pitchfork Pond N of Tupper Lake and hiked the length of the pond, across the carry to Spectacle Ponds, then another carry to Wolf Pond and across it to the N end and the base of a mountain range we had not previously climbed. Following a stream bed NE around a bend, we climbed N to the top of a ridge and then NW up a nameless peak with an open top and a flat rock to sit on as we had lunch. We were warm in the sun. After lunch we dropped down into a pleasant saddle, where we found fresh porcupine tracks. We traced them to a wide den under a rock. Christa looked up, and there was a fat porky treed above us. She had her camera and maneuvered for a good view as I made the porky move by smacking the trunk with a stick. We then climbed the second peak in the range up the wall of a cirque between craggy buttresses. The view from the ledges of the second peak was stunning, over the length of Wolf Pond to Mt. Morris and Big Tupper Lake. Outlooks on both summits command views of the High Peaks from Alderbrook Mountain in the N to Seward. Returning, we followed a ravine valley between the two peaks back to Wolf Pond. During the day Christa took a roll of film, including animal tracks, bear claw marks on beech trees, and the porky and its den. The brilliant blue sky, the long shadows across the snow, the faint taste of spring in the air, and the promise of it in the fat buds of witchhobble made this a memorable outing. Hiking was easy over packed snow with an inch of fresh powder to soften the impact and make the woods look immaculate, lonely, and grand. As the sun sank in the west, tree shadows lengthened across the wave-like surface.

The academic year of 1967–68 marked an interruption in my outings with the Makoskys. Don was to manage a group of SLU students majoring in German for a year abroad at the University of Vienna. The arrangement was made before Christa discovered that she was pregnant. She and Don had tried to have a baby during the first two years in Canton. Failing, Christa consulted a doctor. After an examination he told her that she could not conceive. By the time I knew her she had decided that she did not want children anyway. Almost three months of disbelief passed before she consulted a local doctor on what was happening to her. In July the bad news was confirmed at an unwelcome time as she was preparing to accompany Don to Vienna.

I have lost some of the letters that she and Don wrote to Ruth and me from Vienna, but do have a few of the earlier ones. Here are some excerpts. On October 5, 1967, she wrote:

I hope you have good weather on your New England trip. Fall hasn't started here yet. Everything is still green. We can expect only brown later on, though; there are no maples. But we have discovered many good hiking areas only a half kilometer from Wien. Der Wiener Wald is just beautiful. Not very high but picturesque. Last Sunday we ended up in something that looked like an Alpine meadow; three kinds of gentians and many other flowers. Unfortunately I can't do all day hikes any more (you would not be satisfied with me, Paul, I would be one of the 'make-do' kind of hikers for you now, like Atwood); otherwise we would explore more. Paul, I think you would be in jail here much of the time, because there are signs everywhere threatening you with two weeks in jail if you leave the marked trails.... Who is drinking your Scotch now? I am still off liquor. Too sad. All wine tastes like vinegar and beer like soap.

November 19. We are still taking off to the woods every weekend. Paul wouldn't be satisfied with me any more (Don probably isn't either, but I don't care in his case. I figure it is at least half his doing!). Three to four hours is about my limit. Often pretty frustrating with all those beautiful trails around....I had a dream the other night that contained most features of a Paul-hike all packed into one: 1) I was not ready when Paul called; 2) then in the hurry I forgot my lunch, so Paul had to share his, which that day consisted of only figs; 3) it was around Floodwood; 4) I was always behind; 5) we reached the peak just before dark, and it was pitch dark on the way back; 6) here it becomes dreamlike, not like Paul, but nightmarish; Paul let me go ahead for a change, a mean thing to do at that point, because I had to feel my way down. It didn't pay off. I lost the path, fell into a crevasse, and woke up with a scream! You see, Paul, you are still with us, in our subconscious.... Saw *Merchant of Venice* in Burgtheater, superb performance, and Verdi's *Falstaff* in der Staatoper. Vienna has superb theater and opera, much better than Munich.

December 11. Paul, you would not like my figure any more. As a matter of fact, I must look rather grotesque, as Sunday hikers always crane their necks after me. [Here she made a sketch of her altered figure]....My primitive stove without a thermostat scares me, but I did a chicken successfully for company the other day. It came with head, feet, and a fair amount of feather still on it. I am getting more confident in entertaining our new friends, treating them to our old Canton stand-bys. They seem to enjoy them, including Beefeater martinis. We try to keep our place between 70 and 72 degrees F, a luxury for Viennese.

February 15, 1968. I am back from the hospital about a week. Mother [Johanna Pusch, from Hamburg] is here to help. The birth was fast but hell....I walked out of the hospital like a Giacometti figure. [Here she drew two versions of herself, one in a round bath basin on the floor and the other clothed for the street.]...The villa is completely unsuited for an infant. The place looks like camp art, the Jugendstil furniture draped with diapers, clothing, bedding, chamber pots, wash basins (the bathroom is too cold in winter). Getting through these first few weeks and months will be depressing. But I am counting on a nice spring and summer....Paul, too bad the new prof is only an armchair woodsman. Well, we'll see what kind I'll be. Giving birth was like climbing Marcy, Haystack, Gothics and Colden all in one day. That's how worn I am! I am about Clayton's speed now. I am looking forward to painting with him again, while Helen [Clayton's wife] cuddles the baby! Helen [her daughter] has a real temperament and eats like a horse.

Christa was a reluctant mother. Having lived for several years under the assurance that she could not conceive, she had directed her life toward self-realization in a variety of ways unrelated to propagation of the species. Now, at thirty-four, just as she was eagerly anticipating a year in pleasure-loving Vienna, her body was seized out of her control by an alien purpose. She suddenly became Simone de Beauvoir's "second sex." "Woman's lot [enslavement of the body to reproduction] is heavier than that of other females in just about the same degree that she goes beyond other females in the assertion of her individuality." But Christa had a sense of humor sufficient to transcend resentment, as those letters of the fall and winter show. In spring and summer she found ways of compromise between self-directed and involuntary roles. Her mother and Don himself were willing baby sitters. Increasingly, in spring and summer, she was able to enjoy life in restaurant, Weinstube, theater, opera, concert hall, and of course the Wiener Wald. The letter of February 15 is the last one I have managed to keep, but as I recall the remaining ones were full of the atmosphere of place. Her German heritage made Vienna congenial to her. These later letters evoked the spirit of nostalgic Strauss waltzes and the sweet-sad melodies of *Der Rosenkavalier* of that other Strauss of Munich.

When they returned to Canton in August, we resumed our outings, but with the difference baby Helen made. Only when Christa's mother was visiting or when Helen Fowler or some other baby sitter could be impressed were both Don and Christa able to accompany me. We agreed to a tradeoff, but since Don often had work to do and Christa was always ready to take advantage of this, more often it was just she and I, sometimes joined by Bernie Lammers. And our outings henceforth were more often canoe cruises as my recreational preference was changing. In between times in the woods Christa and her baby were visitors at afternoon tea or cocktails. Ruth was fond of her. Once Christa expressed the view that Ruth might be jealous, that tales might have reached her of Christa's joking references, among her other friends, to her aged "boyfriend." She was mistaken in this. Ruth was not of a jealous disposition, much less so as a veteran of a forty-year marriage.

Hanna, Christa's mother, was also a visitor on our porch during her summer visits from Germany. She spoke and understood little English. I enjoyed hearing her and Christa and Don talking rapidly together in the monosyllabic German of family matters and affections. In this sphere German is the preeminent language. But when those monosyllables are mashed together to form abstractions, crudities result. A nation founded on a Declaration of *Unabhängigkeit* (independence) might devolve, through sheer aesthetic revulsion, into its antonym, *Unterworfensein* (subjection), if the latter were not equally ungainly.

[ 174 ]

After the Makoskys' return from Vienna my log notes a canoe trip in an area that Christa came to love as much as I did, a glacial outwash plain forty-three miles south of Canton.

September 22, 1968. Another miraculous Sunday of this miraculous September, uniformly warm and sunny now for three weeks. Christa and I explored the Massawepie country, leaving at ten and getting back by six. Paddled across the S end of Massawepie Lake into the two long, narrow parallel bays. Picnicked on a high kame overlooking the Massawepie Mire and the peaks between it and Cranberry Lake. After lunch we paddled down the outlet, a winding, fascinating stream through a marshy corridor of tamaracks. Followed it an hour. Surprised a great blue heron and several ducks. On the way back, we stopped at a bend in the stream Christa wanted to paint. While she painted a watercolor I moved the canoe across a narrow strip of land to Pine Pond. Walking back without the canoe, I noticed a clump of bunchberry plants teased into second bloom by the wonderful fall weather. Pointed this out to Christa when she had finished her painting. Near the bunchberries she spotted a single twinflower plant also in second bloom, bravely holding up on a stiff stem two nodding pink blossoms, which seemed the leitmotif of this perfect fall day. Paddled across Pine Pond to a sandy beach now in full afternoon sun. Water felt warm enough to swim. Changed into bikini and trunks for a last swim of the season. Carried to the big lake and crossed it to my car.

During that fall I realized I was falling in love with Christa. Till then a sympathetic sharing of perceptions had been all. Now her physical presence excited me as she slipped into the car seat next to me, another golden day in the woods before us (was this moment of anticipation not the happiest of all states?); as her lovely hands with the long tapering fingers and freshly lacquered nails played over a watercolor at a site that had taken her eye; as an adorable fold creased her stomach as she sat in bikini against a tree; as her supple figure ahead of me on a trail heavily shadowed by hemlocks aroused the impulse to take her in my arms, risking all. But the consciousness of a sexagenarian is double. A *doppelgänger* who had been attending me for some time now and professed to have lived knowingly in the world, advised me with an ironic smile to hold off and see the ridiculous side of this business of love by December for, if not May, at any rate June.

Unlike youth, age can love without craving; love at last can be contemplative. But I knew that this state of suspension would change with physical contact. Once while we were canoeing I told her that I was falling in love. "Then why...?" she broke off. "Why I have not made a pass?" I guessed at her question. She nodded a little hesitantly. "Because there is no future in it." "Yes," she said.

Another advantage of age is the hard-earned lesson that every human being is an island, autonomous and ultimately unknowable, with other interests and feelings than your own. Youth thinks that love can compel love and is outraged when it does not. Age knows better. I have only vague inklings of Christa's feelings toward me but am sure that love had no part in them; not for a man more than twice her age and looking it. But sympathy and understanding did exist. Europeans are better than Americans at communicating across generation gaps. Christa and her mother talking in their rapid German monosyllables could pass for sisters exchanging confidences. Christa was at ease with me and enjoyed my company in the woods. Other than that, there is the slightly patronizing inscription in her gift of an album of her cartoons prompted by our outings: "For 'Uncle Paul' on his 66th birthday. Keep it up, Paul." It would be presumptuous to conclude that the quotation marks are meant to define my relation to little Helen her daughter and not to Christa herself. After all, there are limits to the advantages that age has over youth.

The remark that "there is no future in it" proved to have another sense than the one intended. Just twenty-one months after the return from Vienna, Christa's doctor warned her that she had a tumor in her left breast that would have to be removed. One of our last carefree outings took place on May 3, 1970, when we cruised the Raquette in spring flood stage between Axton and the Tupper Lake launching site. It was a day of variable cloudiness and chill (40–45 F) but no rain. Christa wore longjohns for the canoe and I winter woolens. We drove in two cars to simplify the shuttle. The river was in a grand state of uncontainment, sprawling wide over floodplains up to a half mile and drowning trees and even the posters on the left bank—a scene reminiscent of the Everglades. The four-foot banks of summer were under water. Only the submerged posters and streamers from the reddening buds of swamp maples designated the main channel. Often, however, the current was not in the main channel but through thickets of maples and evergreens. It was a novelty to cut off the bends and bushwhack by canoe through woods and undergrowth, well afloat but having to part brush or ride over a floating log. We were able to cut at least a mile off the normally meandering ten-mile reach between put-in and take-out. We had a leisurely lunch in the shelter of a boulder overlooking a lagoon and the great bulk of the Seward Range.

Shortly after this trip Christa learned of the possibly cancerous growth, and in early June she was operated on in Ogdensburg. Before the operation she had been what I believe is called a perfect 36. The loss of a breast was a blow to her pride as a woman. But she had a saving grace of humor. One of her cartoons depicts her in a proud bikini wading in water up to her knees and labeled "Before," with a smiling Paul looking on; the "After" side, with a frowning Paul as eavesdropper, shows her in water of the same depth but wearing a short smock to conceal a lopsided chest.

[ 176 ]

For a while that summer it seemed that the cancerous growth had been caught in time. But then her lymph gland became affected. Another growth, which also had to be removed, appeared on her neck. By summer's end Christa knew that she was doomed. She treated this lightly in company, jesting that she was born fifty years too soon. In that time, she said, medics will have found a cure. Underneath the brave exterior something else was going on—the tragic sense of life of her European heritage. Earlier she had visited the hospital room of another young faculty wife who was slowly dying of cancer. Christa had described to me what a pitiable figure that woman was as body and spirit wasted away.

On September 26 I had my last outing with her, about a week after the removal of the second tumor. Don's mother was visiting, and this time both Don and Christa were able to go. We spent the whole day, a Saturday, in the Deer River State Park. While Christa made a watercolor of a cascade in the river, Don and I left her briefly for a short canoe trip downstream and back. Christa was weak and Don had to assist her over rough places in the trail to our lunch site. Early in the day she seemed despondent, but her spirits rose later on in that familiar but much loved park with its variety of riverscapes. Three days later she, Don, his mother, Gertrude, and little Helen visited us for cocktails. Christa was cheerful, and it was a happy occasion.

Ruth and I shortened our New England tour that fall to one week, October 2 to 9. Our homecoming was noted by Idella Warner, who crossed the street to tell us the news of Christa's death the day before. Cancer had spread to her liver, and she had been hospitalized again on October 7. The next morning she was found in her private room, a suicide. She left a note saying that the cause of death was KNC, the symbol of potassium cyanide, which, as a chemist, she well knew. In this way she had averted the prolonged wasting away of a lovely body and spirit. She had chosen the best solution left open to her.

The memorial service on October 12 was prepared and spoken by George Frear. There were readings from the Psalms, Ecclesiastes, Keats, Yevtushenko, and Rilke and a eulogy:

She was unique—a lover of beauty and the natural world, but also a forthright friend and a wonderfully witty and incisive talker. She loved good wine and good talk. She had an inborn artistic gift, and in her own home and in many other places we can look at what she has left us—ceramics, watercolors, oil paintings, tables, the whole interior decor of her house. She had a fine, clear mind for science, languages, literature, and the practical matters of life. If long life were based on the amount of craft and joy a person had in it, she would surely have lived twice as long....

Her eye was just as sharp as her mind. Someone has said that walking in the

*Cartoons by Christa*

Paul on a "hike".
with CHRISTA
Paul, Paul, where are you??

Before
After

woods with her was like walking with Thoreau. She never failed to see the secluded wildflower or the nest of the ovenbird. She has left photographs of Adirondack flowers that preserve the record of her vision....

She lived intensely. Perhaps it could be said that her perceptions and actions were so quick and deep that she lived twice as much each hour as most of us, and so had packed one good lifetime into thirty-six years....

In her last illness she was frank about her condition, but she took care to be kind, becoming gentle towards everyone. She took pains to talk to her mother about her German friends, trying, it almost seems, to gather together all her good memories and beloved friends at the end. For she did the same affectionate naming of so many of the Canton group, like a final blessing on them.


Of the readings, the Yevtushenko poem, "People," in translation, touched me most deeply.

> To each his world is private....
> Not people die but worlds die with them....
> They perish. They cannot be brought back.
> The secret worlds are not regenerated.

A secret world died with Christa, a world of depths and complexities that intimacy could never fully probe. Like the Adirondack forest, she aroused a sense of mystery. "Something hidden. Go and find it." Walking in the woods with her, you were in the presence of two mysteries.

Hanna, in Germany, outlived her only offspring by eleven years. It is a sad thing when the daughter dies first.

Christa left me, besides memories, a living legacy in Bernie Lammers. He joined the SLU faculty in the Government Department about the time I retired. I might never have known him except for Christa's inviting him to participate in some of our outings during the last two years of her life. Bernie and I are Midwesterners in origin, though his native city, Louisville, is on the opposite side of the Mason-Dixon Line. Midwesterners, north or south, have much in common, and even more after they settle in the East. We have differences too. He is a devout Catholic and one-time novitiate in a monastery; I, an atheist. We are able to ignore these vagaries in each other. Love of the woods is the chief bond between us. Our ancestors trekked westward into an untamed wilderness. In going back east, Bernie and I have found a remnant of that virgin continent known to our forebears. This link with America's past is our link to each other. In the woods we have just one irritating difference. My idea of a leisurely lunch is a half hour, his an hour and a half. He likes to go into what he calls, after Warren Harding's example in the White House, a postprandial trance. We usually settle for something like fifty minutes. Otherwise we have achieved symbiosis. In the woods he keeps a respectful silence

and lets me talk; going and returning, he does virtually all the talking, while I keep
an ear open for a free education in political parties, advantages of parliamentary
government, evils of militarism, constitutional and environmental law. Declining
energy during the last eight years has curtailed my active life in the woods, but
fortunately not Bernie's. About the time I began to fail him, he found a replacement as much younger than he as I am older, in Jane, an outdoor girl.

## XVII  PEN AND PADDLE

FROM 1965 TO 1968 I assisted Atwood Manley of Canton in writing the biography of one of Canton's four notable figures: Silas Wright, statesman; Frederic Remington, artist; Irving Bacheller, writer; and J. Henry Rushton, craftsman and canoe builder. In the former year Atwood gave me for appraisal the manuscript of his original draft of Rushton's life from birth to death. I commented as follows.

This is interesting and important—a story only you could tell. Though it needs much editing in word choice, grammar, etc., I don't think any major changes in organization are called for, except perhaps leaving out a few passages as indicated in my notes or bridging them over by short summaries. A few more personal anecdotes about Rushton would help in projecting his personality (particularly stories about his relations to townspeople), but you have probably scraped up everything of this kind that is still available. Maybe you could do more with boats other than canoes. Is Rushton's work on guideboats important enough to merit a few more pages and some comparisons with other guideboat makers?

When an editor goes to work on this Ms, he will probably tone down your language in some degree, removing some of the metaphors and the superlatives. If you want to avoid yells of pain when this happens, you might disarm him by doing some rewriting of your own and thus keep the whole job under your control. It seems to me that you make too many episodes "historic," shoot Rushton into orbit too many times (making him groggy with weightlessness), claim too many turning points in his career, and use too much inflated language generally. In the end this diminishes the stature of the really important things because you have no new metaphors or superlatives left in the bag and simply repeat the old ones. They lose carrying power. Your style needs modulating, with stretches of plain prose between the flossy patches. But this book is going to be a real contribution.

Atwood asked me to do the editing. I soon discovered another fault in his manuscript. As former editor of the local weekly newspaper, Atwood was accustomed to writing on the fly without due regard for accuracy. On checking his references, I found inaccuracies and misinterpretations of his sources. In the end I checked all of his references, the majority of them to *Forest and Stream* magazine, a complete file of which we had in the college library. In this research I turned up some new material. So my job became that of an assistant writer, correcting inaccuracies, adding new material, toning down Atwood's writing considerably, and elevating slightly the fervor of my own contributions to make a seamless fit. I think I was reasonably successful in this. *Rushton and His Times in American Canoeing*, published jointly by the Syracuse University Press and the Adirondack Museum in 1968, has been hailed as a classic in canoeing history. I enjoyed immensely my association with Atwood. While our work was in progress, we sought inspiration by paddling his *Vayu*, an all-wood Rushton canoe, on many waters in the Adirondacks. I have told this story in "Atwood, Rushton, and the Chickaree," reprinted in the collection *Adirondack Pilgrimage*.

A year after the publication of Atwood's book another association began with a book manuscript I was asked to appraise and then to edit, Herbert Keith's *Man of the Woods*, again jointly published by the Syracuse University Press and the Adirondack Museum, 1972. There were crudities in the manuscript, but the writing was spirited and the story unique. It was the story of Wanakena, a lumber camp that grew into a hamlet and a hamlet that can no longer grow because it is surrounded by Forest Preserve; of the guides of the upper Oswegatchie River and Cranberry Lake; and of the folklore of natives at the northern edge of the Five Ponds Wilderness Area, where the largest block of virgin timber in the Adirondacks is located.

Herbert Keith was that rarity, the year-round resident who writes a book about his life in the woods. Natives generally leave book writing to outsiders and summer residents. Seventy-five when he presented his manuscript, Herb had passed most of his life in Wanakena and as part-time guide at his camp on the Oswegatchie Inlet. The chief breaks were his boyhood in New York City and his service in World War II, which extended beyond the Armistice while his duty was to identify the bodies of American soldiers killed in southern Europe. There he met and married a Bulgarian artist and piano teacher, Mimi, whom he successfully introduced to the backwoods. Having survived him, Mimi still gives piano lessons in Wanakena and paints in oils. In frequent talks with Herb about his book, I came to know both of them well and to enjoy their company. The house that Herb himself built is the southernmost in Wanakena at the edge of twenty-one miles of unbroken Forest Preserve. The trail to High Falls begins at his property line. It is never dull at the Keith place. People and animals come and go at all hours. Herbert was the genial host to this traffic, advising hikers and feeding the birds and animals. The family cat played host to a family of raccoons that visited for their supper, after which it strolled with them to the edge of the woods to bid goodnight. In our talks Herb was full of yarns and nostalgia. He used to say, graciously including me though I was eight years younger, that we had seen in our lives the best times America will ever have. Those times ended about 1930 with the opening of State Highway 3 that brought the casual tourist into the Oswegatchie–Cranberry Lake area.

After Herb's death in 1978 I wrote to Mimi: "None of us who knew Herb can ever forget him. He was a rare human being in his perfect sincerity, his gift for story telling, love of the woods, human warmth and dignity....I guess we needn't regret his passing too much. He had a long life and a good one and he left a lasting memorial of both."

Early in 1972 Grant Cole, executive director of the Adirondack Mountain Club, asked me to prepare a canoeing guide to the Adirondacks. Three of my articles on canoeing in the park had appeared in the club's periodical, *Adirondac*. After considering the proposal for some time, I agreed in a letter of July, 1972. My first intention was to deal with all five major watersheds, but this was too ambitious for the time frame proposed. I decided to limit coverage to the two north-flow watersheds, the Lake Champlain basin and the St. Lawrence River basin, the latter being the largest of the five. My book would then be followed by another on the Hudson, Mohawk, and Black River basins. Alec Proskine later prepared a guide to those watersheds.

During the next three years I devoted most of my time to this congenial workplay. From ice-out to ice-in I scouted, sometimes by solo canoe, more often in tandem, the rivers, other navigable streams, lakes, and chain ponds in the central and northern Adirondacks. I was often on the waters three days a week and utilized the other days to write descriptions from the notes I had taken. Coincidentally the Adirondack Park Agency was engaged in scouting Adirondack rivers under a legislative mandate adopting the recommendation of the Temporary Study Commission for a state Wild, Scenic and Recreational Rivers System. I knew two of the men on the APA survey team, Clarence Petty and Gary Randorf. As we proceeded simultaneously with field studies, we exchanged findings. I submitted to Clarence a copy of my preliminary manuscript. Clarence in turn corrected some errors of mine in measuring distances. The APA field summaries in pamphlet form have a continuing value in supplementing my own study of each river.

*Paul and his sister Mary at the end of a November cruise, 1983*

*Adirondack Canoe Waters: North Flow* was ready for publication by the Adirondack Mountain Club in 1975. It was favorably received, not only as a guidebook but a celebration of the Adirondack landscape. Sales through 1991 have reached thirty-five thousand. Revisions appeared in 1977, 1981, 1984, 1986, 1988, and most recently in 1991. In the third edition of 1988 a co-author, Donald Morris, joined me, enabling me to retire from most active scouting. His advanced whitewater skills neatly compensate for my deficiency in this regard. Don and I project a major overhaul in a fourth edition, probably for 1993, taking into account recent developments that open several river segments long closed to the public by private owners in the park.

*(Photo Lois Wells)*

The situation just alluded to has occupied much of my attention for the last twenty years. It is surely an anomaly that in a park dedicated at the founding in 1892 "for the free use of all the people for their health and pleasure" twenty-five navigable rivers (1972) were closed, in part or in whole, to public navigation because they flowed through the sixty percent of the Adirondack Park that was privately owned. This closure contravened common law, under which a public easement exists on all rivers navigable in fact. In the New England states and in New Jersey common law has prevailed to keep all rivers open to navigation. Indeed, this is true in most of New York State outside the Adirondack Park. Why not in the park itself? This situation seemed to me intolerable. The wonder was its passive acceptance by the public for nearly one hundred years. I believe I was the first to document this injustice in a series of letters-to-the-editor, letters to DEC officials and the Governor, and articles in *Adirondac* and *Adirondack Life* magazines. The opener, a rather fumbling treatment before I was fully informed through work on my canoeing guidebook, was in the form of an open letter to the magazine *Conservationist*, July 7, 1969.

Dear Editor:

The foot traveler in the Adirondacks has God's plenty at his disposal. If the thousands of miles of trails in the Forest Preserve and easements over private land are not enough, he can bushwhack in a dozen wilderness areas. It is the small-boat traveler that is underprivileged today. There were more open waterways before the creation of the Forest Preserve in 1885 and the Adirondack Park in 1892 than there are now. Most of the four hundred pages of E. R. Wallace's *Descriptive Guide to the Adirondacks* (1872–1899) trace boat tours open to everyone in the last century. In the 1860s and 1870s "Adirondack" Murray ranged everywhere among the lakes and ponds, rivers and navigable creeks of the central and western regions. "For weeks I have paddled my cedar shell in all directions," he wrote, "an easy and romantic" mode of travel that made the Adirondacks a paradise, "above all its rivals, east or west." Unfortunately, hundreds of miles of the waterways described so winningly by Murray, Wallace, Headley, Hammond, Stillman, Emerson, Street, and other travelers of the last century are no longer accessible.

For a canoeist nothing is more inviting than chain lakes or winding rivers in hill, forest, and whitetail country. But he is due for a frustrating experience if he tries to match Wallace's boat tours with present realities. Many of the most attractive routes are now closed. This is true, for instance, of the greater part of the Bog River, including all of its system of lakes. A chain of lakes and carries from Raquette Lake to Big Tupper which used to make possible a popular circular trip when combined with the Raquette River is no longer open. One must go both ways on the Raquette. The most interesting stretch of the St. Regis River, the thirty miles below Keese Mill, was once open to navigation. Wallace recommends especially the "Sixteen-Mile Level, this grand secluded reach of boatable stillwater." On a recent trip over the Blue Mountain–Brandon Road with canoe on my cartop, I found this section of the river, like others downstream, blocked at both ends and at a bridge crossing in between by posters and other means. Likewise with a fifteen-mile stretch of stillwater on the East Branch of the St. Regis beginning a mile and a half below Meacham Lake....

Here at the top of the state, outside the Blue Line, where nearly all land is private, we boat freely on our rivers with access and exit at any highway bridge. It puzzles many of us that this free access is denied in many parts of the Adirondack Park. There is a widespread belief that the rivers of the state are public highways.

The closing paragraph posed three questions, the answers to which by a Conservation Department official amounted to an admission without a resolution. I was better informed when I wrote the first of a series of articles on this subject for the May-June *Adirondac*, 1971. "Lapsed Paradise" was a carefully documented survey of how this situation evolved and of the great extent of the restricted waterways in the park.

The Adirondack Park is unique in the nation in combining a mountainous terrain with a vast network of waters, as if Venice were stretched out over Switzerland. The latest count is over three thousand lakes and ponds of a half acre or more. Thirty river systems flow from interior elevations to the perimeters of the dome-shaped uplift. Those main-branch rivers have numerous tributaries, also navigable, some of which form cross-grained interconnections, so that geography makes possible cruises of a hundred miles or more in all directions, as W. H. H. Murray pointed out in 1869. All of this network was open to the public in the nineteenth century till about 1890, when posting began in earnest in private parks and corporate timberlands.

"Lapsed Paradise," reprinted in *Adirondack Pilgrimage*, lists some of the lost opportunities for the public of today in Murray's paradise of waters. It brought several responses in letters I received from readers. The most interesting was from Hector Prud'homme, mentioned earlier as a guest I met at the Hochschilds' some months after our exchange of letters. He argued that, strictly from the standpoint of preserving the natural environment, it may be fortunate that much of the Adirondacks is in private hands. If all the waterways were open to the public, you would encourage the invasion and trashing of streams and stream banks. The public would leave refuse and spoil places once scenic and wild. These, I felt, were the typical arguments of large landowners bent on preserving privacy in their twenty to fifty thousand acres estates. They were good reasons, not the real one.

July 29, 1971

Dear Mr. Prud'homme:

Thank you for your interesting, pertinent letter in response to my article in *Adirondac*. I agree that preservation of the natural environment is the most desirable goal, even if public use is to be restricted. But I don't think that private ownership is the best way of preserving wild forests and streams.

Private owners come and go, and each has whims that may or may not accord with true preservation. One owner may clear thirty acres or so to build a gaudy tourist trap such as Storytown. Another is just now beginning to sell a hundred lots for a colony of summer cottages on Thirteenth Lake, at the edge of one of the prime wilderness areas of the park. Septic tanks will drain into the lake and motorboats will swarm over it. Another type of owner, representative of the largest of privately owned tracts in the Adirondacks, practices "managed" forestry. The Whitney and Litchfield parks are honeycombed with logging roads, as well as the holdings of International Paper, St. Regis Paper, and Finch, Pruyn. Lumbering operations are not pretty while they are going on or for some years after. Bulldozers are the worst litterbugs.

It is true that some private owners have preserved beautiful tracts of forest, mountain, and lake. Mr. Hochschild is one of them. The Ausable Club is another. In these two instances public use is permitted on a limited basis. Eagle Lake is part of the chain that is kept open for the enjoyment of canoeists, and the public is freely admitted to the mountain trails of the Ausable Club. But these cases are exceptional. By and large, the state, bound by one of the most effective preservation laws in the country, the "forever wild" amendment to the constitution, is a more trustworthy custodian than private owners.

In spite of much evidence to the contrary, I still believe it possible to educate the public. The conservation movement is beginning to make an impact across the country. Outdoor clubs are publishing leaflets on manners in the woods, holding briefings for camp counselors, and organizing clean-up crews. This summer, it seems to me, the trails and camp sites I have observed are a little cleaner than in recent years, in spite of ever-increasing use.

Another answer to the littering problem is zoning, as recommended in the recent report of the Temporary Study Commission that Mr. Hochschild chaired. The classification "wilderness" for fifteen areas of ten thousand acres or more would automatically limit access to those willing to expend some energy in getting there, afoot or by canoe or rowboat. Such people are more scrupulous about leaving things as they found them than the casual tourist. They know the value and the fragility of the thing they are seeking.

On the question of educating the public, my hopes go up and down. The following note to *Adirondack Life* magazine was written during one of my more pessimistic moods during the debate over a bottle bill (finally adopted) for New York State.

To the Editor:

I have evidence that our only salvation is a strong bottle bill. Education is not enough. *Slobus americanus* not only thrives today but has a long notorious history. The impulse to litter the forest floor is ingrained in the national character, even in the cream of our society, from way back. On the picnic points of Raquette Lake the beer bottles of today were matched, a century ago, by the champagne bottles of William West Durant's rich friends. The intellectuals of that age were no better. Take Philosophers' Camp, that Adirondack outing of the sages of Concord, Boston, and Cambridge in 1858. On Emerson's return to Concord, Thoreau recorded in his journal for August 23: "Emerson says that he and Agassiz and Company broke some dozens of ale bottles, one after another, with their bullets, in the Adirondack country, using them for marks! It sounds rather Cockneyish." Rather, indeed. Yet Emerson and Stillman indulged themselves in lyrical descriptions of the beauty of their wilderness camp on Follensby Pond.

Only archaeologists, looking for the exact site of Philosophers' Camp, can rejoice in those shards and heaps of broken 1858 ale bottles on Follensby shore. For those of us who have put our faith in education, Thoreau's diary of August 23, 1858, is profoundly troubling: Ralph Waldo Emerson, Harvard graduate, philosopher, nature poet, and litterbug.


Well, the trash problem is far worse, I am told by my traveling friends, in third-world countries than here at home. Maybe we have come a little up the scale of decency and are capable of further progress. Few canoeists, at any rate, descend into Cockneyism. They are disciples of Thoreau.

To return to restricted waterways, I have felt for the last twenty years that this is an issue worth a persistent crusade. Some of my friends might disagree. Bernie Lammers would say that I should join him in opposing a bloated defense budget or in holding peace rallies on the village green rather than squandering the finite wisdom and energy of old age on a secondary issue. But opening Adirondack canoe waters is the crusade nature and experience have designed me for. A legacy of untrammeled forest recreation, it seems to me, is about the best thing one can pass on to future generations. As Americans inheriting a once virgin continent, we have a little of Francis Parkman in our nature: "haunted with wilderness images day and night" to such an extent that his monumental history of the French and English in America became for him, essentially, a history of the American forest.

Henry James went abroad to be humanized. His brother William stayed at home and went to the Adirondacks for the same purpose. Spending a sleepless moonlight night in a lean-to above Panther Gorge, William experienced "a state of spiritual alertness...as if the Gods of all the nature-mythologies were holding an indescribable meeting in my breast with the moral Gods of the inner life....The intense significance of some sort, of the whole scene...its utter Americanism...was indeed worth coming for, and worth repeating year after year." In my youth I was a follower of Henry's way for a brief period, but after settling in northern New York at a corner of the Adirondacks, I turned to William's way. To an American the forest is humanizing. Personal relations flourish there. No matter how divisive our interests are in civilian life, in the forest we have our heritage of wilderness in common. We connect.

# XVIII  PIECEMEAL GAINS

IN THE NINETEENTH CENTURY the Adirondacks was the nation's favorite region for small-boat travel. But in the twentieth, the boat traveler is hobbled by posters in river corridors and the threat of being ticketed for trespass if he ventures to run some twenty-five rivers from the head of navigability to confluence or to the Blue Line. What could be done about this situation? In the early 1970s there seemed to be only one feasible way of opening restricted river segments—purchases of fee title or easements by the state or by an organization like the Nature Conservancy. At that time I felt that changing state laws and regulations was too formidable an undertaking. The DEC pamphlet on the posting law declared that under the Environmental Conservation Law landowners could post "both lands and waters." Private park owners and game clubs latched onto this provision as guaranteeing their exclusive privileges in river corridors. Gradually, however, my views changed on these alternative courses. Purchases of key river segments seemed too piecemeal, slow, and haphazard as funds from state bond issues became available. And then the bond act of 1990 was narrowly defeated in the polls. Preservationists had looked to this as the opportunity to protect thousands of acres of timberland through outright purchase or easements. The failure of the bond act to pass was a severe setback to those of us committed to opening waterways piecemeal and at the same time preserving open space in the park. The other alternative, changing laws and regulations, began to look more promising. But for several years my efforts were directed at initiating and supporting acquisitions piece by piece.

The first opportunity arose in 1973 in a talk with Harry McManus, owner of a 529-acre tract at Everton Falls on the East Branch of the St. Regis River. This river was so heavily posted that a previous writer of a canoe guide to New York State rivers was discouraged from scouting any part of it; he simply omitted it from his guidebook. Defying the no-trespassing signs, I ran the East Branch for fifteen miles from Rice Brook to Everton Falls and found it a highly enjoyable cruising stream.

*Paul Schaefer and Paul Jamieson at Everton Falls, 1974*

So I asked Harry McManus whether he would consider selling an access easement at Everton Falls, which would open an upstream flatwater round trip of eighteen miles, along with about one mile downstream from the falls. An elderly man in declining health, he said that he would prefer to sell all his land except for a parcel around his camp. A year earlier I had joined the Adirondack Committee of the Nature Conservancy (AC for Adirondack Conservancy). This beautiful river corridor of 1.7 miles and forested mountain slope seemed in keeping with the Conservancy's acquisition policies at that time. I proposed purchase to Timothy Barnett, the executive director of AC. He met me at the site on July 6, 1973, to examine the property and talk with McManus, who agreed to granting an option to buy at one hundred dollars an acre. AC trustees Winifred La Rose and Paul Schaefer also came to inspect the property; Paul took photos. And in early 1974 the purchase was concluded with funds borrowed from the revolving capital of the home office in Arlington, D.C. Several months later the following announcement appeared in an AC bulletin.

The Everton Falls Preserve of 529 acres in northern Franklin County is the AC's first major fund-raising effort towards property that it will own outright and manage for public use. It was the brain-child of Dr. Paul Jamieson, retired professor at St. Lawrence University in Canton, who saw the 1.7-mile stretch of the wild East Branch of the St. Regis River as a nature preserve for canoeists and fishermen, surrounded as it is by wilderness and teeming with birds and animals.

The original purchase price of the tract was $52,900; gifts in the amount of $28,490 have been received by AC toward this acquisition, but $24,410 still remains to be raised for repayment to the Nature Conservancy, which loaned the money for the original purchase.

Among other gifts, AC is happy to report that Dr. Jamieson's home chapter of the Adirondack Mountain Club honored him last year by contributing the price of several acres of the tract in his name. Another gift which is particularly happy comes from a long-time friend of Dr. Jamieson, Eleanor Brown, editor of *Adirondac*, who wrote: "I'd like to add that this gift is made out of respect to Paul

Jamieson as well as to the Nature Conservancy. I value my past association with him, and I value any project the more knowing he is behind it." Mrs. Brown and her husband, John F. Brown of Schenectady, contributed over $4,000 worth of ITT stock.

The balance due the Nature Conservancy home office was raised by the end of 1975. I managed the Everton Falls Preserve for ten years. My first act was to clear and mark a one-hundred foot canoe-carry trail from the Red Tavern Road to a good launching site above the falls and another below to invite public use of a ten-mile stretch, nearly half of the river's course to confluence with the main stem of the St. Regis. The attractions of the preserve are not limited to boating. The wide expanse of ledges at the divided channels of the falls, a drop of about eighteen feet, invites loitering and picnicking, and the woods on both sides of the river and Red Tavern Road invite nature study. Following instructions of the Conservancy, I prepared a brief history of the site and a management plan, while biologist Paul Hafer made a natural-history inventory. With the help of the Laurentian Chapter of the Adirondack Mountain Club, I posted the perimeter of the tract and the frontage on the bisecting Red Tavern Road with signs welcoming the public for the harmless kinds of recreation approved by the Conservancy. Paul Hafer and John Green assisted me in routing two nature trails, one along the river and the other in the interior of the woods, and in selecting stations of special interest. I wrote a pamphlet guide to the trails for distribution at the site. Once annually the Laurentian Chapter of ADK schedules a clean-up, usually in May. The most arduous labor is clearing the two nature trails every spring, and indeed throughout the summer and fall, of undergrowth and windfalls. As I turned eighty, this physical labor became too taxing and I turned management over to the three men who had been most helpful, Lewis Weeks and Perry Yaw of Potsdam and Duncan Cutter of Nicholville. Duncan has the advantage of living just fifteen miles from the preserve and of treasuring its woods and waters for his own recreation.

The ten miles of waterway thus opened to the public is a tiny fraction of the mileage that remained closed in the park. But this first success encouraged further initiatives.

Sixteen miles south of Canton on the main stem of the Grass River is Lampson Falls, a broad sixty-foot drop over sloping Precambrian rock. The pool below the falls is almost enclosed by a terraced spit of bedrock that makes an ideal overlook and picnic site in the shade of white pines. Sixty years ago, shortly after I moved to Canton, I discovered Lampson Falls, then owned by a power company that never developed the falls for hydro power. There was a gate over the access road, but the owners made no effort to exclude visitors on foot, a small number of local people. For nearly two decades Lampson Falls was an almost private swimming and picnicking place for my wife and me and chosen friends. Then after World War II the power company sold its land to three local men, who built a hunting lodge at the head of the falls and sold memberships in a small hunting club. The whole tract was now heavily posted and patrolled.

Lampson Falls heads a 1.8-mile reach of extraordinarily beautiful riverscapes. Flatwater continues for about three-quarters of a mile, and then begins a dramatic series of nine cascades in the next mile, some abrupt, others flume-like, and some in divided channels, composing a museum gallery of rock and greenery. To me this segment of wild river is the dearest place in the world. I resolved to do what I could to open it to the public under the protective mantle of the Nature Conservancy or the State Forest Preserve—all the more resolved in that a twelve-mile canoe route would then be opened from the Degrasse State Forest to Russell.

I knew one of the owners, Clayton VanBrocklin, by way of having asked his permission to make two nostalgic visits to the tract. Now I addressed the following letter to him, with copies going to the other two owners, Clayton's brother Mason and Kenneth Giffin.

August 3, 1972

Dear Mr. VanBrocklin:

I am writing to ask whether you and the other co-owners have ever considered selling the Lampson Falls tract. Since Kenneth Crowell and I visited the tract as your guests last November, we have talked between ourselves about the desirability of preserving the falls and the shore line as a natural area into the indefinite future.

You present owners are doing a good job of preservation now, but the danger is that the tract may eventually fall into the hands of individual owners less concerned than you are with its scenic value just as it is, without further development.

You have possibly heard of the Nature Conservancy. It is an organization founded in New York State eighteen years ago and now nation-wide, with chapters all over the country. Its sole purpose is to acquire unspoiled tracts such as Lampson Falls and preserve them as natural areas for the enjoyment of future generations. Over fifty such projects have already been completed in this state alone. There is an article on the Nature Conservancy in the *Conservationist* for August-September 1968, page 17. Since the date of the article, the Conservancy has completed other purchases, such as the large Santanoni tract in the central Adirondacks.

Kenneth Crowell and I are local members of the Conservancy. If you might be interested, now or in the future, in selling the tract to an organization that would insure its permanent preservation, we Canton members would be glad to propose the purchase to the Eastern New York Chapter [the Adirondack Committee was not

[ 194 ]

formed till the following year] and the national Board of Governors.

I then had talks with the three owners. I found that the VanBrocklin brothers had grown up in a house, now demolished, on the Clare Road just a half mile from the Lampson Falls tract. Boyhood memories of the river made them very emotional about the property. Over the next seven years they changed their minds several times about selling or not selling and to whom to sell. The third owner, also of a local family, was more objective about the property but was fully aware of its possible value for a second-home development. He was willing to sell at the asking price of $500 an acre for the six hundred acres.

At the time of my approach the owners had another possible buyer, an American diplomat in New Delhi, a graduate of St. Lawrence University, who had seen the tract and coveted it for a retirement home for himself and his friends. My friend Atwood Manley knew the diplomat from some past association and offered to write to him about the desirability of preservation. His reply, in a letter Atwood turned over to me, was all that we hoped for. "A portion of it would have made an ideal second career homesite for me, but I can't be too sorry the Nature Conservancy has decided to acquire it. In fact, it seems to me that all who are fortunate enough to live in the vicinity will profit greatly if that magnificent stretch of land is incorporated in the Park. I only hope that there are no plans to develop it."

In 1973 officers of what was now the newly organized Adirondack Conservancy Committee came north to view the property at my bidding. We walked along the most scenic stretch from the last of the cascades upstream to the big waterfall. They were enthusiastic. Tim Barnett, executive director, arranged to have the property appraised, as required by the home office of TNC. The local appraiser was accustomed to valuing properties on the basis of board feet rather than scenery. He put a value of $200 an acre on the tract. That was so far below the asking price that the Conservancy bowed out. It is bound by its rule of not paying more than the appraised value.

Our next recourse was the DEC. Funds for land purchases were then available from the Bond Act of 1972. Kenneth Crowell had taken some color photos of the cascades and the falls. His wife, Marnie, was to attend a meeting at which Commissioner James Biggane of the DEC was to be speaker. She showed him the photos. He agreed at once that this portion of the main stem of the Grass just inside the northwest corner of the Adirondack Park should become part of the Forest Preserve. He would issue orders to seek acquisition. We now had high hopes.

Negotiations with the owners, conducted by the county DEC office here in Canton, were long and devious. The VanBrocklin brothers changed their minds several times. During intervals of willingness to sell, they still dreamed of large profits through a sale to a developer of second homes. But finally they agreed to

*Lampson Falls (photo Edward Pierce)*

sign a contract giving the state first refusal at a compromise figure per acre. Subsequently they sought release from that agreement when a developer did turn up who was willing to pay more than the state's bid. The state refused to release them from the signed contract, and finally, in 1979, six years after DEC negotiations started, the Lampson Falls tract became part of the Forest Preserve as the Grass River Wild Forest. A year or two later this unit was expanded by another six hundred acres on the north, comprising Harper's Falls on the North Branch of the Grass and opening another stretch of wild river, just above confluence, to the public, as well as the twelve miles on the main stem. Throughout these negotiations I visited the DEC office here in Canton once or twice monthly to lend moral support and see that there was no relaxing of effort.

The success of this initiative has given me more satisfaction than any other undertaking of a lifetime. Purchase by the state not only opened a fascinating canoe route but also preserved in its natural state an outstandingly beautiful forest and river corridor for the enjoyment of future generations. During the last twelve years it has drawn an increasing number of visitors, some of them from distant points. It is especially popular with the college students of the county. Shortly after its purchase I nailed markers on a trail downstream from the falls on the east bank, across a logging bridge (later replaced by a footbridge), and down the west bank to the last of the nine cascades. Appealing to the Laurentian Chapter of ADK, I arranged for spring cleanups. These have continued to the present, though such is the public's respect for the tract that little trash is found, other than debris washed down the river in spring floods and beached on the floodplain below the falls.

Lampson Falls has historical interest in that it was once owned, along with much of the town of Clare, by the most famous woman of the European continent in Napoleon's time, Madame de Staël. She never visited her holdings in northern New York, but once thought of migrating there with her son. This story is told in my article "Lampson Falls" in *Adirondack Pilgrimage*.

In a letter to Herbert McAneny, dated August 18, 1979, I described my canoe trip down this newly opened section of the Grass. Herbert had asked about my current activities.

The highlight was a scouting trip on a newly opened canoe route of twelve miles on the main stem of the Grass, partly in and partly outside the Blue Line. Early this year, after my urgings over seven years, the state finally bought the Lampson Falls tract, the last 2.9 miles of the river before its final exit from the park.....Not just the big waterfall but the whole corridor is a cornucopia of riverscapes. It makes up the middle of a canoe route that begins in meandering flatwater five miles above the falls and ends outside the Blue Line in the village of Russell. The first carry is at Lampson Falls. Then comes nearly a mile of flatwater in a gorge. The dynamics resume with nine cascades of four to fifteen-foot pitches. We were a party of three the last day of May, two of us paddling tandem in my Old Town and a skilled kayaker. The latter ran six of the cascades, while we laboriously carried or lined all of them. It took us two hours to get through the Lampson Falls tract. But the last 4.5 miles were fast and effortless through almost continuous Class I and II rapids in a deep trough between wooded hills. I told Ruth afterwards that this trip was the climax of my canoeing. Maybe also near the end of it. Those carries were tiring to my seventy-six years. When I go back to Lampson Falls now, it is on foot to admire seasonal variations in the wildwater, June's masses of lady's slippers and bunchberry, and August's profusion of cardinal flowers in rocky niches along the stream.

Madame de Staël, mistress to an age as a recent biographer calls her, the age of the French Revolution and the Napoleonic empire, once owned most of the town of Clare including Lampson Falls. Her folly was to buy it as an investment for her children, thinking that rapid settlement would boost land values. Today the town of Clare has only ninety-seven inhabitants, mostly woodsmen. Madame de Staël never visited America and never dreamed that the real resource of her land was scenery. For that river corridor of six hundred acres the state paid nearly eight times what she had paid for her 26,000 acres.

In 1972 the main stem of the Grass was not the only part of the river system under threat of second-home development. Early in March the Horizon Corporation announced a plan to build a virtual city of second homes along the North Branch of the Grass, a scheme envisioning an eventual population of twenty thousand and a radical restructuring of the natural environment. Two or three days after this announcement I addressed to the editor of Canton's weekly newspaper, the St. Lawrence *Plaindealer*, a letter opposing this project. Since the site was virtually in our backyard here in the northwestern Adirondacks, I felt it was up to the people of St. Lawrence County to lead in the opposition.

March 9, 1972

Dear Editor:

St. Lawrence County residents should think twice about the proposal of out-of-state capitalists to develop a colony of second homes in the Adirondack woods above South Colton. The economic benefits would be a brief shot in the arm, shorter lived than those which once excited us when the St. Lawrence Seaway was proposed. We do not need short-term jobs that end with the completion of a development. What we need is light industry that will not pollute our air and water but will provide steady jobs and keep money circulating in the county, not going largely to swell the profits of out-of-state entrepreneurs.

We all know State Route 56, that lovely, lightly traveled road that winds upward through the Cold Brook gorge onto the Adirondack plateau and into the big woods. For generations it has been the way in to a different world—a wild forest land of space, freedom, relaxation, and adventure. The road has changed over the years, but there is still little development in the nineteen miles from South Colton to Sevey Corners—just a few farmhouses, hunter's shacks, and a tavern. But now a developer proposes to change all that by building a network of roads through the woods, damming the water of the North Branch and making artificial lakes, and erecting vacation homes on 24,300 acres on the west side of Route 56 above the Plains and the Huggard Farm, in Grandshue and Hollywood townships in the town of Colton and spilling over into the town of Clare.

At present this land is all wild forest. Recent lumbering has stripped it of much marketable timber, but it is still excellent habitat for deer, with wintering yards in the swampy headwaters of the North Branch. These swamps would be flooded. The winter yards would go, and the resulting lakes would warm the waters of one of the best remaining trout streams in the county, not to speak of inevitable pollution from even the most advanced of sewage systems.

[ 198 ]

The site is within the Blue Line of the Adirondack Park. Here at the northwest corner of the park we are unfortunate in having little state-owned Forest Preserve. There is one small block of state land at Church Pond and another tract on both sides of the road approaching Sevey's. Most other tracts are owned either by Niagara Mohawk or by timber companies which lease hunting and fishing rights. The alliance between lumber companies and game clubs does not preserve wilderness, but it has worked reasonably well to hold development in check, make favorable conditions for most species of wildlife, and keep traffic light on our road into the woods and mountains.

Now one of the lumber companies intends to break this pattern by selling out to developers willing to pay nearly $100 an acre for cutover land. It is a high price. It is going to raise the hopes of all the lumbering interests along Route 56. What we have to look forward to, if the proposed development is successful, is colonies of vacation homes all the way from Cold Brook gorge to the tract of state land below Sevey's.

The legend of Sunday Rock is probably known to everyone in the county. The boulder beside Route 56 at South Colton has been a proud landmark for over a century. It divides, we say, the developed part of the county from the wilds of South Woods, as we used to call the Adirondacks. The rock means different things to different people because an aura of emotion clings to it. Father passes the legend on to son and daughter. Sunday Rock is a link with our past and a hope for our future. That hope (for most of us in the county, I think) is that South Woods will remain the proper home of the deer, the bear, the coyote, and the beaver, a place where man is only a temporary visitor.

Twice, when Route 56 was widened, the people of the county, and even some outsiders who knew our legend, have rallied to save Sunday Rock from the dynamiters by moving it a few yards from its original stand. Now the time has come to save Sunday Rock again; not the rock itself but all it stands for in our feelings and memories.

Let's revive the Sunday Rock Association and address petitions to the Adirondack Park Agency and Department of Environmental Conservation. Let them know that we do not want South Woods developed by Horizon Corporation of Tucson, Arizona, or any other group.

I meant this letter as a rallying cry. Whether it was or not, an organization quickly sprang up of people in the two central villages of the county, Canton and Potsdam, and soon spread throughout the county and then to the state at large and some out-of-staters with ties to the Adirondacks. My suggestion of a name was rejected for the more comprehensive appeal of Citizens to Save the Adirondack Park, a name not dependent on knowledge of a local landmark. Maximum membership over the next two years reached nearly three thousand. And when another development scheme, Ton-da-Lay, north of Tupper Lake, was proposed, Citizens broadened its scope to oppose that one too. The publicity that our organization engendered was of assistance to the newly created Adirondack Park Agency in thwarting both developments. Horizon Corporation was eventually forced to abandon its plans and to sell its land back to the timber companies. Open space along Route 56 and a free-flowing North Branch were thus preserved.

The defeat of these two development plans encouraged me to think that something might be achieved in opening restricted Adirondack canoe waters to the public. An organization like the Citizens would probably have brought quicker results, but I had neither the skill or the inclination to work through an organization. I preferred to carry on the campaign alone and with what individual support I could muster along the way. For the next seventeen years it was simply a matter of opening a segment here and there of restricted river corridor through recommending purchase of fee title or easement by the state or the Conservancy or through persuasion of landowners. Fred Hackett, president of the Adirondack Mountain Club in the early 1970s and attorney in Suffolk County, Long Island, assisted me not only with legal advice but also by intervention with the DEC and landowners. Bog River Flow was a desirable waterway to open. Two Scout councils controlled most of it and restricted public access, much to the resentment of local residents, whose property taxes were higher because of the thousands of acres of exempt Scout land in the town. Fred had supported the Suffolk County Council of Scouts with generous donations. He now threatened to withhold this support unless the Council agreed to open its waters to public canoeing. The threat was effective, but the conditions were so stringent that few paddlers ever chose to take advantage of them. It was not till thirteen years later that a large purchase by the state finally succeeded in opening this incomparable waterway.

A fourteen-mile canoe route on the Raquette River in the town of Piercefield was also opened for several years through personal influence. The tract of 21,000 acres was then owned by Paul Smith's College. Wayne Byrne, a former president of ADK, co-chairman of the Adirondack Conservancy, and a friend of mine, was also a trustee of this college. He was able to persuade the administration to open this segment of the Raquette to canoeists. The college had hesitated because of the risk of incurring liability for injury in the considerable whitewater sections of the river. This opening was only a temporary victory. In 1980 the College sold the entire Piercefield tract to International Paper, and soon after the sale IP again closed the river. Recently, however, in a change of policy, IP has said that it will "not interfere" with recreational canoeing. Its lessees in the camps along the stream are not yet reconciled to this change of policy. They continue to tell canoeists that they are trespassing.

[ 200 ]

In contacts with landowners and with the game clubs that lease large corporate timberlands, I found that liability was often cited as a reason for excluding canoeists. On consulting the state's General Obligations Law, I noted a provision that protects from liability any landowner who permits certain recreational activities on his property. He is not responsible for keeping his premises safe and cannot be held liable unless proved to have "malicious intent" to harm, a very hard thing to prove. Canoeing, however, was not specified among the permitted activities. So I asked the Assemblyman and Senator from my district to introduce an amendment adding "canoeing" to the list. This amendment was adopted in 1977, and for a brief period I hoped it would be effective in persuading landowners. The Adirondack Park Agency also hailed the amendment in a press release "as a major benefit to private landowners and recreational canoeists in the Park." But these hopes proved hollow.

The river of top priority on my list was the South Branch of the Grass, all forty miles of which inside the park were posted. The largest tract was owned by the St. Regis Paper Company (later Champion International) and leased to game clubs, the largest of which is the Twin Falls Club. Correspondence with the secretary of this club elicited just one reason, liability, for refusal to open the waterway to the public. Armed now with the 1977 amendment, I addressed another request to the officers. Several months passed without a reply. Finally I drove to the clubhouse off the Tooley Pond Road to question the caretaker. Yes, my letter had been received and considered. But now a host of other reasons were offered for opposing public navigation—littering, breaking into hunting cabins, overnight camping, careless camp fires, rowdy behavior; in short, canoeists were painted as vandals and roughnecks unworthy of any privileges. The real reason, as I came to realize from this and other contacts, was desire for absolute privacy. One completely honest landowner admitted this; he did not seem to know that under common law there is a public easement on all rivers navigable in fact.

My file of correspondence on restricted rivers, rights of passage, acquisition of river corridors or easements dates from August 1969 to the present (1991) and is several inches thick. The first letter is simply a request for DEC regulations on recreational use of rivers. The answer by the then superintendent of land acquisition formed the basis for part of the preface to my canoeing guide. As I became better acquainted with the great extent to which canoeing had been curtailed in the park, I found it hard to restrain a sense of outrage reflected in a letter of December 13, 1972, to J.O. Preston, director of lands and forests in the Albany DEC office.

Dear Mr. Preston:

Thank you for your letter of December 6 on Adirondack canoe routes closed to the public. I welcome your assurance that canoe travel will be one of the factors considered in establishing a priority list of properties desirable for easement rights or full fee title.

The manager of a large private park on which there is a restricted river tells me, "The state can do whatever it wants to." I hope he is right, for the sake of restoring to public use the "paradise of waters" that Adirondack Murray and contemporaries were able to enjoy. There is a precedent in such established canoe carries over private land as the Marion River, Raquette Lake to Forked Lake, Raquette Falls, Bear Pond to Upper St. Regis Lake, etc., not to mention numerous fishing rights easements on other rivers. There has been a tremendous growth of interest in canoeing in recent years. A camp owner near the foot of Long Lake counted sixty-six canoes passing downstream in a five-hour period of an August day last summer, headed for the outlet. If other rivers besides the Moose-Raquette-Saranac were open, some of this congestion might be relieved, and canoeists would get a fairer break.

When I tell friends from New England or the Midwest that long navigable reaches of Adirondack rivers are closed to the public, they are incredulous. Indeed, it is hard to explain why rivers once declared public highways for commerce are not now open for recreation. And this in a state park. Is New York so crassly materialistic that it can't provide to mild-mannered canoeists the same riparian rights that it gave log drivers, who made a mess of the shores?...

My subsequent letters, I hope, show some moderation in tone and sophistication. From the bulk of this correspondence I quote the following selected excerpts:

September 10, 1975

Mr. F. M. La Duc, Land Development Manager
St. Regis Paper Company

In April this year the Adirondack Mountain Club published my guide, *Adirondack Canoe Waters: North Flow*. Preparations are under way for a revised printing. I would like to say that canoeing opportunities have improved in the northwest sector of the park. Because of the gentleness of the northwest slope, this is the best cruising area, suitable for novice as well as expert. At the same time, however, it is the region with the greatest number of blockages to navigation....

The St. Regis Paper Company, through its lessees, is a major factor in restricting public canoeing in the northwest: 1) a 16.5-mile segment of the South Branch of the Grass from Route 3 to Newbridge on the Tooley Pond Road....Your lessee in the town of Clare refuses to open carries around Brumagin Rapids and Copper Rock Falls; 2) 11.5 miles of the Middle Branch of the St. Regis in the town of Waverly....; 3) 15 miles of the Deer River from the Red Tavern Road to the Deer River State Forest....

In much of the United States riverbeds to the high water mark are in the public domain, or carry easements are established by custom or prescription. The chairman of the canoe guidebook of Appalachian Mountain Club tells me that in all six New England states carries on all rivers are established by custom. Most Americans take right of passage on navigable rivers for granted. It comes as a shock to them to learn that private owners in the Adirondacks prevent passage by posting the carries....

I hope that the St. Regis Paper Company will see fit to reserve public right of passage in negotiating future leases on the above-mentioned rivers....

Mr. La Duc's answer was noncommittal. Several years later, however, St. Regis Paper did open the Deer River on condition that the Adirondack Mountain Club assume liability. Three of us members of the Laurentian Chapter of ADK were allowed to brush out carry trails around rapids and falls. This arrangement lasted for two years until liability insurance rates were so greatly increased that the Club withdrew from the agreement and the Deer River was again closed.

June 3, 1978

Commissioner Peter A. A. Berle
NYS Department of Environmental Conservation

This letter is a follow-up to our luncheon conversation on May 25 at the Camp Topridge conference on Cultural Heritage in the Wilds. A substantial part of that heritage is exploration by small boat. Adirondack writings of the nineteenth century are eloquent on the amenities of this mode of travel. "The novel and romantic peculiarity of this wilderness," wrote W. H. H. Murray in 1869, "is its marvelous water communication....One can travel in a canoe or light boat for hundreds of miles in all directions through the forest."

Murray's small-boat waters have suffered drastic contraction in the twentieth century....Many reaches of Adirondack rivers are locked up in private parks and corporate timberlands leased to game clubs. Though there is no title to running water, state regulations make it possible for landowners and lessees to prevent access to a navigable stream and to deny passage by posting carry trails at waterfalls, dams, and heavy rapids or by prohibiting use of the riverbed (usually in private ownership in New York State) for tracking a boat through shoals.

Restoring the waterways to the public is fundamental to preserving the cultural heritage of the Adirondacks. Moving waters carve museum galleries through the forest in which landforms and the community of plant, animal, and bird life are on display as nowhere else.

Canoeists and kayakers are a growing portion of recreationists. Many of them find more hospitable reception elsewhere than in the Adirondacks: Algonquin

[ 203 ]

Park, the West, the Boundary Waters, the New England states....Wisconsin is forthright in guaranteeing public rights to waterways. From an attorney attached to the Department of Natural Resources, James Christenson, I have this statement: "The navigable waters are held in trust by the State for the public to guarantee and safeguard their right to enjoy all incidents of navigation. Such incidents include but are not limited to boating, fishing, hunting, and swimming."

When lumbering was the principal industry, Adirondack rivers were declared public highways for log driving. Now that tourism and recreation are the principal industries, perhaps it is time to declare Adirondack rivers public highways for small-boat travel. Right of passage includes, at a minimum, access to a river and use of the riverbed and foreshore to the extent necessary for navigation....

I am attaching a list of canoeable north-flow streams that are either inaccessible or blocked at one or more points by posted carries; also a list of river corridors selected for their outstanding character and promise of early practicability for purchase.


October 29, 1979

Mr. Norman VanValkenburgh, Director of Lands and Forests
NYS Department of Environmental Conservation

I should like to urge that you reconsider state purchase of part or all of the Paul Smith's College tract in the town of Piercefield....I am not alone in putting a high value on this segment of the Raquette, which, if publicly owned, would insure right of passage on a continuous 114-mile canoe route from Raquette headwaters to the Blue Line above South Colton. In the study of Adirondack rivers made by the Bureau of Outdoor Recreation for potential inclusion in the federal system of wild and scenic rivers, this segment (extended to Carry Falls Reservoir) was one of only seven choices, as listed in a survey dated October 1975....

This is a long-established small-boat route, though in the present century right of passage has been denied under some owners. In the last century and early years of this, hotel guests at Gale's Pond View House and the Childwold Park House used to cruise this segment in guideboats and canoes. Hotel guides were skilled at running the rapids. An Assemblyman, Martin Ives, remarked of this route in the 1890s: "I will venture to say that there is no trip just like it in America, but when once enjoyed it will never be forgotten."...

The Temporary Study Commission singled out the Raquette below Piercefield as an example of what the state should do to extend recreational boating in the park. "There used to be more miles of canoe routes open to the public than there are today. Private landowners have denied access to several rivers and lakes once open to canoeists.... One prospective canoe route is the Raquette River downstream from Piercefield."

[ 204 ]

The opportunity to carry out this recommendation may not arise again for a long time if the Piercefield tract passes into the hands of another private owner.

The Piercefield tract did pass into the hands of another owner, the International Paper Company, which outbid the state by a few dollars an acre, and soon after boating on this route was again closed. Throughout the decade of the 1980s, having lost out once, the state has been negotiating with IP for sale at a much higher figure for either fee title or an easement in this river corridor. So far no final agreement has been reached.

January 30, 1981

Mr. H. D. Phillips, Woodlands Manager
Northern Timberlands Division, St. Regis Paper Company

Your advertisement in the Watertown *Daily Times* of January 29, "Serving Man and Nature," rings hollow to the canoeing fraternity. Locking up scenic, navigable streams is a queer way of serving man or man's place in nature. You permit your lessees to post the carries around waterfalls and heavy rapids and to prosecute "trespassers" (or threaten to do so), thus denying right of passage.

I believe that this practice is open to challenge in the courts or by state agencies. There is no title to running water in New York State, and state laws assert a public right to navigate inland waters. To quote the Navigation Law: "The right of navigation is a public right, belonging not to towns, villages, and cities as corporations but rather to all citizens in severalty" (Chap. 941, Art. 3, sec. 30, par. 1). The interpretation of this law is as follows: "Whatever the rights of the owner of lands bordering on or within the waters of a navigable river, they must yield when the powers of government are called into exercise for a general public benefit in the improvement of navigation."

As writer of a canoe guide to Adirondack waters, now in its third printing, I have been obliged to say that St. Regis Paper is ultimately responsible for closing to the public two of the finest cruising streams in the northeast Adirondacks: the Deer River in Franklin County below the Red Tavern Road and the South Branch of the Grass to Newbridge on the Tooley Pond Road. The Red Tavern Club and the Twin Falls Club post these routes. In addition, the Middle Branch of the St. Regis is posted in the town of Waverly through what I believe is your company's game club.

These acts show callousness to the public interest and belie the slogan of your ad. Timber companies in the Adirondacks were successful in the last century in getting the state legislature to declare public highways for logging practically all navigable streams. Now that your industry no longer uses them for that purpose, you might consider returning the favor to the public. A free will gesture would be

[ 205 ]

more in the spirit of your ad than a reluctant response to the pressures that, sooner or later, will be brought to bear.

Mr. Phillips replied that the company's policy of leasing was a justifiable one in that it helped to defray the carrying cost of timberland, especially the tax burden. The above-mentioned segment of the Deer River, however, was opened briefly to the public for two years, 1984–1985, through an agreement with the Adirondack Mountain Club.

July 31, 1984

Henry G. Williams, Commissioner
NYS Department of Environmental Conservation

Thank you for your letter of July 26 and your action in referring the question of canoeing rights to your General Counsel....I hope Counsel will address the issue of access within the highway right of way at bridges. Canoeists all over the country take for granted legal access at bridges on public roads as well as at parks. Many existing canoe routes in this state depend on bridge access alone. If they have to be scuttled, canoeists at least are not going, in the words of the song, to "love New York."

A DEC official in the Ray Brook office, Mr. Huyck, speaks of laws that limit use of the right of way to highway purposes alone, not transporting a canoe around bridges. I have looked in vain through the consolidated laws of New York for such a provision. The only thing I found that seems relevant (Transportation Law, Art. 2, par. 14-e) is that the commissioner of transportation is empowered to secure easements for a right of way providing multiple use. "Multiple use" would seem to include carrying a canoe around bridges, along with all the other uses motorists freely engage in, such as berrying, botanizing, changing a tire, snacking, napping, etc.....

Another point I hope Counsel will address is the need for clarification of DEC's question-and-answer folder on the Posting Law. It declares without qualification that a landowner may post "both lands and waters" against trespass. This leads many landowners to think that they "own" all waters, running as well as landlocked, and can therefore prevent navigation even on streams where there are no obstructions to require the use of the shore for carries. I have had several arguments with landowners and lessees over this point, though in this neck of the woods a recent county court ruling has disarmed them.*

---

*St. Lawrence County Court overturned a conviction for trespass on the West Branch of the St. Regis River on the ground that "the stream is not privately owned, neither [riparian owner] can be found to own the water flowing in front of the premises. A person boating on the water is, therefore, not a trespasser." *The People* v. *Waite*, 1979.

[ 206 ]

In my experience DEC personnel have shown an inclination to support riparian landowners in their claims of privacy over the public right of navigation. This tendency dates back to the last century. All waterways in the Adirondacks were open to boating till posting began in the late 1880s. E. R. Wallace's guidebooks from the 1870s through the 80s describe established small-boat routes on virtually all Adirondack rivers and even several minor streams such as Big Brook and Quebec Brook, both now closed to the public. A Forest Commission's annual report of the early 1890s blandly remarks that the Beaver River is the latest small-boat route to be closed to the public by posting. Yet at that time the Commission could have invoked the public right of navigation under common law, including the right of passage around obstructions by portages on the foreshore.

I have been obliged to report in my guidebook that more than half of the boating streams in the northern Adirondacks described by Wallace are today closed to the public in part or in whole....The Beaver River is still closed from a point below Lake Lila to the Stillwater. During negotiations for the recent purchase from the Webb heirs, the state was in a position to apply leverage to open a continuous canoe route on the Beaver. It could have been part of a traverse of the park from west to east by the Beaver, the Bog (also closed in its upper reaches), the Raquette, and the Saranac.

I admire the dedication of DEC officials and have many friends among them. But in one respect the Commission is less than sedulous—in safeguarding and extending public rights on navigable streams.

April 3, 1985

Henry G. Williams, Commissioner
NYS Department of Environmental Conservation

Thank you for forwarding a copy of your March 29th letter to George Davis. I am especially interested in the closing paragraphs affirming the Department's plans to upgrade existing canoe routes and develop new ones.

As for the general acquisitions policy, I am still inclined to agree with George that it is too narrow in scope....Though one man's opinion doesn't bear much weight, a recent purchase at a high figure seems questionable to me—the 88 acres of Camp Vigor in the town of Parishville. True, this inholding consolidates surrounding state land. But most of the purchase price went for an elaborate complex of buildings in an area of little natural scenic attraction. The small pond is isolated (not part of a chain), and the shores are featureless, like most of the surrounding preserve land. Some inholdings are vital for both the Department and the public, such as Buck Pond in the Five Ponds Wilderness—but not Camp Vigor and its expensive buildings.

To balance accounts, I'd like to commend another recent purchase—the 650 acres of the 400 Club in the town of Clare. This opens a canoe route on the lower North Branch of the Grass, making possible a carry around Harper Falls. Last Saturday some whitewater friends of mine made this trip from the Clare Road and pronounced it one of the best.

Much of the upper Bog River or Bog River Flow, as it is called, a unique area which once harbored active golden eagle nests and may again, is up for sale. This would make an essential link in a chain of waters from west to east across the park if two other bottlenecks could be eliminated....

I am attaching a list of canoeable streams in the northern Adirondacks which are closed in part or entirely. Several years ago I sent this list to Commissioner Berle, who initiated the program you refer to.

State purchase of 9,248 acres on the Bog River Flow later in the year 1985 made a fitting celebration of the Forest Preserve Centennial and opened most of the headwaters of this river to the public. Several years later the state acquired from the International Paper Company a tract on the lower Bog and thus opened the entire river system except for one headwater pond. The Bog is not only an attractive waterway in itself but also valuable as a cross-grained link between watersheds.

June 28, 1986

Thomas E. Brown, Regional Director
NYS Department of Environmental Conservation
Watertown, New York

On June 19 three paddlers were ticketed for trespass at Newbridge on the Tooley Pond Road, town of Clare, St. Lawrence County. In three solo canoes they had put in at the bridge, paddled upstream a mile and a half to the foot of Copper Rock Falls on the South Branch of the Grass, and returned to take-out at the same bridge. There a forest ranger and a conservation officer were waiting for them. A third car drove off, probably driven by the caretaker of the Twin Falls Club, who regularly patrols the road. The paddlers explained their conception of legal access—the right of way on a public road.

R. W. Matzell, the conservation officer (who is also a member of the Twin Falls Club), told them that the right of way on the Tooley Pond Road is limited to the blacktop. Since this seemed unlikely to the young men, they questioned the county Highway Department. They were told that the right of way is standard for a town road and that in the early 1960s, when Newbridge was relocated, a wide strip had been purchased from the St. Regis Paper Company, now Champion International.

If the Clare justice finds them guilty of trespass when they appear before him on July 10, I am going to urge them to appeal. A ruling on bridge access on town,

[ 208 ]

county, and state roads is needed. Canoeists across the country assume that they have this right. In my experience some DEC officials deny it. If such access is illegal, many, probably a majority, of the canoe routes of the state would be eliminated.

The three paddlers, led by Chris Angus, did appeal their conviction by the Clare justice, who fined them $25 apiece. The St. Lawrence County Court overturned the conviction, ruling that there was a failure at the trial to prove beyond a reasonable doubt that the paddlers were trespassing on private property. This was not the comprehensive ruling I had hoped for, affirming the right to carry around bridges on public roads. But the case became celebrated in the press and in two documentary films and may have influenced the DEC to change policy.

July 1, 1988

Governor Mario M. Cuomo
Executive Chambers, State Capitol

I wish to urge that the state purchase the 96,000 acres, in detached parcels, currently offered for sale by Diamond International. All of this land is in or adjacent to the northwestern sector of the Adirondack Park. It includes boreal spruce-fir forests in four river corridors. If the state loses this opportunity, the land will fall into the hands of a developer or a consortium, as has already happened to Diamond holdings liquidated in Vermont and New Hampshire.

As writer of a canoeing guide to the Adirondacks, I represent the interests of public recreation in the park. In the northwestern sector twenty navigable rivers and streams are wholly or partly closed to public access and passage, although this is the best region of the park for river cruising....

A directive from your office is important in an emergency like this. Many of us have concluded that the DEC is inclined to favor private over public interests in the park, in its endless delays, its refusal to use the power of eminent domain, and historically in its failure, under common-law prescription, to keep all Adirondack waterways open to navigation, as they were from the arrival of the first tourists in 1840 to about 1890. Although the park was created in 1892 for "the free use of all the people for their health and pleasure," this is the situation today: Many rivers rising in the park are closed to navigation, whereas the same streams are fully open once they cross the Blue Line. This is a major frustration to those of us who prefer beaver dams to barbed wire fences, whitetail to holstein country.

The state failed to act in time to purchase the Diamond International land, and the entire 96,000 acres fell into the hands of a developer, Lassiter Properties of Atlanta. This disaster, however, had its good side. Public outrage was so great that

[ 209 ]

Governor Cuomo made two decisions, one to negotiate with Lassiter for a substantial portion of the tracts it had just bought and the other to establish a commission on the Adirondacks. Late in the same year the state announced the purchase from Lassiter of fee title or easements of 55,000 acres, at $18 an acre more than Lassiter had paid originally. This purchase opened a segment of the Middle Branch of the Oswegatchie to canoeists and made access to the Jordan River easier.

## XIX  THE COMPREHENSIVE WAY

BY 1988, AFTER EIGHTEEN YEARS of slow progress in opening a river segment here or there through purchase or persuasion, I concluded that legislation was the better way to go for the many rivers still under restrictions. In an article in the May-June issue of *Adirondack Life*, "Rights of Passage," I wrote: "The quickest and most effective solution would be legislation to bring clarity into the confusing, inconsistent mixture of common law, statutory law, and case decisions concerning inland navigation." This, my fifth magazine article on the subject, may have had some influence in rallying the support that now became manifest. Others more skilled than I at legal analysis, lobbying, and propagandizing through two documentary films that were aired statewide joined in the campaign and pushed it to what now (summer of 1991) is the verge of a comprehensive resolution through passage of a rivers bill before the state legislature, adoption of new regulations by the DEC based on a policy change, or both.

July 26, 1988

From Charles C. Morrison, Director
Land Resources Planning, DEC, Albany
Dear Paul:

I want you to know that your continuing efforts to re-open Adirondack rivers to public navigation are appreciated. I am attempting to pursue this again in the Department from a couple of directions. As you may recall, I started to do this in the early 1980s but there was a feeling then that all such rights had to be purchased, one by one. A lot has happened since then with respect to the public trust doctrine and I think that there is a greater receptivity currently. Also, there is some interest in the Legislature in this subject.

August 1, 1988

Charles C. Morrison, DEC, Albany
Dear Charlie:

Many thanks for your encouraging letter of July 26 about public navigation on Adirondack rivers. I am glad that you are back on the job of promoting this.

Legislation would certainly be the quickest and most effective way. It would have to come over the determined opposition of North Country legislators, who consistently support private over public interests in the park, as do some DEC officials in regional offices.

It seems that for every gain (such as Bog River Flow) there is a loss somewhere else. The latest threat concerns a popular whitewater run on the Saranac between the bridge on the Silver Lake Road and Clayburg. In 3.5 miles the river drops off the plateau in sustained, challenging rapids. Paddlers come from out of state to run this. It is extraordinarily attractive because the volume of water usually remains adequate well into summer. Lately landowners at the bridge have posted the four corners and say they are combining to engage an attorney to support their contention that, since each of them owns to the center of the bridge, a paddler carrying around the bridge is a trespasser. (I own to the center of Jay Street but can't halt traffic.) Canoeists across the country assume that they have the right of access at bridges on public roads. A DEC official at Ray Brook denies this....

January 20, 1989

From John A. Humbach, Professor of Law and
Associate Dean, Pace University

Mr. Charles Morrison at DEC suggested to me that you might like to have a copy of my survey *Public Rights in the Navigable Streams of New York*. In it, I have attempted to provide a comprehensive resource for anyone doing legal research on stream-bed ownership and the public right of passage on navigable fresh waters.

I have for many years admired your writings for and on behalf of the paddling community. I hope that you will find the enclosed to be interesting and useful.

January 25, 1989

John A. Humbach, School of Law, Pace University
Dear Professor Humbach:

Thank you very much for the copy of your survey *Public Rights*. It is considerably more comprehensive than the previous surveys that have come to my attention. Chapters 4, 5, and 6 are especially pertinent to problems in the Adirondacks. I hope that your book will be widely circulated among DEC personnel in the regional offices, legislators, and large private landowners in the park.

Your study reënforces my conviction that what we need, instead of the welter of case decisions, with their lacunae and inconsistencies, is a statute spelling out the right to use the bed and foreshore for passage on an otherwise navigable stream. As I read Chapter 4, there is ample ground for such a statute.

Thanks again for your excellent study.

The DEC had requested this analysis by Professor Humbach, who is himself a canoeist. Issuance of this study was a turning point. Its influence in the Albany

[ 212 ]

office of the DEC and among legislators was very great, as the following letter testifies.

February 27, 1989

From Charles C. Morrison

Dear Paul:

John's report has met with great enthusiasm at the highest levels within DEC and we are taking initial steps to establish policy direction, begin a program of public education on this issue that will include recreationists, landowners, enforcement officers and the courts, and submit legislation.

We will follow up with the Division of Fish and Wildlife on the DEC folder on the posting law. You have been calling that to our attention for years and we have done nothing about it because we didn't have the legal analysis we needed on this issue. With John's report in hand and considering the high level support by the Commissioner and other top officials in DEC, I feel that we finally have the basis for ensuring this will be corrected.

John's research conclusion is that a "public servitude or easement, in effect" exists on *all* rivers which are navigable in fact (as contrasted with those which have been declared by law to be navigable). This servitude or easement is held in trust by the State. John says no private landowner may extinguish this easement by taking adverse possession, no matter how long the rights have been unused. (It would be like claiming adverse possession for land occupied by a State highway.)

Further, in the process of exercising the rights associated with this easement, a person who is traveling on a river that is navigable in fact not only may walk, pole or line his vessel through a rapid but also may carry around the rapid or around any obstacle in the river, such as a dam, and this may be done either above the mean high water mark or below it. Also, if a river is not navigable in some reaches and navigable in others that does not preclude the entire river from being navigable in fact. Nor is a river that is navigable only seasonally excluded from being navigable in fact.

I believe I have stated John's conclusions correctly. At least I have not heard anyone with any legal understanding of the issue refute him on these points.

We fully agree with you about the need for State legislation which will reaffirm the existence of these public rights. We are working on this, probably as an amendment to the Navigation Law.

If we make the final breakthroughs on this issue, much of the credit will belong to you for keeping after it for so long and so effectively. You have been my conscience on navigation rights ever since I got your message in the Northwest Flow guide....

All best wishes. Keep the faith.

[ 213 ]

July 29, 1989

Honorable Ronald Stafford
New York State Senate

My research has shown that the Adirondacks is the one area of the Northeast where many navigable rivers are closed, in part or in whole, to public navigation. All New England rivers have been open to both commercial and recreational travel since Colonial times. This is also true in most of New York State. And from 1840, when the first tourists began arriving, to about 1890 it was true in the Adirondacks as well. Since then private landowners have arrogated to themselves, with the oversight or complicity of state agencies, exclusive use of many river segments, though there is no title to running water. In two cases, the West Branch of the St. Regis and the South Branch of the Grass, the entire 40-mile reach of each river inside the Blue Line is closed to public navigation.

A bill recently introduced in the Assembly (No. 8334) and the Senate (No. 5985) would guarantee public travel on navigable streams. Though it does not give paddlers the right to cross private property to gain access or exit, it does insure right of passage once one is legally on a stream. Right of passage is the major problem in the Adirondacks, where necessary portages are posted against trespass.

This bill puts in statutory form public rights of navigation under common law. It is based on an exhaustive study of common law and case law, *Public Rights in the Navigable Streams of New York* (1989), by John A. Humbach, professor of law at Pace University...

I hope that you will use your considerable influence in the Senate to bring Bill 5985 to the floor and that you will be able to support it, without crippling amendments. I would welcome your views on this issue. Though not a voter in your district, may I presume on a slight acquaintance dating from your student days at SLU?

Senator Stafford, deputy majority leader in the Senate, replied that he shared my views and would support the bill. In 1990, after the Rivers Bill passed the Assembly, it was held up in the Senate. Senator Stafford believed, as did others, that certain amendments were needed, especially concerning the matter of liability. The Rivers Bill never reached the floor of either body during the 1991 session because of a prolonged hassle over the budget. But it is still very much alive.

January 2, 1990

Mr. David L. Newhouse, President
Association for the Protection of the Adirondacks

When the Association for the Protection of the Adirondacks moved to broaden its membership a few years ago, I joined in the hope that it would broaden its

[ 214 ]

policy positions to reflect public interests even when they diverged from private ones. Historically, it has represented wealthy private landowners and clubs. It has performed good service in preserving the integrity of the Forest Preserve, and to that extent it has served the public interest. But there are areas of conflict.

When the Summer 1989 issue of the *Association News* strongly endorsed the Rivers Bill (A. 8334 / S. 5985) now before the Legislature, I took this as vindication of broadened policies. The Fall/Winter issue, however, backtracks in ambiguous language equivalent to little or no support for the bill. One clause is clearly at variance with the facts: "the landowners who hold fee title to the streams passing through their lands." In New York State there is no title to running water; the bed of a stream may be in private ownership but not the water flowing over it. The statement as a whole hedges by asking for clarification of existing law. Ample clarification has been available since January 1989 in the 69-page *Public Right of Passage on New York Waters* by John A. Humbach, professor of law at Pace University.

For a century the Adirondack League Club has prohibited public navigation on a major portion of the South Branch of the Moose. Now certain members of the Association representing this club or other private interests have formed an ad hoc committee to oppose rivers legislation and have engaged an attorney to challenge the constitutionality of the Rivers Bill. Robert Stern's memorandum contends that susceptibility to commercial, not recreational, traffic determines whether a river is navigable in fact. Professor Humbach has pointed out that this memorandum is faulty in overlooking many cases that have accepted recreational use as proof of navigability.

Furthermore, in his ignorance of Adirondack history, Attorney Stern entraps himself. Adirondack rivers in the last century were open to both recreational and commercial use. "The smallest streams, stretches of dried rocks in summer," writes W. C. White in *Adirondack Country*, "served to move logs in spring....In time every Adirondack river became a highway for logs." Alfred Donaldson's *History of the Adirondacks* corroborates: "Sending logs down narrow, rock-riven streams was first tried on the Schroon River....No sooner had this method been successfully tried than it came into general use and led to early legislation declaring certain rivers public highways....Every lake or stream of any size in the Adirondacks has probably played some part in the story of lumbering." It is conceivable that a severe gasoline shortage might once again bring these rivers into service for floating or rafting logs. At any rate, proof certainly exists that they are susceptible of such use.

Norman Van Valkenburgh, in his letter of October 5, 1989, addressed to you, makes some pertinent suggestions for verbal changes in the bill. But his bias toward the presumed rights of riparian owners is reflected in the sweeping statement, unsupported by specifics: "If the rights of the riparian landowners were not already at risk, they certainly are in these concluding sections of the bill. Clearly, these four sections, if implemented as written, constitute a taking of rights from the upland owner."

Historically, the "taking" is all on the other side. During most of the last century, all Adirondack waterways were open to both recreational and commercial use. About 1890 private landowners, with the acquiescence of state agencies, began posting river corridors and chain lakes and ponds, a practice that made a mockery of the founding principle of the Adirondack Park in 1892: "for the free use of all the people for their health and pleasure."

In common law there is a public easement on all rivers navigable in fact, and this easement is held in trust by the state. The state has the obligation to safeguard right of passage. I am informed by the chairman of the canoe guidebook committee of the Appalachian Mountain Club that no restrictions on navigable waterways exist in the New England States, where common law has prevailed to keep them open since aboriginal times, including the use of portages on private shores where necessary. Yet New York, alone in the Northeast, has permitted private owners to close all or parts of twenty navigable rivers in the Adirondacks.

Must New York canoeists continue to go to Maine for unhampered wilderness canoeing when we have an incomparable network of wilderness waterways at home? Is the Association for the Protection of the Adirondacks about to take a position inimical to the public interest?

Cc:  Governor Cuomo
      Peter Berle
      Thomas Jorling
      Norman Van Valkenburgh
      Charles Morrison
      Neil Woodworth


In a speech to the young at the New York State Fair Governor Cuomo is quoted as saying: "If you walk away from politics you get hurt. This is a system that punishes aloofness and rewards involvement. It is very much a system, frankly, where the squeaky wheel is apt to get the grease." Maybe the young people who heard him were as heedless as I would have been at their age. But the lesson has finally sunk in. I have done a lot of squeaking in the last twenty years. Enough of it has brought results to convince me that the Governor is right.

## XX  WHY OLD MEN WRITE AUTOBIOGRAPHIES

**M**OST OF US are solipsistic. We give little heed to the private worlds of others. Eleanor Brown is an exception. She has the art of making the Other feel authentic. She is a student of human nature and knows that the mainspring of an old man's happiness is vanity. If fame is the last infirmity of noble mind, vanity is the pervasive weakness of baser ones. It is the impulse that causes many old men, and women, to write autobiographies. Even those who try to conceal it usually fail. David Hume thought he could do so by limiting "My Own Life" to seven brisk pages. "It is difficult," he wrote, "for a man to speak long of himself without Vanity. Therefore I shall be short." But he is not short enough. Vanity flourishes in his last paragraph. Observing that failure in what may be the shortest of all autobiographies, I have been at no pains to write short. Let vanity hang out if it will. Eleanor Brown is right in taking it for a harmless peccadillo of old age. So she contributes to the sum of human happiness by a letter like the following.

July 10, 1988

Dear Paul—

I want to let you know how grateful we are to you for involving us with eskers—particularly with the old snowmobile route, now canoe carry, from Ochre to Fish Pond. We spent a lovely four-day Fourth of July weekend in the Saranac/St. Regis area, accompanied as always by your canoe guide and *now* by your *Pilgrimage* as well, and after some judicious pre-trip reading John [her husband, a chemist with General Electric] decided the Little Clear/St. R. Pond/Ochre/Fish trip was the one we shouldn't miss—and we're delighted we didn't! My spirits were down briefly, as we were bushwhacking around Ochre through the usual jungle-cum-insects (it was hot and we wanted to avoid the two long carries and *both* enjoy the esker!)—but first, we came on the rusty-colored spring (diagnosed by John as due to iron-oxidizing bacteria) that could have given Ochre its name, and then, of course, we hit your beautiful giant-tree-clad ridge, and I would have gone through many jungles to see that! Not a soul at Fish Pond—only a few canoes on St. Regis Pond (& two bicyclists—they'd come in on the fire truck trail)—but several loons and myriad mergansers. We swam in St. Regis P. en route back without a soul in sight.

We also tried out the new Hitchins Pond/Bog River route as far as Lows Lake, which you have been promoting for so long. Don't you have an enormous feeling of satisfaction in seeing this great ground-swell in most of the Adirondack conservation groups toward reopening the canoe routes you've recommended? I do think ADK's present conservation chairman is the ideal person to be spearheading the political side of this effort, following your terrific job in setting the stage and bringing the possibilities to public attention. Neil Woodworth is savvy, energetic, and such a devoted canoeist himself that the cause is one of pure joy for him. With a little luck (i.e., cooperation from NYS) I think great things will happen! You keep bowing to Wallace [author of a nineteenth century guide to Adirondack waters] about these routes—but the other movers and shakers bow mainly in the direction of Jay Street, Canton! Affectionately, Eleanor

Of course, there are qualitative gradations in the centers of vanity. Rousseau wrote three volumes of his *Confessions* to show how different (*autre*) he was from other men, and that difference loomed large over the next hundred years of the Romantic Movement, producing all manner of aberrations in life and literature in contrast to the stuffy Age of Reason. My vanity rests on lesser consequences. It rests on four little things: 1) having got Everton Falls and Lampson Falls into the public domain; 2) calling attention to the one-hundred-year-old locking up of Adirondack waterways from the public and having some influence in righting this injustice; 3) bringing eskers into the consciousness of Adirondack recreationists; and 4) contributing to Adirondack letters, where competition is not severe enough to dwarf my three books. Compared to Rousseau's worldwide influence on posterity, these quadrilateral achievements are pea sized. But vanity helps to magnify them. Forest recreation, I tell myself, is the key to the American heritage, and anything that promotes it is good for Americans. As a young man I was a Europhile. Through forest recreation I have come all the way home to America.

I got involved with eskers in the 1970s. By that time I had climbed all the mountains I wanted to, except for an occasional repeat, and was looking for tramping ground more suitable to advancing age yet unkempt enough for the bushwhacking I was reluctant to give up. I was also engaged in scouting canoe waters, and eskers often parallel watercourses. These ridges are at most 150 feet tall in the Adirondacks (the Five Ponds one) from base and often much less. But they meander engagingly from side to side like a curvaceous stream and soar and dip like a roller coaster at the fair. They are beloved of the whitetailed deer, which beats out paths on their crests. Scats at lookout points serve as trail markers in summer; in winter, deep troughs in the snow, along with the occasional imprint of

*Rainbow Lake Esker dividing the waters (photo Bradford Van Diver)*

a siesta-taking deer on a south-facing slope where direct rays of the sun serve as an electric blanket. I share with the whitetail an affinity for eskers.

So did Verplanck Colvin, Adirondack surveyor, though he didn't know their origin or their name. "This ridge [between Rock Pond and the outlet of Sand Lake] by the way, was one of those long narrow dunes which had so interested and perplexed me in the Bog River section....Open and picturesque with superb white pine trees here and there upon it, with numerous deer paths deeply stamped, leading through its carpeting of moss and whortleberry bushes, the beautiful lake on one side and the shallow winding river on the other, made it far more entrancing than the choicest ramble of guarded park." Even before Colvin wrote that passage in 1878, Louis Agassiz was in America explaining the latest findings on glacial geology. Colvin apparently hadn't read Agassiz' article on eskers in Maine in the *Atlantic Monthly* a decade earlier. It would have dispelled his perplexity about this landform.

An esker is a long, narrow, winding ridge of sand, gravel, cobbles, and even small boulders with edges rounded by being trundled down a swift subglacial stream. Eskers were laid down during the wasting process of the last ice cap about twelve thousand years ago. They were formed in stream tunnels at the edge of the ice mass; or the straighter ones may have originated in crevasse fillings. They can be single, double, or triple, like the braided channels of a river. And they are often undulating like a riverbed. Some have tributaries. They range in length from a tenth of a mile to ten miles or more. The longest, somewhat discontinuous, is eighty-five miles long and crosses the Adirondacks from the North Branch of the Saranac River to the Beaver River in the west. Geologist Buddington calls it the "Adirondack Esker."

In the 1970s I fell in love with this landform, so widespread in the central and northwestern areas of the park. The closest is only six miles south of Canton, and they become numerous in such glacial outwash plains as Massawepie Park, the area between the Oswegatchie and the Beaver rivers, and the Paul Smiths area. I introduced them to my hiking companions, a few of whom also became addicted. One reason they fascinate me is that they are so much like rivers, the subglacial streams that laid them down. They are rivers solidified, turned bottoms up, concave to convex. A second reason is the forest cover they bear, especially in places undisturbed by loggers. Their mineral soil and sunny exposure make them ideal habitat for pine, both white and red, the most magnificent tree of our Northeastern forests. Here and there, on the Cranberry Lake, the Five Ponds, the St. Regis, the Osgood River eskers, are aisles of pine trees as old as the Forest Preserve or older. An object of my rambles was to locate these stands. And a third reason is a kind of proprietary right I have to celebrate this landform because a St. Lawrence University professor was the first geologist to show how prevalent eskers are in the Adirondacks and to map them.

George H. Chadwick published his article "Adirondack Eskers" in the December 30, 1928, issue of the *Bulletin of the Geological Society of America*. His findings remained buried in the files of that scholarly journal for fifty years till I unearthed them in an article with the same title for the November-December 1978 issue of *Adirondack Life*, reprinted in my book *Adirondack Pilgrimage*. The article reproduced Chadwick's map of some eighty eskers. Topographical maps of today are more accurate than those available to Chadwick, and it has become possible to identify many more than those known to him. At least a dozen additional ones have come to my notice through map reading, scouting on the ground, or hearsay from an esker friend, Michael Kudish of Paul Smith's College, whose survey of the vascular plants of the Adirondacks necessarily obliges him to pay attention to soils and therefore eskers. I am certain many others will be found, including those of low elevation (twenty feet or less) not apparent in map reading.

Natives used to call these ridges "hogbacks," "horsebacks," "serpent ridges," or, like Colvin, "sand dunes." Now Adirondackers are calling them by their standard name, the Gaelic word for "ridge," first suggested in the 1860s. Bringing "esker" into the popular language of the region, as my article and my canoe guide seem to have done, and getting people "involved with eskers," as Eleanor Brown puts it, are not much to pride oneself on unless one values this landform as much as I do and enjoys speculating on the subglacial streams that formed them deep in the ice mass of that landscape architect.

Four years after my retirement, in 1969, Frank Piskor became president of St. Lawrence. My relations with him over the next twelve years of his presidency were naturally distant but wholly agreeable. He

*Mary (sister) on a Massawepie esker, 1991*

was deeply interested in the Adirondacks. In 1971 he initiated annual conferences on the Adirondack Park in the pleasant setting of the University camp complex on Upper Saranac Lake, Camp Canaras. Vice President Allen Splete organized and chaired the conferences. The speeches and other proceedings were taped and then transcribed, rather inexpertly, by Splete's secretaries. For the next several years I edited these transcripts for publication.

At the Homecoming ceremony in October, 1974 the University awarded me its North Country Citation for "achievements and services in the field of Adirondack Literature and Environment." Six years later at Convocation in September, 1980, I received the honorary degree of Doctor of Humane Letters. Helen Ellison, a former student of mine and of Ruth's (known as Aitchie in her undergraduate days) and then a trustee of the University, "presented" me to the Dean and President.

When Dr. Piskor retired in 1981, his friends and associates were asked to write memorial letters. I was happy to write the following letter because of the splendid new library erected under his regime. The Piskors are still living in Canton, and I have frequent chats with them on my afternoon walks, for they take the same route.

May 11, 1981

Dear Frank and Anne:

Ruth and I had retired from the faculty several years before you and Anne came to Canton. Our view of your administration is therefore detached from the daily flux of campus life and even from some of the big events and achievements of the last twelve years. It is a composite of significant trivia: hearing from Helen Ellison after your appointment what wonderful people you are and how lucky St. Lawrence was going to be; attending one of your informal talks on Robert Frost before a circle of students in a residence hall; meeting Canton's most happily

[ 221 ]

married couple, arm in arm, on evening walks or cultivating a flower bed on the village green; sharing in the collective embrace of genial hosts at the Christmas dinners for faculty; hearing your recent talk on the adventures of a book collector; and your visiting my home to tell me of the honorary degree.

You are an offprint collector too. Going through files a couple of years ago, I came across a letter from the desk of the vice president for academic affairs at Syracuse University, dated August 27, 1962, and signed "Frank Piskor." It was a request for an offprint of my article on Robert Frost as a mountain poet.

At the time I turned up this letter the new library was nearing completion. This conjunction pointed up the paradox of a man hard enough to raise large sums for the University and soft enough to love American poetry to the extent of tracking down its most obscure critic.

To an emeritus, the outstanding tangible memorial of these twelve years is the most seductive of college libraries. It has lured me back into scholarly habits and seems to be having similar effects on students.

The intangible memorial is the humane spirit with which you have imbued the campus and the community.

**B**AD THINGS HAPPEN to good people, a soap psychiatrist on TV assures those who want to think well of themselves in spite of adverse fortune. I prefer to take the truth about a contingent world without the soap but in the suggestive imagery of "Dover Beach."

> ...we are here as on a darkling plain
> Swept with confused alarms of struggle and flight,
> Where ignorant armies clash by night.

Yet Ruth and I were not prepared for the affliction that overtook us in the last five years of her life: Ruth, because she had some remnants of faith in providence left over from family years; I, because I had grown accustomed to an extraordinarily long run of good luck that I wore like a habit, as if a truce had been called between those ignorant armies of the night. Our marriage had been happy. We had mutual interests. We enjoyed each other's company. We had had rewarding careers, without separation, in the same institution. In retirement the good times continued with a sharing of travel, music, literature, art, friends, and the presence of a winsome cat in the house. Ruth took up sketching and watercoloring. A few of her paintings side by side with our Robert Plumbs do not suffer by comparison. She continued expert knitting for hospital and church bazaars. Her sweaters were much in demand. Though she was not strong enough to join me on hikes and paddles, she enjoyed drives through the Adirondacks, picnics on shorelines, and sketching from the car window while I took short turns in the woods. Year after year the good days succeeded one another as if we had some charmed immunity from the slings and arrows of outrageous fortune. America provides a favorable milieu for relative immunity with its two great shielding oceans and a fair playing field for individual fulfillment. Even so, things can go terribly wrong.

The affliction was almost imperceptible at first but grew in virulence for five years. Looking back now, I can trace the first signs of it to 1984 when Ruth, shopping at a supermarket, would forget where she had parked the car and fall into a kind of panic till a friend took her in hand and reminded her to look on her registration card for the license number. Then she had a small accident involving another car and decided to give up driving. At first I thought these were normal symptoms of aging. But other signs of dementia followed and grew in intensity. Parts of her life and personality slipped away one by one, not to be recovered. She ceased reading, sketching, painting in watercolors, doing the crossword puzzles in the Sunday New York *Times*, listening to music. Saturday afternoon opera broadcasts on public radio became noise to her and she wanted them turned off. Knitting was a last resort. For three years following 1984 she was seldom without a knitting needle and yarn. But she finished no single piece. After completing two or three inches, she would discover a mistake and either unravel all she had done or discard the fragment. I joked that she was Penelope, holding off suitors by unraveling by night all she had done by day. Then in the last two years she gave up knitting altogether and simply passed the idle hours sitting in the blue velvet chair across the living room from where I was reading. By this time she could no longer do her share of household chores but surrendered them all to me. She forgot how to dress conventionally and how to care for her person.

Most distressing was her loss of the past we had shared. What few memories remained were of her early life and even those were inaccurate, as I knew from her earlier confidences. I came to realize how much personality depends on one's past, on the accumulation and recall of experience. Ruth's personality disintegrated, the richness of her being slipped away.

In the last year she became irritable. We had never had a serious quarrel till now, when she fought against the medical attention I insisted she have. Each trip to the doctor or dentist was a crisis heightened by long waits in the outer office. "Why am I here?" she kept reiterating.

By the fall of 1986 it was clear that Ruth was suffering from Alzheimer's disease. Her doctor had screened out the other possibilities for which some remedial measures can be taken. For Alzheimer's no cause or remedy was known. I read books and pamphlets about it, and they enabled me to cope with the affliction a little better than I could otherwise have done and to keep Ruth at home. She had never passed a single night in hospital in the fifty-eight years of our marriage till the last night of her life. On the night of September 14–15, 1989, she had a stroke, and the next day she was unable to stand or walk unassisted. I summoned her doctor. It was evening before he was free to come. After examining her, he pronounced it a mild stroke. The effects would pass, he thought, with a few days of rest in hospital. I called an ambulance and followed it to the Potsdam hospital. After seeing Ruth comfortably installed in a private room with a nurse in attendance and promising to return next day, I left. I was soon to regret not having spent the night by her side, for next morning at seven, September 16, the doctor on duty phoned to tell me that Ruth had died that morning and that attempts to resuscitate her had failed. She was two months beyond her eighty-eighth birthday.

Once the initial shock passed, I could not grieve. For the next few days it was relief I felt that the long ordeal was over for both of us. But soon after, and still now twenty months later, my head bent over a book in the evening, I have a sense of her presence and of my need for it and that if I looked up and across the room to the blue velvet chair, there she would be reading some book in French, perhaps Colette, whom she loved, or knitting a baby sweater for a bazaar, all intact— memory, sensibilities, *esprit clair*.

Ruth had ceased to be herself before she died. The gradual loss of her companionship over five years eased the transition to living alone, except for my aging Himalayan cat. By nature I am self-sufficient, a defect from one point of view, a boon when circumstance leaves no choice.

It is now a delightful spring in 1991. May has always been my favorite season in the North Country, and this year it is near perfection. One fine day recently I drove to the Cranberry Lake vicinity to meet Don Morris and to flag a new carry trail from the South Branch of the Grass River to Highway 3 so that paddlers could bypass a mile or more of shallow rapids. Entering the woods beyond Sunday Rock, I had a renewed sense of well being, a surge of joy at being alive. At higher elevations along Highway 56 spring was a week more retarded than in Canton. The canopy was a harmony of pastel color—pale green, yellow, mauve, pink—as leaf buds, catkins, and flowers unfurled. At the edge of the woods shadbush and witchhobble were in bloom, just as they were sixty years ago when I first visited these woods and as they will be for future generations. It is said that though space lets us return, time does not. Yet in May woods my sixty Adirondack years are as one. Past is present, and present, future as the wheel of the seasons turns to shadbush and witchhobble bloom and canopy of pastels.

Even in world affairs the 1990s is a good time to be alive. Just how fortunate we are in this decade I realized in reading the three volumes of Harold Nicolson's diaries and letters. His life spanned the first sixty-eight years of the century. "What turmoil I have lived in since 1914!" he wrote in 1954. The turmoil continued through most of the 1980s in the Cold War and various hot spots in this troubled, violent century. In 1948 Harold Nicolson and his political friends debated the desirability of a preventive war while America had the atomic bomb and the Soviet Union not quite yet. Opinion then was that as soon as Stalinist Russia had nuclear capability it would embark on world conquest; it would destroy Western Europe, then occupy Asia, and finally provoke a death struggle with the United States. Though this outcome seemed probable to Nicolson, he argued against a preventive war. It might be, he admitted, that such a war would be successful and usher in a Pax Americana, an admirable thing to contemplate. But the outcome remained doubtful. There was just a frail chance—"not one [chance] in ninety. To make war in defiance of that one chance is to commit a crime. A preventive war is always evil. Let us rather die." Such was the state of desperation among well-informed Western Europeans and some Americans in the middle decades of the century.

Well, Nicolson's one frail chance is now a reality. The Cold War is over and done with. And in Desert Storm, a short war conducted with surgical precision, the United States confirmed its role as administrator of a Pax Americana. We still have lessons of restraint and wisdom to learn. But the spectacle now is that of a worldwide movement toward peace, democracy, and human rights. In a contingent world things sometimes work out for the best. The 1990s promise to be a good time to spend one's last years in.

World affairs I leave to my friend Bernie Lammers. My endeavors are in the narrow sphere of the Adirondacks, this land I love for what it can do for the spirit. Here too things are going well for the solace of an old man. Just yesterday, May 30, I received from my friend Charles Morrison in the Albany office of the DEC the copy of a directive to all offices and personnel of the agency that at one stroke puts to rights an injustice of a century's duration, the locking up of Adirondack rivers by private interests. I still hope that the Rivers Bill will pass in the near future. But the DEC directive accomplishes all that the Rivers Bill is designed to do and perhaps more, in that it contemplates a role for the DEC in enforcing the public right of navigation against private owners who attempt to prevent it; it is a public nuisance for a landowner to obstruct, annoy, or hinder the right of passage on navigable waters.

This new DEC policy must still be tested in the courts. I am confident about the outcome. I expressed that confidence in the following essay on the future of the Adirondacks which I wrote early this month at the request of the Katonah Museum of Art as part of a 1992 celebration of the centennial founding of the Adirondack Park.


In 1990 Neal Burdick, editor of *Adirondac*, invited several people he considered qualified to respond to the question: What will be the greatest difference between the Adirondacks of today and of the year 2000? Ten responses brought ten different viewpoints. The fact that they differed so widely on a mere decade of change is a lesson in humility for anyone forecasting the next one hundred years. The Commission on the Adirondacks in the Twenty-first Century has rendered its report. Its 245 recommendations have now entered the realm of politics and compromise, the final results of which no one can confidently predict. Even if all major recommendations should be adopted, forces beyond state control, such as acid rain and the greenhouse effect, also impinge on the park. In view of all these variables, one is forced to a subjective opinion: Within the realm of probability, what kind of park would I, based on my own experience and values, like to survive into the twenty-first century?

I am an outsider. My experience over the last sixty-two years has been that of going in, year round, for a day, for a camping trip of several days, or, accompanied by my wife, just for a drive through the park and sojourn at a motor inn. My favorite recreations are observing nature, trail hiking, bushwhacking, snowshoeing, and canoeing. Once, when an attractively sited camp came on the market, I was strongly tempted to buy it. But on reflection I decided not to....

I prize the Adirondacks as a refuge of peace, serenity, and adventure. In this I believe I have much in common with the seventy million who live within a day's drive. Even those who never go in derive satisfaction from knowing the park exists, a remnant of our national heritage of wilderness. They want the Adirondacks to be as different as possible from the place where they earn a living.

There is a mystique about going in. It is symbolized on one entrance road by a large boulder known as Sunday Rock. For many generations the rock has been legendary as the division between two different worlds, the workaday, civilized one and the free, playful world of the

*Paul, 1989 (Photo Nathan Farb)*

great woods, where there are no obligations of a Sunday or any other day. Passing the rock, going in, is a ceremony of transition. We leave the world of linear time, which governs most of our lives in growing up, marrying, working for a living, raising children, growing old and dying. In linear time there is no return. But in the woods we can experience a brief immersion in the cyclical time of nature and the cosmos, "a playful spin." William Chapman White beautifully expresses this immersion in his *Adirondack Country*: "As a man tramps the woods to the lake he knows he will find pines and lilies, blue heron and golden shiners, shadows on the rocks and the glint of light on the wavelets, just as they were in the summer of 1354, as they will be in 2054 and beyond. He can stand on a rock by the shore and be in a past he could not have known, in a future he will never see. He can be part of time that was and time yet to come." As long as the Adirondacks offers this kind of experience, we can be hopeful about its future.

A poll sponsored by the Adirondack Museum in 1990 shows that a majority believes environmental conditions have deteriorated in the last ten years. Most of Neal Burdick's respondents are equally pessimistic about the next decade. The gift of silence will be further eroded, they say, cuteness will take over the roadsides, additional second homes and condominiums will reduce the park's grandeur, the park will become another Vermont, political compromises in implementing the Commission's report will satisfy no one, and the Adirondacks will become increasingly a rich man's playground.

These are plausible views of the immediate past and future. Yet they seem to me one-sided in their pessimism. I cannot foresee a time when the kind of experience described by White will be impossible to come by. Safeguards are firmly in place in the forty-three percent of Forest Preserve land in the park, protected under the forever-wild constitutional amendment of 1894, the strongest preservation law in the country. The enchantment of cyclical time may require more physical effort and ingenuity to attain than at present. It may not be available at all to those who simply drive through the park. But it will be there in the recesses of the Forest Preserve, particularly in the million acres classified as wilderness, for those who seek it and know how to find it.

It is desirable, nevertheless, to make the enchantment available to the casual visitor. The two new Interpretive Centers recently opened are a step in this direction. The recommendations of the Adirondack Commission of 1990 would enlarge the Forest Preserve by some 650,000 acres of choice timberland and conserve open space in the private lands of the park. Legislative approval of a substantial portion of the 245 proposals would go far to guarantee the preservation of the Adirondacks as the foremost wilderness area east of the Mississippi.

Preservation of open space is the key to the future. Risk factors differ among the four categories of space—travel corridors, settlements, back country, and waterways. Awaiting the motor tourist are hundreds of miles of roads bordered by dark conifers or by a mixed forest that awakens each spring in delicate pastel colors and subsides in fall in flaming brilliance. Driving through this wall of trees brings a sense of freshness and linkage to the natural world. Here and there the wall opens to modest views of mountain, lake, or river. The Commission report of 1970 listed forty scenic vistas. In the last twenty years a few of these have already been lost to vegetation or development. One of the finest, the view of Whiteface Mountain across a broad expanse of Lake Placid, is now blocked by condominiums. Travel corridors are at high risk because most of the land they traverse is private and subject to development.

Back country is at risk because of the desire of second-home buyers for seclusion and for the very aesthetic features most threatened by increased development. Over seventy percent of all vacation homes in the Adirondacks are located on lakes, ponds, or rivers. The Commissions of both 1970 and 1990 address this issue by seeking to divert development toward the settlements and away from back country. It will not be easy to accomplish this. The isolated beauty of back country is a popular attraction for subdividers and summer residents. Yet every new subdivision, each new vacation home, diminishes the open space that is the park's essential character. Adoption of the zoning provisions of the 1970 Commission's report has not prevented the creation of thousands of new building lots in the last twenty years. The 1990 Commission seeks a more drastic remedy in the transfer of development rights from back country to settlements. At this time it is too early to predict success. The second-home buyer will not easily be persuaded that he can enjoy the park without owning a choice piece of it.

I am more optimistic about the future of the waterways. Some twelve hundred miles of Adirondack rivers are zoned against harmful development under the state's Wild, Scenic and Recreational Rivers Act. And there is a good chance for passage of measures that restrict development on lake shores. But most promising for the future is the opening to public navigation of Adirondack rivers where right of passage has been denied for up to one hundred years.

Water is the most important recreational resource of the Adirondacks. The park is unique in the lower states in combining mountainous terrain with an intricate network of waterways. Besides 2,759 lakes and ponds greater than a half acre in surface area, thirty river systems flow from interior elevations to the perimeter of the dome-shaped uplift. Those main-stem rivers have numerous tributaries, many of which are navigable and form cross-grained interconnections, so that geography makes possible cruises of a hundred miles or more in all directions. All of this network was open to the public in the nineteenth century. The Adirondacks was then the nation's favorite region for small-boat travel.

About 1890, however, the owners of large private parks, with the acquiescence of the state, began to post river corridors and chain lakes against trespass. In the present century this practice was also followed by the game clubs that lease corporate timberlands. Boating opportunities have been sharply curtailed for up to one hundred years.

Now the situation is changing. A professor of law at Pace University, John A. Humbach, in an exhaustive study of common and case law on navigation on inland waters, concludes that there is a public easement on all rivers navigable in fact, and that this easement is held in trust by the state. The Department of Environmental Conservation has adopted this study as a guide to future policy. It has issued orders to field personnel to cease ticketing boaters for trespass on navigable streams, and it is preparing regulations that name the navigable streams of the state and affirm public right of passage on them. At the same time, awaiting action by the legislature, is a rivers bill that will give the force of statutory law to right of passage.

Valid reasons can be found to deplore the outlook for the park in the increase of the noise level, overuse of mountain trails, invasion of the back country by summer residents, increased traffic and development in travel corridors, acidification of high-altitude lakes, etc., but for this writer recognition of the public's right of passage on navigable rivers and streams opens a whole new realm of recreational enjoyment. Wild river corridors are the museum galleries of the natural world. The supreme kind of forest recreation is paddling a canoe in tandem down a winding balsam-spired stream or across a lonesome pond bordered by piny eskers. This is the outlook for the twenty-first century, just as it was a reality in the nineteenth, when W. H. H. Murray hailed the Adirondacks as a paradise for boaters beyond all rivals, east or west.

*The charm of female companionship in beautiful places. Mary's visit in 1991.*
*Mt. Jo, Elk Lake, Saranac River*

POSTSCRIPT

AS I END THIS MEMOIR in the fall of 1991, my urologist gives me an expectancy of two or three years. At age eighty-eight that seems generous enough even without a cancerous prostate. I do not dread dying. I am not built on the heroic scale of my old friend Atwood Manley, avid for tomorrow's news. Approaching his ninety-sixth birthday, he roused from a coma to announce to Unitarian Powers: "I, G. Atwood Manley, am not ready to die!" I am ready. Death is a terminus in my philosophy. Expectancy of an after life is a delusion of grandeur. I hope I shall continue, as in writing this memoir, simply to be glad for what was.

Victorian novelists contrived a resolution in last chapters; characters were either done for or presumed to live virtuously and happily ever after. Iris Murdoch, in our cranky century, impugns resolutions in the postscript to her novel *The Sea, The Sea*: "Life, unlike art, has an irritating way of bumping and limping on, undoing conversions, casting doubt on solutions." I am with the Victorians in this matter. In eighty-eight years one ought to be able to contrive a resolution of sorts, given a fair amount of luck.

My affairs are in order. My debts are paid. My cat, last dependent, died a few months ago after an easy life of eighteen years. The competence I shall pass on to my beloved sister, an eager consumer of life's pleasures, will help to prolong her still youthful joy of life. As Charles Lamb said of his pension from the East India House and earnings from his writing, "Competence to age is supplementary youth."

Retirement is a resolution in itself. Mine has lasted for over a quarter century. At times I have shared Santayana's sense of well-being after his retirement: "Never have I enjoyed youth so thoroughly as I have in old age." I am at ease in the world. Time is no longer a regimen of obligations. It is playmate, not master. It moves fast or slow or around as I will it. I have been free to devote it to what I enjoy most, exploring the woods, peaks, and waters of the Adirondacks, studying the past of the region, and looking out for its future.

A resolution in a negative sense is that I go less often to the woods now that stiffening joints, weakening muscles, and unsure balance have set in. On the positive side, I have a small reputation as regional writer. My three books may remain in print a few years after I am gone. An even longer niche in posterity is the archives of the University's Owen D. Young Library, where my Adirondack collections are to be stored.

I would not describe my present existence in Iris Murdoch's terms as bumping and limping. A reprieve of health allows me to enjoy the quiet pleasures of age: reading and listening to music; visits to and from my Canton friends; living here in the open spaces near world's end; walks to the Canton College campus and Bend-in-the-River Park; the ease of writing my memoirs, story line and characters all ready made and emotional involvement in the past; the mellowing effect in late afternoon of three ounces of Scotch as indulgence, not habit; the annual visits of my sister; and revisiting with her the places I have loved.